NEW UNIVERSITIES OVERSEAS

A. M. CARR-SAUNDERS

NEW UNIVERSITIES OVERSEAS

ILLUSTRATED

LONDON
GEORGE ALLEN & UNWIN LTD
RUSKIN HOUSE   MUSEUM STREET

FIRST PUBLISHED IN 1961

OC OO224825

DS

ᴄ

PRINTED IN GREAT BRITAIN
in 11 on 12 point Bell type
BY SIMSON SHAND LTD
LONDON, HERTFORD AND HARLOW

PREFACE

At a meeting of the Inter-University Council in 1957 Miss Margery Perham suggested that an account might be written of the recent expansion of university education in British overseas territories. The suggestion was welcomed, and a search was made for an author. The search was unsuccessful, and at a later meeting I was asked to undertake the task. By that time I had retired, and as I had been one of the warmest supporters of the proposal, I had no excuse for refusing the invitation though the difficulties involved in carrying out the work were only too obvious to me.

When writing the book I found it necessary to ask for the assistance of many people in Great Britain and overseas; to all my requests for help I have received the most generous replies. I have been furnished with facts, and I have benefited greatly from the observations of those who have read drafts of chapters. To all of them, too numerous to mention, I acknowledge my sincere thanks.

A. M. C.-S.

CONTENTS

TABLES

ILLUSTRATIONS

(between pages 64 and 65)

ABBREVIATIONS USED IN THE TEXT

IUC   Inter-University Council for Higher Education Overseas

COCAST   Council for Overseas Colleges of Arts, Science and Technology

CD and W   Colonial Development and Welfare

INTRODUCTION

This book sets out to describe the latest phase of the long story of the rise and development of universities in territories which are, or have been at some time, under the British crown. Most of these territories are now independent, some within and some outside the Commonwealth, while others still have colonial status. It is with territories which had colonial status in 1945 that this book is concerned. In most of these territories, when this story opens in the middle of the second world war, facilities for higher education were little developed. During the war thought turned to their future; concern over the lack of higher educational facilities was growing before the war, and it was realized that the post-war agenda should include a programme under which higher education in these territories could be rapidly advanced. This led to the appointment of the Asquith Commission which sat from 1943 to 1945 and produced a plan designed to promote that end.

Under this programme the British universities, with financial help from the British government, were to foster the evolution of universities in the territories, helping the institutions then existing and creating others where none existed. The impulse to development was to come from Great Britain, and the task, though officially approved and financed, was to be promoted by the British universities. This plan was approved by the government, and it may fairly be said that it was imaginative in conception as well as novel in procedure. Thus the British universities set out on an adventure, and venturousness is not usually associated with universities by common repute. It is now appropriate to survey what has happened during the fifteen years during which the plan has been in operation. It was devised for colonial territories advancing to independence; they have now reached, or are about to attain, self-government, and the end of the present phase is at hand.

The first chapter gives a brief account of the situation before 1945 and of the factors which led to the appointment of the Asquith Commission; the second chapter describes the programme formulated by the Commission, while the third deals with the measures taken in order to carry it out. The next two chapters contain a sketch of each of the universities and colleges from 1945 to the present day; each institution has a personality of its own, and the territories served by them differ vastly in extent and in regard to the accomplishments and needs of their populations. Therefore some such sketch must be attempted; it would have been possible to go on and tell the full story of each of them, but to have done so would have brought up many times in succession the problems which face them all, such as finance, form of government and appointment of staff. To avoid such repetition, the succeeding chapters are devoted to these topics, while the last two chapters review the plan in the light of experience and consider the prospect which is opening out.

A very large number of men and women have played a part in this adventure; it would be invidious to single out some of them for mention in the text from which therefore names have been omitted. Appendix I gives a list of all who are or have been members of the Inter-University Council, and Appendix II a list of the holders of the principal offices in the overseas universities and colleges.

CHAPTER 1

THE BACKGROUND

The dispatch written by Sir Charles Wood in 1854 on behalf of the directors of the East India Company and addressed to the Governor-General of India in Council marks the first occasion on which an initiative coming from Great Britain was directed to the foundation of universities in a dependent territory under the British crown. In accordance with the recommendations of the Commission on Higher Education in the Colonies which reported in 1945 (called the Asquith Commission after its chairman Lord Justice Asquith) a programme was put into operation for the development of university education in those British territories which had dependent status at that date. This was the second occasion on which an initiative directed to this end was taken in Great Britain, and it is the object of this book to describe the programme and the developments which have taken place under it. The Commission made a survey of the facilities for higher education in the colonies as they existed in 1945, and based their recommendations on what they found. This chapter gives a brief outline of the growth of these facilities in the territories in question.[1]

The Royal University of Malta—the appellation 'royal' was conferred in 1937—is an ancient institution. In 1592 the Society of Jesus founded a college in Valetta with the co-operation of the Order of St John of Jerusalem; the college conferred degrees by virtue of the degree-granting power with which the Society was endowed by the pope. When the Society was proscribed in 1768, the college passed into the hands of the knights and acquired university status by papal bull. In 1798 Napoleon occupied the island and abolished the university; it was reopened by the British in 1800, and at the same time the School of Anatomy and Surgery, founded in 1674, was transferred to the University. During the following century the constitution of the University underwent a rapid and bewildering series of changes; at certain times it was autonomous, at other times it was directly subject to the government. When the island was granted responsible government in 1921 the University became in effect a government department; under a statute of 1935 it obtained a measure of autonomy, but as regards appointments and finance its governing body had only advisory functions. The organization of studies was formerly on the lines of a continental university with faculties of arts, theology, law and medicine. The degree in medicine was recognized by the General Medical Council in 1904; in 1915 a faculty of science and a faculty of engineering and architecture were added. The University lived on a minute income, £13,000 in 1936-7 of which the government found £10,800, and £18,000 in 1945-6 of which the government found £12,000. The penury of the University forced it to resort to two expedients; almost all the members of the teaching staff held part-time appointments, and students, intending to follow a degree course, were only admitted every third year. The latter arrangement reduced expense by limiting the number of separate lectures and classes for which provision had to be made each year, but it implied a period of waiting for admission, inflicting hardship on most of the student body which numbered 250 in 1944-5, of whom 212 were working for degrees. In spite of the difficulties arising from inadequate income the University maintained its ancient and honourable traditions as a seat of learning; moreover, unlike the situation in other territories, it was almost the only resort of students, few of whom frequented universities abroad.

The Royal University of Malta was founded before the British acquired the island. The other universities in territories which had colonial status in 1945 were founded after the British had taken possession. As in so many other cases at home and overseas, the earliest institution for higher education in Hong Kong was a medical college; it was set up by Sir Patrick Manson and Sir James Cantlie in 1886; Sun Yat-Sen was among its first students. About 1905 there was talk of a university, and the idea was discussed in the local press. Lord Lugard, when governor of the colony, took up the idea, and in 1911 the University of Hong Kong was incorporated by local legislation; with it was amalgamated the medical college. From the beginning the aim of the University was to maintain standards equal to those of British universities. The Government of Hong Kong presented a site of 36 acres, but the people of Hong Kong provided the capital, one local benefactor paying for the main building, others contributing to the cost of additional buildings and to an endowment fund. Other gifts made later increased the endowment, and in 1931 the University received £265,000 from the Boxer Indemnity Fund. Among the objects of the University was 'to promote a good understanding with the neighbouring Empire of China'. Thus there was a political element among the objects, and this element was mentioned by Lord Lugard in his speeches. The establishment of the University was welcomed, he said, by those 'who are interested in the maintenance of British prestige in the Far East'. The use of English as a medium of instruction would 'promote British interests', and indeed one of the reasons for using English was that 'British influence in the Far East may be extended'.[2] These remarks have evoked the just comment that if they 'were taken to mean that the University was to regard itself as an instrument of propaganda or that the nature of its work were to be determined by political motives we should think them unfortunate'.[3] But whatever hopes British officials entertained about the political importance of the University, these considerations did not enter the minds of the local people who supported it; nor has the work and teaching of the University been shaped by them. The University, as a centre of western learning, did attract students from the mainland, but not at first in such numbers as might have been expected if the Sun Yat-Sen movement, which led to the downfall of the Chinese Empire, had not engendered nationalist fervour tending to keep students at home.

The governors who followed Lord Lugard seem to have shown little interest in the University; the population of the colony was less than half a million in 1911, and to the government of Hong Kong, which had to find most of the money for recurrent expenses, it was an unwelcome burden. Between the wars the proportion of students coming from outside Hong Kong, mostly from Malaya and China, increased, and in 1941 of the 600 students only little over a half were from Hong Kong. Thus the government was called upon to bear the greater part of the running costs of an institution many of whose students were not its direct care. It was difficult for the government to give adequate support, but the support it did give (about £22,000 a year) was less than it might well have been, and the University carried on in a state of chronic poverty. Moreover the University was isolated, and not only geographically, since there is no evidence that university or official circles in Great Britain took any interest in it.[4] Nevertheless, in spite of all these difficulties, the University had by 1941 provided for a wide range of studies; there were faculties of arts, science, medicine and engineering; the medical degree was recognized by the General Medical Council, and the standards were equivalent to those prevalent in Great Britain.

Ceylon was still a colony in 1945, but independence, granted in 1948, was round the corner. The work of the organization created in 1946, which is described in the next two chapters, was limited during its early years to the colonies, and therefore no close relations were built up with the University since it was anticipated that they must soon cease. However, in order to complete the account of higher education in territories which had colonial status in 1945, a sketch of the history of the University of Ceylon is given in Appendix 4.

Malaya is a geographical term for an area which now includes the Federation of Malaya and the Government of Singapore. In 1819 the British acquired Singapore, then an uninhabited island, at the initiative of Sir Stamford Raffles who founded a trading settlement which, as a free port, attracted Chinese merchants and became world-famous for its business activities. During his last days in Singapore, Raffles, a man of vision, called for the establishment of a college which would be 'a monument of light'; 'education', he said, 'must keep pace with commerce in order that its benefits may be ensured and its evils avoided . . . Shall we not consider it one of our first duties to afford the means of education to surrounding countries and thus render our stations not only the seats of commerce but of literature and the arts?'[5] An institution was founded, but there was no one who had the understanding or energy to carry out Raffles's plans; it passed through many vicissitudes, its property was mostly frittered away, and in 1903 the remnants of the foundation were taken over by the government which used them to found a secondary school under the title of Raffles Institution.

The islands of Singapore and Penang, together with certain areas on the mainland, forming the so-called Straits Settlements, came under the Presidency of Bengal until 1867 when they were transferred to the Colonial Office. The greater part of the mainland fell within either the Federated or the unfederated Malay States. Early in the present century there was a movement to found a medical school. A fund was raised as the result of a public appeal, and in 1905 the Straits Settlements and Federated Malay States Government Medical School was opened; in 1912 it took the title of the King Edward VII Medical School in recognition of a grant from the King Edward VII Memorial Fund; in 1921 the name was changed to the King Edward VII College of Medicine. The College was a part of the government medical service and the members of its staff were government servants; its diploma was recognized by the General Medical Council in 1916, and it won a high reputation for its standards and for its contributions by research. Before the second world war its income was about £34,000, derived from a government grant supplemented by interest on an endowment given by the Rockefeller Foundation; about 60 students were admitted annually. The next step in the provision of higher education was taken after the first world war. In 1918 a movement was set on foot to celebrate the centenary of Singapore; a fund of £128,000 was raised by public subscription, and it was a fitting decision to use it to found a college of arts and science and to name it after Sir Stamford Raffles. Raffles College was opened in 1929; the fund, supplemented by a grant of £268,000 from the governments which also gave the site, met the capital cost and provided the nucleus of an endowment fund. In 1940 its annual income was about £36,000 of which the governments contributed about £18,000, and there were about 300 students. Unlike the Medical College, it was not a government institution; it was controlled by a council on which the governments were represented, while academic matters were in the hands of the senate. Again, unlike the Medical College, whose standing was recognized by the medical world in Great Britain, the work of those responsible for the high standards achieved at Raffles College long remained without adequate recognition overseas. The appointment in 1938 by the Secretary of State of a Commission on Higher Education in Malaya (called the McLean Commission after its chairman Sir William McLean) provided the first evidence of interest in Raffles College in Great Britain. The Commission recommended the fusion of the two colleges into a university college; this new college would continue to award the medical diploma, but there was to be a board of examiners in England which would grant diplomas to students of arts and science, a strange recommendation involving remote control and indicating some failure to appreciate the standards reached at Raffles College.[6]

Before 1945 there were few facilities for education in Africa at post-secondary level. In response to an appeal by Lord Kitchener, a fund of £100,000 was raised to build a college at Khartoum, and in 1902 Gordon Memorial College was opened.[7] Apart from two notable gifts from Sir William Mather and Sir Henry Wellcome the capital and recurrent costs of the College were borne by the Sudan government; in 1944 the government grant for recurrent expenses stood at £E.74,000. Up to 1944 the Director of Education was the titular Principal of the College. Until the end of the first world war the College housed a primary school, a teachers' training department, an instructional workshop and an upper school, the last-named attended by 86 boys. In 1924 it was decided to convert the College into a secondary school, and in 1930 there were 555 boys following a two years' course of secondary education and another two years of vocational training. In 1936 the government established a separate school of law under its legal department and planned to set up other professional schools. The Commission on Higher Education in East Africa (called the De La Warr Commission after its chairman Lord De La Warr) visited the Sudan in 1937. They approved the policy of creating professional schools, and recommended that in due course the College should cease to provide secondary education and should become responsible for post-secondary professional courses. The College would thus presently become 'of university type', and ultimately a university. These recommendations were accepted in principle; the government set up schools of agriculture and veterinary science in 1938, of science and engineering in 1939 and of arts in 1940; in 1942 these schools were linked together under a higher schools advisory committee.

There was already separate provision for medical education in the Sudan. After Kitchener's death in 1916 an appeal was issued for a fund to build a medical school as a memorial to him. The appeal had little success in Great Britain where only £2,000 was subscribed; it had greater success in the Sudan where £11,000 was raised. The appeal was renewed in 1923, and this time enough money was received, including a gift by a local merchant of Persian origin of all his property for the benefit of poor students, to make possible the opening of the Kitchener School of Medicine in 1924. It was originally proposed that the school should form part of Gordon College, but it came into existence as a separate institution, having its own board of management of which the director of the Sudan medical service was the most important member; the government gave a grant to cover recurrent expenses. The school awarded a diploma for which the course of training was gradually lengthened, and in 1940 an important arrangement was made with the two Royal Colleges of Physicians and Surgeons. A visitor appointed by them supervised the final examination for the diploma, and those who gained it became admissible to the final LRCP and MRCS examinations; thus, though the diploma was not recognized by the General Medical Council, its holders could sit for a registrable qualification.

Passing to British colonial territories in East Africa, there is nothing to record until after the first world war. In 1921 the government of Uganda established a technical school on Makerere Hill outside Kampala for the training of artisans. In the following year its scope was enlarged, and a wide range of vocational and professional training was gradually made available, in medicine, surveying, engineering and teacher training; in 1928 the courses for artisans were transferred elsewhere. In 1933 courses leading to the Cambridge School Certificate were introduced, and preparations were made for post-secondary work. From the beginning the ultimate aim for the college had been set high; the report of the Uganda Education Department for 1925 said: 'this year has been devoted principally to organization; the only government educational system has been the College at Makerere, which is destined to become the University College for the Protectorate'.[8] The De La Warr Commission which visited the College in 1937 grasped the importance of building up a university for East Africa and displayed imagination, unusual in enquiries of this kind, when they recognized in the College, as it then was, 'the beginnings of a university'.[9] This being in their view the proper goal for the College, they recommended that the site and buildings should be planned to that end from the outset, remarking that it would be most unfortunate if it were fettered 'for good to a restricted site in increasingly urban surroundings'.[10] They further recommended that the constitution of the College should be revised and that post-secondary courses should be introduced. The difficulties arising from the site and the steps taken to overcome them after 1945 will be described in Chapter 6; the other recommendations were carried out at once. The College, hitherto administered by the Uganda government, was remodelled in 1938 as an independent inter-territorial institution to serve the needs of higher education in the East African territories as a whole under a governing body on which the governments concerned were represented. The government of Uganda, which had met the cost (£105,000) of the buildings, including an Anglican and a Catholic chapel, handed them over to the College; an endowment fund of £500,000 was raised to which the governments of the United Kingdom (£100,000), Uganda (£250,000), Kenya (£50,000), and Tanganyika (£100,000) contributed, and in 1943 the College had an income of nearly £31,000. When the war came, the College was offering post-secondary courses in arts and science leading to diplomas, and was also providing sub-professional courses open to those who had gained diplomas. In 1946 there were 176 students including 10 women.

Contact between West Africa and the outside world had begun earlier and had become closer than in the case of East Africa. School education was much further advanced; secondary schools had been founded as long ago as 1845 in Sierra Leone by missionary effort. Moreover, 'University study by West Africans', it was said in 1945, 'has been for generations in full swing. African doctors, African lawyers, African teachers, African churchmen have for sixty years and more, in small but increasing numbers, passed into, and through, the universities of Great Britain, Europe and America'.[11] Yet in Nigeria, the largest of the four West African territories, there were only two institutions which could be said to offer any facilities for higher studies, Yaba Medical School founded in 1930 and Yaba Higher College founded in 1931, both situated in the neighbourhood of Lagos and maintained by the government at a cost in 1943 of about £13,000 and £17,000 respectively. The former was the only centre for medical training in British West Africa; the buildings, on a site adjoining the Higher College, were wooden structures poorly suited for their purpose. The school offered a four-year course leading to a certificate as medical assistant; no attempt was made to reach medical standards recognized in Great Britain. There were 20 students in 1939 and 30 in 1943. Yaba Higher College offered courses in teacher training and also courses, usually lasting two years, which prepared students to pass into professional schools organized by government departments. The total student body was under 100, and the buildings, though more substantial than those of the School, were on a restricted site. At the opening of the College Sir Donald Cameron had said: 'We look forward to the time when it will be possible for men and women to obtain at Yaba external degrees of a British university'.[12] But when war came, no progress whatever had been made in that direction; indeed students were discouraged from sitting for the external degree of London University.

In Ghana there was an institution, founded in 1924, of a very different kind, Achimota College situated about six miles from Accra; it had spacious grounds and good buildings including a library with 16,000 books, by far the best college library in British West Africa. The College was governed by an independent council on which members of the staff were represented. The government of the colony provided the whole cost of the College, about £600,000, and made an annual grant of over

£50,000. Sir Gordon Guggisberg, in a speech in 1924, said: 'Achimota, as I see it, will be more in the nature of a university college than a secondary school. . . . Achimota College is the stepping stone towards the university which it is the ardent desire of the African to have'.[13] But things did not turn out this way. The College grew up as a composite institution, making coeducational provision for all stages of education, with a kindergarten at one end and a university department at the other; there was also provision for teacher training courses. The attention given to the earlier stages of education held back the growth of university studies; in 1939 there were 679 pupils of whom only 32 were in the university department which prepared students for the external degree in engineering and for the external intermediate examinations in arts and science of the University of London. In 1944 this large programme was curtailed when the kindergarten and the primary school were disbanded; thus, when the war ended, the College embraced a secondary school, a teacher training section and a university department.

At Freetown in Sierra Leone there was an institution of yet another type, Fourah Bay College, founded by the Church Missionary Society in 1827 which owned and controlled it. Its original purpose was to train ministers and lay workers. In 1876 it was affiliated with the University of Durham and began to prepare students for certain degrees and diplomas of that university. The government of Sierra Leone gave only a small grant to the College for its degree work, but paid for the teacher training courses which the College provided; in 1942–3 the income of the College was £3,755. The number of students was always small; in 1932–3 there were 29 students of whom 16 were university students; in 1937–8 the corresponding figures were 30 and 17, and in 1942–3 25 and 20. A considerable proportion of the students came from outside Sierra Leone; in 1942–3 the proportion was 50 per cent. The importance of the College was far greater than these figures suggest; it opened the way to university education for students from all British West Africa and it was the only institution which set out to satisfy the 'ardent desire' of which Sir Gordon Guggisberg spoke. Entries would have been greater if the failure rate in the matriculation examination, resulting from the poor facilities for secondary education, had not been so high; in the six years 1938 to 1943 only 26 candidates out of 65 passed. It is remarkable how many Africans, prominent in public life in West Africa, have been educated at the College for which they entertain strong feelings of loyalty as shown by their continued support; it is also noteworthy how highly the connection with Durham University was esteemed.

During the last two hundred years many plans were made in the British West Indies under which higher education was to be offered, but, with the exception of that for Codrington College, they all failed.[14] Christopher Codrington bequeathed certain properties to the Society for the Propagation of the Gospel, and in 1741 a College called after him was opened in Barbados. In 1875 it became affiliated to the University of Durham, but did not develop in the same manner as Fourah Bay College. The number of students has always been small; nearly all prepare for the ministry and few aim at degrees. Though Bermuda does not count as part of the West Indies, passing mention may be made of Berkeley's plan for a college in that island put forward at about the time when Codrington College was founded. After emancipation a number of schemes were propounded; one for a university in Jamaica was due to a Baptist missionary, Phillippo by name, who had full faith in the capacity of Africans for university education. Another plan resulted in the establishment of Queen's College in Jamaica which was opened in 1873, but it soon came to an end, and yet another plan produced Jamaica College which conducted some university work for a few years. Among other schemes that of Keenan for a university of Trinidad, serving all the islands, deserves mention. In 1921 the Imperial College of Agriculture was established in Trinidad; its dual function was to provide post-graduate training for cadets from Great Britain selected to enter the colonial service as agricultural officers, and to offer diploma courses which were mostly followed by West Indians. Between the wars local ambition for a university was manifest; in 1929 the first West Indian Conference considered the possibility of setting up a university; in 1938 the government of Jamaica appointed a committee to examine the project, and in 1943 the Legislative Council of

Jamaica passed a resolution in favour of founding a university. That was as far things had got in 1945 in which year over 350 West Indian students, having no university of their own, were studying in universities overseas.

This sketch of the growth before 1945 of facilities for higher education in those territories, which had colonial status at that date, has not revealed evidence of any official interest in Great Britain in these developments until 1936 when the De La Warr Commission was appointed. It remains to indicate how this interest was aroused since it led ultimately to the appointment of the Asquith Commission. In 1923 an Advisory Committee on Native Education in Africa was set up by the Colonial Office; this move followed, and was no doubt prompted by, the publication of the report of an enquiry under the auspices of the American Phelps-Stokes Fund in 1922, since the author of that report, Dr Thomas Jesse Jones, attended the first meeting of the Advisory Committee. This report was a comprehensive and farseeing document; while mostly concerned with school education in Africa it made reference to higher education. 'It seems probable that for some years to come African colonies must depend upon Europe and America for university training. It must be recognized, however, that Africa should have its own colleges as soon as the elementary and secondary schools are able to supply a sufficient number of students to warrant the organization of colleges'.[15] In 1929 the Colonial Office Committee was transformed into the Advisory Committee on Education in the Colonies, and in 1940 the Colonial Office appointed an educational adviser. In its first decade the attention of this Committee was focused on the earlier stages of education, but from time to time problems of higher education came into view. In 1932 Raffles Colleges raised the question of degrees which led to a discussion by the committee; in the same year the committee received a document from the East African directors of education which, among other matters, referred to courses for matriculation; a sub-committee was set up under the chairmanship of Sir James Currie which produced a remarkable report in which was laid down a plan foreshadowing in many ways that later worked out by the Asquith Commission.[16] This report was accepted by the Advisory Committee and was submitted to the

28

Secretary of State in 1934; but twelve years passed before a scheme worked out on similarly imaginative lines got off the ground. The interest of the Advisory Committee in the problem of higher education in East Africa led, however, to a recommendation for the appointment of the De La Warr Commission; in a similar fashion the Advisory Committee became interested in the problems of higher education in Malaya, and on their recommendation the McLean Commission visited Malaya in 1939. In 1940 the Advisory Committee had under consideration the proceedings of the West African Governors Conference which made mention of university development in West Africa. Again a commission was recommended, and the recommendation was accepted.

Two months later the Advisory Committee received from one of its members, Professor H. J. Channon, a memorandum which stressed the need for an overall review of the problem of university development overseas and of the extent to which the universities of Great Britain could help in its solution; he had been a member of the McLean Commission, and his memorandum seems to have originated as a pendant to the Commission's report. The discussions on higher educational problems in different parts of the world in 1940 led the committee to give a warm welcome to the memorandum, and the proposal it contained met with the approval of the Secretary of State, who announced in 1943 the appointment of two Commissions, the Asquith Commission which was to make a general review of the problem, and the Commission on Higher Education in West Africa (called the Elliot Commission after its chairman Mr Walter Elliot) which was to report on the special problems of West Africa. There was overlapping membership between the Commissions, and it was understood that the particular proposals for West Africa would fall within the general scheme put forward by the Asquith Commission.

The story of the development of educational facilities as a whole in the colonial territories is outside the scope of this book, which is concerned only with higher education, and therefore this is not the place to discuss the policy pursued in regard to school education. But now that these territories are assuming the responsibilities of independent nationhood, it may be asked whether the delay in making provision for university education, and the consequential lack of citizens educated to the point where these responsibilities can be assumed, does not indicate neglect by the metropolitan power.

When we consider the Far Eastern dependencies whose peoples, inheriting ancient cultures, were eager for western knowledge and demonstrated their willingness to raise funds, we find that, apart from an occasional governor or senior official who welcomed this eagerness, there is little evidence of sustained and informed sympathy with these ambitions on the part of British officials on the spot. The one partial exception is the recognition of the value of medical education by the governments, which is best illustrated in Singapore. The enthusiasm of West Indians for higher education had been manifest since emancipation and was encouraged by some missionaries and others who drew up schemes for colleges none of which, however, bore fruit; but there is little evidence of support for these plans from British officials. West Africa provides a somewhat similar case; there again we find young people, as in the West Indies, resorting in numbers to universities in Europe and America, a marked sentiment of gratitude for the limited facilities which Fourah Bay College could supply and a growing sense of frustration at the lack of local university facilities. A governor of the type of Sir Gordon Guggisberg, who understood the situation and did his best to promote higher education, was a rare figure, and without the sustained interest of British officials such men could achieve little. It is paradoxical that in the Sudan and East Africa, where school education was at a lower level than in other territories, there was more evidence of official recognition of the need to advance towards the higher ranges of education. The government of the Sudan has a good record in this matter, and the advancement of Makerere College, made possible by the government of Uganda, is to the credit of the latter.

What needs explanation is the general lack of interest in higher education shown by British officials. If they had appreciated the need for higher educational facilities they might have encountered serious financial obstacles in the days before the Colonial Development and Welfare Acts. But they displayed very little sympathy with local aspirations for university education. They had usually graduated at one of the older universities from which they carried away agreeable memories rather than professional accomplishments or enduring intellectual interests. They had little understanding of the part played in the modern world by universities and of the importance of the professions for which universities are a preparation, and to them the idea of transplanting to the regions where they worked the only type of university known to them doubtless seemed fantastic. Between British officials with this background and the young and ambitious local intellectual elite there was little or nothing in common; certain virtues, probity, justice and devotion to duty, were widely exhibited by the former, but understanding of, and sympathy with, the student class were not among them. Moreover in Africa and also in Malaya British officials put their trust in the traditional social structure as exemplified in the policy of indirect rule. But the intellectual elite was in revolt against these traditional forms; in consequence the officials, regarding themselves as responsible for the simpler elements which made up most of the population of which the student class were not representative, came to think of this class as their opponents, if not actually subversive. This is what lies behind the remarks of Lord Lugard when he said in 1920 that 'it is a cardinal principle of British colonial policy that the interest of a large native population shall not be subject to the will of a small class of educated and Europeanized natives who have nothing in common with them and whose interests are often opposed to theirs'.[17] The same applies to Sir Hugh Clifford's views when he said that 'it can only be described as farcical to suppose that . . . continental Nigeria can be represented by a handful of gentlemen drawn from a half dozen Coast tribes—men born and bred in British administered towns situated on the seashore—who in the safety of British protection have peacefully pursued their studies under British teachers'.[18] Such being the attitude of the most senior British officials it is not surprising that they and those who served under them did not exert themselves to provide what the 'educated and Europeanized natives' wanted, namely facilities for university education. But it was into the hands of the latter that the responsibility for these territories was destined to fall, and time alone can show how far the failure to push ahead with higher education will endanger the stability, efficiency and liberality of the successor regimes.

NOTES

1. The Sudan, though never a colony, was included in the survey at the request of the Foreign Office.

2. Quoted in *A Report on the University of Hong Kong*, 1953 (by Sir Ivor Jennings and Sir Douglas Logan), p. 11.

3. *Ibid.*, p. 11.

4. When Lord Lugard had brought the legislative council of Hong Kong to the point of making a grant of $50,000 to the University, the Colonial Office intervened and forbade the grant. Margery Perham: *Lugard: The Years of Authority*, 1960, p. 346.

5. Quoted in the *Report of the Commission on University Education in Malaya*, 1948, p. 134.

6. The Asquith Commission made mention of the Hebrew University of Jerusalem. This University was within the ambit of the plan, but Israel became independent before conversations between the University and the I.U.C. could lead to action.

7. The nature and scope of Lord Kitchener's interest in educational problems is not clear. According to his latest biographer 'Kitchener found it impossible in practice to take any genuine interest either in Gordon College or in education. . . . He needed a supply of reliable native clerks'. (Philip Magnus: *Kitchener*, 1958, p. 146.)

8. Quoted by J. E. Goldthorpe and M. Macpherson, 'Makerere College and its Old Students', *Zaire*, Vol. XII, 4, 1958, p. 349.

9. *Report of the Commission on Higher Education in East Africa*, 1937, p. 80.

10. *Ibid.*, p. 85.

11. *Report of the Commission on Higher Education in West Africa*, 1945, p. 17.

12. *Ibid.*, p. 33.

13. *Ibid.*, p. 39.

14. See Lloyd Braithwaite: 'The Development of Higher Education in the West Indies', *Social and Economic Studies*, Vol. VII, No. 1, 1958.

15. *Education in Africa*, a Study of West, South and Equatorial Africa by The African Education Commission under the auspices of the Phelps-Stokes Fund and Foreign Missionary Societies of North America and Europe, 1922, p. 48.

16. This report was not before the Asquith Commission. Sir James Currie's committee and the Commission arrived independently at very similar views.

17. Quoted by James S. Coleman, *Nigeria: Background to Nationalism*, 1958, p. 156.

18. *Ibid.*, p. 156. It was only in 1937 that the government of Nigeria reversed its opposition to education abroad and granted scholarships for study in Great Britain. (*Ibid.*, p. 124.)

CHAPTER 2

THE PROGRAMME OF 1945

The Asquith Commission was set up in August 1943, and its report was published in June 1945. The terms of reference were: 'to consider the principles which should guide the promotion of higher education, learning and research and the development of universities in the Colonies; and to explore means whereby universities and other appropriate bodies in the United Kingdom may be able to co-operate with institutions of higher education in the Colonies in order to give effect to these principles'. The Foreign Office invited the Commission to extend their recommendations to the Sudan which was never a colony and was at that time subject to an Anglo-Egyptian condominium. The Commission were asked to deal primarily with 'principles'; they did not interpret this request as meaning that they should confine themselves to a bare recital of generalities; they decided that they ought not to ignore the special application which any general principles must bear to larger problems of university organization and work. This chapter, however, deals only with the most general recommendations of the Commission, namely those relating to the establishment of new university institutions and to the manner in which they and existing institutions might be helped and advised by United Kingdom universities. Their other recommendations concerned staffing, finance, constitution, entrance qualifications, syllabuses, professional education and a host of other matters; what the Commission recommended and what has been done in each of these fields is best left to later chapters.

After taking note of the facts set out in the last chapter the Commission urged 'the early creation of universities so situated that, as far as is compatible with geography, the remaining areas of the Colonial Empire shall be served by one of them'.[1] 'The main consideration in our minds', the report went on to say, 'is that His Majesty's Government has entered upon a programme of social and economic development for the Colonies which is not merely the outcome of a desire to fulfil our moral obligations as trustees of the welfare of Colonial peoples, but is also designed to lead to the exercise of self-government by them. In the stage preparatory to self-government universities have an important part to play; indeed they may be said to be indispensable. To them we must look for the production of men and women with the standards of public service and capacity for leadership which self rule requires. It is the university which should offer the best means of counteracting the influence of racial differences and sectional rivalries which impede the formation of political institutions on a national basis. Moreover, universities serve the double purpose of refining and maintaining all that is best in local traditions and cultures and at the same time of providing a means whereby those brought up in the influence of these traditions and cultures may enter on a footing of equality into the world-wide community of intellect. In short, we look on the establishment of universities as an inescapable corollary of any policy which aims at the achievement of Colonial self-government. We believe that there can be no more welcome proof of the sincerity of this policy than the provision at an early date of facilities for university education in the Colonies themselves.'[2]

The Commission then elaborated their recommendation for the early creation of universities. 'We regard as practicable, and indeed as urgent, the immediate setting up of university colleges. By a university college we mean an institution of higher education at university level which is not empowered to grant degrees. We believe that there should be no undue delay in converting these colleges into universities.'[3] In other words they recommended that the procedure, then employed for bringing new universities into existence in Great Britain, should be applied in the colonies. The Commission had a special reason for recommending this procedure. Owing to the remoteness, inaccessibility and unfamiliarity of the regions which the new foundations were to serve, doubt might well have arisen concerning the claim of new universities so situated to stand on an equal footing with established universities. 'An institution with the status of a university', the Commission wrote, 'which does not command the respect of other universities brings no credit to the community which it serves.'[4] Therefore university colleges should be founded whose students would work for the degrees of another university commanding prestige; this would demonstrate that standards were high. In this way the colleges would build up their reputations with the result that, when they received degree-granting powers, their degrees would attract the respect of other universities.

The Commission next considered at what degree the students should aim. They discussed a plan under which the Inter-University Council, a new body recommended by them and described later, would seek degree-granting powers and make its degrees available to students of the colleges. This plan was rejected on several grounds, one being that colonial students, for whom alone the degree would be open, would certainly think that they were to be offered an inferior award. The thoughts of the Commission then turned to London University, whose degrees had been available to overseas students for more than a century. Appendix 5 gives some account of the earlier history of London University; it suffices here to outline the position which has obtained since the University was remodelled in 1900. The University is a federation of colleges all of which must be situated within the administrative county of London. Students who attend these colleges are called 'internal' students and can sit for 'internal' degrees. Since the University has no power to affiliate colleges outside this area, it was not open to the Commission to propose that students of colonial colleges should work for 'internal' degrees. But the University also has power to award 'external' degrees to 'external' students, and to prescribe the conditions which such students must fulfil. The University prescribes the minimum qualifications necessary for acceptance as an external student. But there is no limit to the conditions which the University may prescribe, and it has laid down that students seeking external degrees in engineering or pharmacy must attend institutions which it has inspected and approved; it was only after inspection had taken place and approval had been given that it was possible for students of Achimota College to study for the external degree in engineering as was mentioned in the last chapter. As will be explained in the next chapter the University had made further use of this power in a manner which plays a most important part in the programme. But apart from these exceptions the University is not concerned with the manner in which an external student has prepared for an examination; he may have attended some institution, he may have taken a correspondence course or he may have studied at home. Moreover he may live in any country. To this there is one point to add; if external students in other countries had to come to London to be examined, few of them could take advantage of these facilities, and therefore the University is prepared to open local examination centres if asked to do so by the appropriate local authority—usually the department of education in the case of commonwealth countries.[5]

Therefore it was open to the Commission to recommend that students of colonial colleges should work for London external degrees. Since the standards demanded for external degrees are exactly the same as those demanded for internal degrees, this would mean that students would be working for an award carrying international repute. But the Commission saw two difficulties. The London syllabuses were drawn up with the needs of British students in mind; the University had made some concessings, permitting, for example, students born in Asia to substitute an oriental classical language for Latin or Greek. These concessions were valuable but, in the view of the Commission, did not go far enough; the need was for syllabuses drawn up to meet the needs of colonial students. The second difficulty was connected with the procedure for setting papers and marking scripts. This was carried out wholly in London, as was inevitable since external students did not study under a body of teachers with whom the University could collaborate. If this procedure were applied to the colleges it would, in the opinion of the Commission, not give their teachers the experience which it was desirable that they should have in order to prepare for the day when the colleges would become universities, set their own examinations and award their own degrees. The Commission put these difficulties to the University and

37

learnt that the University was prepared to put into operation a scheme under which it would take into special relationship colleges which fulfilled certain conditions and applied to participate in it. This scheme was designed to overcome both difficulties and is described in Chapter 3; the Commission regarded it as entirely satisfactory and recommended that students of the colonial university colleges should work for London external degrees.

By accepting this scheme the Commission assigned to one British university a special function relating to the proposed university colleges. In its terms of reference the Commission were asked to explore means whereby the universities of the United Kingdom as a whole could assist colonial institutions of higher education, and it remained to consider how the home universities jointly could be of help, not only to the colonial colleges, but also to the colonial universities. To this object the Commission attributed the greatest importance; 'the success of any scheme', they said, 'for the development of higher education in the colonies depends on the active interest and co-operation of the home universities'.[6] With this end in view, they proposed the creation of a body to be called The Inter-University Council for Higher Education in the Colonies. It was to have two distinct functions, that of co-operating with existing colonial universities and that of fostering the advance of colonial university colleges to full university status. Each home university would nominate a member, and there would be power to co-opt persons with special knowledge of colonial problems. 'The first task of the Council would be to acquaint itself with the present position and needs of the colonial university institutions.'[7] This acquaintance must be at first hand and kept up to date, and could only be gained by visits of members of the Council to the institutions. The Council would be a purely advisory body, giving advice, whenever asked to do so, on any of the numerous problems which face the overseas universities and colleges. In particular it was thought that the Council could assist by helping the institutions to fill vacancies on their staffs, and that it could 'foster the feeling that for those who go to the Colonies there exists at home an authoritative academic body interested in their careers'.[8] It was very much the intention of the Commission that through the work of the Council the colonial institutions should be brought within the family of Commonwealth universities.

Mention may be made here of the views of the Commission on certain broad questions of policy. 'It is essential', they wrote, 'that Colonial universities should be autonomous in the same sense in which the universities of Great Britain are autonomous.'[9] They would not be subject to any control from Great Britain, and their relations with their governments would be those which are maintained between the British universities and the British government. It was no part of the duties of the Commission to prescribe courses of study, but they did address themselves to the problem of maintaining a balance between two extremes of purpose. 'The education provided', they wrote, 'must be neither rigidly directed to the training of recruits to the professions nor so disdainful of practical needs that its products are unequipped for useful service to the community. . . . There is pressing need for men and women trained to undertake work in social administration, in medicine, in the teaching profession or in one of the other several fields of service. If the choice lay between the two extreme objectives . . . , there are some who might be inclined to regard this need as paramount; for the production of an educated or semi-educated class divorced from the community as a whole and unlikely to secure employment in it would be disastrous. We are convinced nevertheless that concentration on professional training would be almost equally regrettable.'[10] They stressed the importance of a wide range of teaching as helping to achieve the needed balance, and went on to recommend that the universities and colleges should be residential. 'No other single condition', they said, 'can serve so well to give the students a broader outlook or a higher general level of education.'[11]

Thus the aim was to create colleges with the teaching strength, buildings, equipment and other elements of the material background which would place them on an equal footing with western universities. They would not assume university status at the outset since the world at large might not be willing to credit them with the standards that should accompany this status; but when enough time had passed to allow them to demonstrate these standards they would become universities.

As to existing universities the aim was to enable them to enlarge their facilities and in particular, by the development of personal relations, to bring them within the family of Commonwealth universities.

The Commission foresaw that 'the development of higher education in the Colonies must depend on the grant of substantial financial aid from Great Britain'.[12] They did not, however, think that the Council should be asked to render advice on the allocation of funds to colonial institutions. 'We consider that the Council would have greater influence with Colonial institutions if its function were in the main confined to consultation and advice on the academic aspect of any projects of development put forward.'[13] Therefore they recommended the establishment of a separate body, the Colonial University Grants Advisory Committee, on which the Council would be represented, and assumed that the Council would be consulted 'as a matter of course, on the desirability from the academic point of view of the projects for which financial aid is sought'.[14]

'We are fully aware', the Commission wrote, 'that the recommendations we are making contemplate the expenditure of very substantial sums both from United Kingdom and from Colonial funds'. University education, they went on to say, is always expensive, and in the colonies would be more expensive than in Great Britain. For this there were many reasons; the institutions would be small at first and overhead costs would in consequence be high; the institutions would be residential; a large proportion of students would be working in the relatively more expensive subjects such as medicine; from the nature of their situation the institutions must be self sufficing in respect of libraries and equipment to a greater extent than would be necessary in Great Britain. 'All these things', the Commission said, 'we freely admit. But we do so without any sense that our attitude needs excuse. The university education which we seek to provide for the Colonial citizens of the Empire must be fitted for the purpose for which it is designed. Its aim is to give to these Colonial students an opportunity for self-development which will enable them to fit themselves for the management of their own concerns; to train themselves for their future responsibilities by gaining the expert knowledge necessary for the service of their own communities; and finally to take their place among those who are contributing to the intellectual life and scientific progress of man'.[15]

NOTES

1. *Report of the Commission on Higher Education in the Colonies,* 1945, p. 10.
2. *Ibid.,* p. 10.   3. *Ibid.,* p. 12.   4. *Ibid.,* p. 13.
5. Appendix 5 describes the origin of the external degree system of the University of London, and also gives some account of the power possessed by most British universities to affiliate other colleges (a power used by the University of Durham in relation to Fourah Bay College).
6. *Report of the Commission on Higher Education in the Colonies,* 1945, p. 30.
7. *Ibid.,* p. 31.   10. *Ibid.,* p. 14.   13. *Ibid.,* p. 32.
8. *Ibid.,* p. 32.   11. *Ibid.,* p. 15.   14. *Ibid.,* p. 33.
9. *Ibid.,* p. 34.   12. *Ibid.,* p. 54.   15. *Ibid.,* p. 56.

CHAPTER 3

THE PROGRAMME IN OPERATION

Those who think that universities are always slow to act should revise their opinions; the organization necessary to carry out the recommendations of the Asquith Commission was created and set to work by the universities immediately after the Secretary of State, who had received its report in June 1945, announced in February 1946 that he favoured the institution of an inter-university council. In March 1946 representatives of the United Kingdom universities met in London and established themselves as the Inter-University Council for Higher Education in the Colonies; the title of the Council (subsequently referred to as the IUC) was amended in 1955 by the substitution of the word 'overseas' for the words 'in the colonies'. The Committee, set up by the senate of the university of London to carry on discussion with the Asquith Commission, had remained in existence and was therefore ready to act as soon as the Secretary of State had approved the report. The Colonial University Grants Advisory Committee, as recommended by the Asquith Commission, was instituted in 1946. The following chapters describe what has been achieved under the programme and the part which these three bodies have played. This chapter is concerned only with the constitutions of these bodies, their main functions and their relations are with another, to which is added some account of the manner in which new university institutions have come into existence.

The IUC consists of representatives of each home and colonial university, one from each, except in the case of London University which has two, together with the educational adviser to the Secretary of State and members whom it can co-opt up to half of the total of representative members. It meets four times a year, appoints its own chairman and an executive committee, the latter meeting at monthly intervals. It is a body, set up by the universities, which enters freely into communication with such other bodies and persons, at home or abroad, as it deems proper in the course of its work. Its income is derived from funds made available under the Colonial Development and Welfare Acts, and its functions are purely advisory. Advice has been requested far more often by the colleges, which have many problems and limited experience when in early stages of development, than by the universities which are well established and have their own traditions.

It is not easy to give a picture of the variety and volume of the work of the IUC. Assistance with the staffing of overseas institutions has involved a large amount of work. The Council is prepared to advertise vacant posts and, if asked to do so, forms selection committees on which it invites members of home universities with special knowledge of the subject in question to serve; the readiness with which many hundreds of busy teachers have accepted these invitations deserves acknowledgment. Committees may have to meet on a number of occasions and, when suitable candidates do not present themselves, may attempt to encourage more hopeful applications; in the end the views of the committees are transmitted to the institutions which have entire liberty to make appointments as they think best. There have been several occasions when the IUC were attempting to find candidates for over 100 vacancies simultaneously, and between 1946 and 1960 it has advertised 2,303 vacancies and has recommended 1,758 candidates. The Council also endeavours to promote the secondment of teachers in home universities to colonial institutions and has set aside a sum of money for this purpose. But the filling of vacancies and the subsequent arrangements for medical examinations and passages are not the only matters relating to staffing which have led the institutions to invoke the help of the IUC; advice has been asked on problems relating to salary scales, grading, promotion, superannuation, children's allowances, home leave and travel expenses. Such problems, in addition to raising difficulties familiar in Great Britain, present special difficulties in the context of overseas conditions.

The Council has attempted to bring to the overseas institutions the kind of opportunities for mobility and interchange which the home universities enjoy. Thus it has interested itself in the Fulbright and Commonwealth Universities Exchange Schemes in their application to colonial areas. It has co-operated with the scholarship programmes of the Leverhulme Trust and the Goldsmiths Company which offer opportunities for British-born graduates of United Kingdom universities to undertake advanced study in overseas institutions. Through the generosity of the Carnegie Corporation of New York it is able to offer fellowships, tenable in universities in the United Kingdom and the United States, to locally born residents in the territories who are recommended for training as future members of university or college staffs.

The advice of the Council has been sought in relation to academic programmes and constitutional problems; among the latter are such matters as the relations of the institutions to governments, and the respective spheres of the governing body or council on the one hand and of the academic board or senate on the other. There are problems relating to site, lay out, choice of architects and the construction and equipment of halls of residence and laboratories. In particular the Council is able to help and advise over libraries and the acquisition of books; in 1947, owing to the generosity of the Carnegie Corporation, it was enabled to appoint a library officer whose salary since 1952 has been borne by its own funds. This officer has visited the institutions and has built up a close liaison with their librarians; he possesses a full knowledge of their needs, helps them to procure books, has secured numerous gifts and operates an extensive microfilm service.

The Council has also initiated discussions on a variety of topics; in particular it has organized meetings of the vice-chancellors and principals of the overseas universities and colleges with financial assistance from the Carnegie Corporation of New York. Such meetings have been held in Jamaica (1955), Arden-on-Hudson, USA (1958), Oxford (1959), and Cumberland Lodge, Windsor (1960). Many other services are rendered by the IUC which it would be tedious to enumerate. If what has been said creates the picture of an organization in London,

44

mainly occupied in keeping up a flow of advice by correspondence, that picture is misleading. From the beginning it has been the intention that relations should be personal; members of the overseas institutions are welcomed in London when on leave, and members of the Council pay frequent visits to the territories. The latter may go to attend meetings of college councils on which they represent the IUC, or they may go on special visits or as members of IUC delegations which sometimes include persons who are not members of the IUC, thus extending among British universities personal knowledge of the institutions. A rough estimate indicates that since 1945 well over 200 visits, financed by the IUC, have been paid by its members and others associated with its work. But this is by no means all; numerous visits have been paid as members of commissions, delegations and working parties in response to requests from, and at the cost of, territorial governments or the institutions concerned. In this way first-hand and continuing knowledge of the institutions and their problems has been built up, and personal acquaintance has been made with the members of their staffs; as a result it can be said that the position of the overseas institutions and of those who work in them is well understood by members of the home universities who are anxious to give such help as lies in their power. It may be added that the relations of the Council with the institutions are not limited to the period of colonial status. After the Sudan had become a republic the University of Khartoum continued to invoke the assistance of the IUC over problems of staffing, and after Ghana had attained independence relations with the University College remained as before except in respect of finance. While the Sudan was never eligible for grants from Colonial Development and Welfare funds and paid for visits made by IUC members and London examiners, the University College of Ghana was eligible for such grants up to independence. Since independence the government of Ghana has borne the cost of visits.

Unlike the IUC the Colonial University Grants Advisory Committee was set up by the Secretary of State and is advisory to him in matters relating to the expenditure of United Kingdom funds on higher education in the colonies. It consists of members appointed by him together with two representatives nominated by the IUC. Its duty is to estimate the needs of the universities and colleges for capital grants over a period and to communicate its views to the Secretary of State, to set aside for each institution a portion of such sum as he may allocate, and to advise him on the merits of each particular scheme submitted by an institution as one to be paid for, in whole or in part, out of its allocation. When setting up the Committee the Secretary of State indicated that it should be 'guided by the opinions of the IUC in regard to the academic aspects of its work'. Since all this expenditure has academic implications, the Committee asks for the views of the IUC whose special concern is that the schemes should fall within a balanced programme of development, and that design and furnishings of libraries, halls of residence and laboratories should take into account recent developments elsewhere. It is the concern of both bodies that costs should not be excessive; but the control exercised by the Committee over expenditure of United Kingdom monies is no greater than, if it is as much as, that exercised by the University Grants Committee in Great Britain.

The third body engaged in carrying out the programme, namely a committee of the senate of the University of London, is concerned only with the university colleges; it maintains close relations with the IUC of which its chairman has always been a member. The committee includes the vice-chancellor, the chairman of convocation, the principal, the chairmen of the three statutory councils, the deans of certain faculties and other members of the University, and acts through the senate on behalf of the University in all matters relating to the colleges which have been accepted into the scheme of special relations. In 1946 the University announced that it was willing to consider applications from colleges which desired this relationship. In order to gain admittance to a scheme a college must show that its staff, resources, equipment and constitution are appropriate to a university institution, and in particular that it possesses an academic body charged with the duty of formulating academic policy. This policy must include the encouragement of a liberal course of education and of corporate life among the students, the promotion of research and willingness to accept the responsibilities of intellectual leadership in the community which it serves. The

University is willing to take into provisional special relationship new institutions which are designed to fulfil all these conditions from the beginning; by so doing it makes it possible for new institutions to begin teaching for degrees from the outset. But in the case of an existing institution, providing some post-secondary teaching but not able to fulfil all the conditions, a period must elapse during which its facilities are being built up before special relationship can be established and teaching for degrees can begin. During this period the University is willing to advise on the steps to be taken in order to qualify for special relations.

One feature of the scheme has fundamental importance. As recommended by the Asquith Commission the students work for the external degrees of the University of London. As explained in the last chapter, the University can prescribe such conditions as it pleases for external students. It has laid down that students working for a degree under special relation must attend for at least three years at that college for which the degree in question has been approved. Thus it comes about that, although candidates for external London degrees are normally under no compulsion to make attendances, this does not hold good for students of colleges in special relation. The scheme is not uniform; arrangements which best suit the circumstances, educational, social and geographical of each college are worked out between the college and the University. Proposals come from the colleges. They may relate to matriculation requirements, suggesting that, because secondary education is not far advanced, these requirements should be less than those normally demanded by London; if approved by London, a lower level at entry carries with it the corollary that the length of the degree course must be extended by a year. They may relate to syllabuses, and in subjects such as language and history the desired changes may be radical. The changes are chiefly in syllabuses; in general the structure of London degrees is maintained. A complete set of regulations, independent of any other set of regulations, is drawn up for each college and approved by the senate. A college can nominate members of its staff to act as examiners who, if appointed by the University, co-operate with the London examiners in the setting of papers and the marking

47

of scripts. The London examiners have the final word, and the standards demanded are those which rule for London degrees.

As in the case of the IUC the relations of London University with the colleges involve personal contact; visits from members of the colleges are welcomed by their opposite numbers in London. Members of the college staffs who act as examiners attend meetings of examiners if they are in London. London examiners, especially when practical tests are involved, fly out to the colleges, and other London teachers pay special visits when full discussions about current problems and future developments take place. In the single session 1959–60 over 50 visits were made to the colleges by members of the London staff acting as examiners or otherwise. The volume of work falling on London teachers has been heavy; in the same session over 180 senior members of the University acted as examiners. Moreover up to date some hundreds of special syllabuses have been agreed; since all syllabuses must be approved by the relevant board of study and by the external council of the university, it follows that the time and attention of a very large number of members of the University have been devoted to the problems of the colleges.

The University has made an important concession in favour of the full-time teaching and research staffs of the colleges who, irrespective of the university from which they obtained their first degree, can work for the PhD degree of London. This concession has encouraged good candidates to come forward when vacancies are advertised. Up to date 66 members of college staffs have obtained the PhD degree, and a further 85 have registered for the degree.

Such are the bodies created in accordance with the recommendations of the Asquith Commission with the object of carrying out its plan. Only the first two bodies are concerned with universities; all three are concerned with university colleges. At the time of the Commission it was foreseen that university colleges would not all have the same background; some would develop out of post-secondary colleges while others would be founded as university colleges. It was not and could not have been foreseen that university colleges would arise with yet another background. This happened in the following manner.

The minority report of the Elliot Commission recommended that there should be territorial colleges in each West African territory serving as feeders to a single West African university college and undertaking other functions such as teacher training. An IUC delegation which visited West Africa soon after the publication of the report did not approve this proposal and recommended that the proposed territorial colleges should have functions similar to those of polytechnics with the title of regional colleges. This idea underwent modification at other hands; eventually there emerged the concept of colleges of arts, science and technology which have been defined as 'colleges which offer courses of general scientific and technical education leading or aiming to lead to qualifications of professional or near-professional standard (not normally university degrees)'. When that stage had been reached the Secretary of State set up a body called the Council for Overseas Colleges of Arts, Science and Technology, subsequently referred to as the COCAST, which is advisory to him on questions of policy and on the expenditure of such money as he may set aside out of United Kingdom funds. These colleges are independent, much as are the university colleges; they differ from one another in respect of the lower limits of their work, but in respect of the upper limits problems have arisen which concern the IUC because they have sought to offer courses leading to degrees in engineering.

In 1954 a COCAST college, the Kumasi College of Technology, applied to the University of London for recognition as an institution preparing students for the external degree in engineering. It follows from the description of the London external degree system given in the last chapter that the University was faced by a dilemma. It would have run counter to its long-established tradition to have refused to inspect the College and, if found satisfactory, to have refused to approve it for this purpose; on the other hand to approve a college supported by United Kingdom funds for the purpose of preparing for the unmodified external degree would run counter to the whole strategy of the Asquith plan under which colleges so supported would work for modified degrees under special relation. In the event the University inspected and approved the College for this purpose, but added a strong recommendation that the University College of Ghana should adopt the engineering department of the Kumasi College as its faculty of engineering, thus bringing it with the special relation scheme. But nothing came of this recommendation. A similar story with a different ending comes from Nigeria. The COCAST college in Nigeria has three branches; in 1957 the branch at Zaria in the Northern Region proposed to offer degree courses in engineering. The facilities were inspected and approved, and in that case the department of engineering at Zaria became the faculty of engineering of University College, Ibadan, not an ideal situation since Zaria is about 400 miles distant from Ibadan. In the latter case a department of a COCAST college became the faculty of a university college; in two other cases, those of the Royal Technical College, Nairobi, and Fourah Bay College, colleges once within the purview of the COCAST became university colleges. How this happened is described in Chapter 5.

CHAPTER 4

THE UNIVERSITIES

All the universities and colleges have similar problems, but they work in very different surroundings. It is the object of this and the following chapter to give some description of them and of the main events in their histories from 1945. The subsequent chapters will take up one by one the problems which are common to them all.

THE ROYAL UNIVERSITY OF MALTA

This university of ancient lineage serves the islands of Malta and Gozo, having together a population of 330,000 and covering an area of 121 square miles. The university building, completed in 1662, is situated in St Paul Street, Valetta; it has historic associations, but judged by the high standards prevailing in Valetta it is not a distinguished building. It is easy of access, but is so hemmed in that extension is impossible; moreover, though some of its rooms and corridors are dignified, it is not well suited for its purpose. The medical school is accommodated in the government hospital. The University has no sports ground and can offer only inadequate accommodation to students for social purposes. The Argotti botanic gardens covering two acres belong to the University and are open to the public.

Maltese and English are the official languages. The former language is the normal medium of intercourse; the students debate in that language and use it for taking minutes of their meetings, but are taught in English. There are some old schools, but the development of the school system on modern lines with sixth forms has only just begun; in 1958 a fifth of the population was said to be illiterate. The University conducts its own entrance examination, and since few grants are available for students, they are mostly drawn from the better-off section of the community. There were 300 students in 1946; numbers rose to nearly 500 but have declined lately to below the figure for 1946. The decline seems to have been due to the emergency teacher training scheme which attracted students who might have entered the University. The medical faculty has more students than any other faculty; nearly a third of the students were in that faculty in 1958.

The University was formerly under the control of the government in respect of finance and appointments; in 1947 with the encouragement of the IUC it obtained a new constitution, similar to those of the newer English universities, which gave it a proper degree of autonomy. Capital grants from United Kingdom funds enabled the University to build and equip a science block not far from the main site. The University was also assisted to build up its library, to strengthen its department of English, and to contribute to the fields of learning in which it has unique opportunities, in particular by surveying the antiquities of the islands and by preserving and restoring the rich collection of archives, and among them are those of the Order of St John of Jerusalem in the Royal Library. But financial support for recurrent expenses from the Maltese government continued to be on a small scale (£28,000 in 1954-5), and the University was in very serious and chronic financial difficulty. In 1957 a Commission, appointed by the government of Malta, issued a report which made many important recommendations, the chief of which was that a statutory commission should be set up to carry out whatever policy might emerge from a consideration of the report. This recommendation was accepted, and under the guidance of the statutory committee several important changes have been and are being made. Biennial entry of students replaced triennial entry in 1959, and the first steps have been taken to replace part-time by full-time appointments to the staff. The financial situation was eased when, after the suspension of the constitution in 1958, the government raised the annual grant for the University to £60,000.

By far the most important recent event was the formulation of a plan to move the University to a site of some 30 acres two miles outside Valetta. The scheme involves the purchase of the old building and the new science block by the government; it is estimated that the sum so acquired, supplemented by grants from United Kingdom funds, will pay for the new buildings. It is also proposed to erect a new building near the hospital where the clinical departments will be situated; the pre-clinical departments will be housed on the new site. If this can be brought about, the University will at length have adequate accommodation in which to carry on its large range of activities in its faculties of arts, science, theology, law, medicine, dental surgery, and engineering and architecture.

THE UNIVERSITY OF HONG KONG

The colony of Hong Kong includes the island of that name 32 square miles in extent, and Kowloon occupying three square miles on the mainland; in addition on the mainland are the New Territories leased from China in 1898 for 99 years and covering 355 square miles. The population, which did not reach a million before 1939 and now numbers close upon three million, is almost wholly Chinese and is concentrated in the city of Victoria on the island, in Kowloon and in certain industrial districts on the foreshore of the New Territories. The people were formerly almost wholly engaged in trading, but recently the growth of industry has provided an increasingly important alternative occupation. Apart from the narrow foreshore the whole area is so steep and rocky that food production is confined to some rice growing and market gardening in valley bottoms and other favoured spots. The island of Hong Kong, rising abruptly from the sea and seamed by tortuous valleys, is a lovely sight. The city of Victoria lies on the north side of the island facing Kowloon across a narrow strait; it is built on a strip of low lying land mostly reclaimed, and on the very steep slope immediately behind culminating in the Peak, 1,825 feet high. Ascending from sea level the Pokfulam Road is reached; it winds along the 200 foot contour and on its south side is the university precinct some 40 acres in extent, rising sharply to a height of about 460 feet. There is hardly a level patch of ground within the precinct; many universities are built on hills, but few, if any, besides

Hong Kong, are built on the flank of a precipitous mountain. Moreover the mountain is formed of granite, in places hard and in places decomposed. Before erecting a building it may be necessary to cut into hard rock; when this is not so, retaining walls must be constructed since the risk of land slides is great; indeed during the rainy season the descent of boulders and tons of earth is a continual menace. It is estimated that site preparation raises the cost of building by 50 per cent. The Queen Mary Hospital, in which clinical teaching is given, lies less than two miles off; on the way to it is a small piece of level ground serving as a playing field for students.

When the Asquith Commission was in session, Hong Kong was under enemy occupation and no information about the University was available. After the recovery of the territory it was found that the university buildings had suffered severe but not irreparable damage, that most of the equipment had been looted or destroyed, but that the libraries were mainly intact. The university authorities displayed great energy and in 1946 admitted students to first year classes on the understanding that the future of the University was uncertain and would depend upon the result of an investigation then being conducted by a committee. This committee was appointed by the Secretary of State to advise him whether the University 'as such should continue to exist'. At that date the population was probably only a third of its present total and the victory of the communists on the mainland could not be foreseen. The committee expressed the opinion that the size of the local population did not justify the re-establishment of the University; they were, however, so much impressed by the need to foster Anglo-Chinese understanding and by the capacity of the University to promote this end that they advised its re-opening, but only on condition that it was established 'on a firm financial basis'.[1] They emphasized this condition because it was clear to them, after reviewing the history of the University, that it had suffered from chronic poverty before the war, and that it would be better not to continue it than leave it without adequate support. The University therefore remained in being, but no plan was made to place it on 'a firm financial basis'. In 1947 the government of Hong Kong made a grant for the repair of war damage, and in 1947–8 the

University was offering degree courses in a number of subjects including medicine; by 1950 there were over 600 students. In 1949 a local benefactor, continuing the long tradition of private beneficence to the University, built and furnished the first hall of residence for women. In 1950 an IUC delegation found that the financial problem had not been faced, that the University was in urgent need of an income double that of which it was in receipt (£80,000), and of very large sums for capital purposes. The need was not merely for additional buildings since much of the pre-war accommodation was either poorly designed for its purpose or out-of-date and ought to be replaced; the three barrack-like halls of residence for men, placed one behind the other on a steep slope, were frightening in their gauntness (they are still standing). A grant of £500,000 was made to the University from United Kingdom funds in 1951, and a sum of £1,000,000, derived from the sale of Japanese assets in Hong Kong, was handed over to the University in the same year as an endowment. A school of engineering and architecture and a chemistry block were erected, but another IUC delegation in 1953 reported that the financial situation was still most unsatisfactory. So serious did the financial implications of meeting the University's requirements appear that later in the same year the government of Hong Kong invited two visitors of wide university experience to report on the whole situation.

Their report has provided the basis for planning since 1954.[2] Its authors remarked that an adjacent area of about forty acres, which the government was willing to put aside for development by the University, seemed unlikely to be suitable for the purpose, and this has proved to be so. Sites have been acquired near the hospital on one of which a new pathology building was erected in 1958; the others will be used for staff housing and a hall of residence. Apart from this all development must take place by making intensive use of the original restricted site. Progress is now being made with the construction of a new library, new premises for the students' union and other work. These developments are made possible by grants from the government of Hong Kong which announced in 1957 its willingness to aid the University with capital supplemented by grants from United Kingdom funds.

In spite of harassing difficulties the University has made great strides; it has re-established its pre-war faculties and has added a school of architecture and an institute of oriental studies. The Universities of Khartoum and Malta also make provision for architecture; in respect of facilities for engineering Hong Kong was a pioneer (1934). Oriental studies, which date from 1932, were organized in an institute in 1952 to which is attached a museum of Chinese art and archaeology; its object is to provide facilities for research in Chinese and Oriental studies for eastern and western scholars. The Chinese section of the main library has over 110,000 volumes; the rest of the main library has more than 100,000 volumes and includes a valuable collection bearing on the relations between China and the west during the Ch'ing dynasty and the early years of the republic. There are 1,405 students of whom a quarter are women; about 30 per cent of the students are in receipt of grants. Among the students there are a few Europeans, Singalese, Koreans and others; but most are Chinese chiefly from Hong Kong, the remaining Chinese coming from other Far Eastern countries. English is the normal medium for social intercourse and is used for teaching except for degrees in Chinese studies when Mandarin is employed. The University has three halls for men and one for women; there are also three attached halls conducted under religious auspices, and there are two non-residential halls for exempted students. Residence in a hall is compulsory unless exemption is granted; over 70 per cent of the students complete full residence, and more would do so if there were more accommodation. As can readily be understood the site of the University is not such as to provide good facilities for sport; but students play soccer, tennis and cricket; indeed Hong Kong seems to be the furthest outpost of cricket in the Far East.

Since 1946, when the committee reported in favour of continuing the University but only on conditions which have taken a long time to establish, the position of Hong Kong has undergone profound changes. Barriers in the way of promoting Anglo-Chinese understanding, which was to have been one of the functions of the University, have appeared; on the other hand the population has trebled and can absorb, it is estimated, well over 200 graduates a year. This increase is largely due to the inflow of Chinese whose acquaintance with English is often not sufficient for entrance to the University; pupils of the Chinese middle schools encounter the same obstacle. To meet their requirements seven non-governmental Chinese colleges have grown up whose full-time students number about 4,000. Standards in these colleges vary; but some of them aspire to university status, and the government is considering how this ambition can be satisfied. At the same time, in order to meet the needs of students with command of English, the government has agreed to an increase of the student population of the University to 1,800 by 1966–7.

The achievement of the University in re-establishing itself as a centre of free western learning and as a well-documented centre for the study of Far Eastern affairs is remarkable. But the past history and present position of Hong Kong are unlike those of other British colonies, and this renders it improbable that its future will be similar, that is to say as an independent state. One fact among others stands in the way of this consummation; when the lease of the New Territories expires, the colony of Hong Kong proper could hardly form a viable economic unit.

THE UNIVERSITY OF MALAYA

As in the case of Hong Kong no recent information about Malaya was available to the Asquith Commission because, at the time when they were sitting, the territory was in enemy occupation. When it was liberated in September 1945, it was found that, though the two colleges (Raffles College and the King Edward VII College of Medicine) had suffered heavy losses of equipment, furniture and books, the buildings were little damaged, and indeed that the Japanese, who used the accommodation for administrative purposes, had added a block to Raffles College, in the same architectural style as the rest of the buildings, which could be used for teaching. The staffs of the colleges had been dispersed, most of them interned or made prisoners of war; the students had been scattered. British military occupation followed Japanese occupation, and it was not until midway through 1946 that the college buildings were freed for their proper purposes. Then the returning staff set to work with remarkable energy, and in the autumn of that year teaching began again. Thus the question was not, as in the case of Hong Kong, whether teaching should be re-established, but how to carry out the decision, taken before the war on the recommendation of the McLean Commission, to unite the two colleges into a university college 'as a first step in the development of a University of Malaya'. This was the problem set before a Commission appointed in 1947. This Commission devised a scheme for uniting the colleges; it also reported that the colleges had reached standards which justified the omission of the stage of a university college and recommended that they should be incorporated forthwith into a university.[3] The Secretary of State accepted the recommendation and expressed the hope that the university would be established in 1948; in the event it came into existence in 1949.

Before the Commission was set up, the organization of Malaya had been so adjusted that the whole mainland with the island of Penang became the Malayan Union (now the Federation of Malaya) under one governor, while the island of Singapore came under another governor; a governor-general was appointed to co-ordinate the policies of the two territories whose combined area is about equal to that of England and Wales. The total population numbering about eight million includes three races, each of which is the inheritor of an ancient civilization, Malays, Chinese and Indians forming respectively 43·5 per cent, 44·5 per cent and 10 per cent of the total; but when the proportions in each territory are examined it is found that in the Federation (total population about 6·75 million) Malays contribute a little under 50 per cent, Chinese 37 per cent, and Indians 11 per cent to the total, whereas in Singapore (total population 1·5 million) the corresponding proportions are 14 per cent, 76 per cent, and 8 per cent. The two territories also differ markedly in other respects. The island of Singapore, in size and shape somewhat resembling the Isle of Wight, is the site of one of the world's great ports, the country lying outside the city being largely suburbanized, whereas the Federation is predominantly a land of forest-clad mountain and hill surrounded by an alluvial foreshore.

In 1947 when the Commission was sitting it was anticipated

that the two territories would draw together. It was with this in mind that the Commission considered the problem of a site for the University which was to serve all Malaya. The two colleges, which were to be fused and so form the University, were about three miles apart, each situated on the outskirts of the city. It was not possible to move one college to the site of the other; moreover, the area owned by Raffles College, about 90 acres in extent, was in part low-lying and swampy, and thus presented serious difficulties in the way of providing the many new buildings which the University would require. Apart from these facts which alone suggested that a new site would be an advantage, the Commission took the view that the University should not be in the island of Singapore which was untypical of Malaya as a whole, but that it should not be far from Singapore with its world-wide contacts and invigorating life. Therefore the Commission, after inspecting many possible sites, recommended the purchase for the University of some 1,500 acres of rolling land bounding an estuary near Johore Bahru, the capital of Johore, which is situated in the southernmost tip of the mainland and is connected by a causeway with the island. The Commission held that this site of great natural beauty, about twenty miles from Singapore, would give the University all the advantages of contact with Singapore and at the same time would associate it with typical Malayan life and scenery.

This recommendation was accepted, the proposed site was purchased and a plan drawn up for its layout. But all this took a long time, and in 1954 it was estimated that the move of the University to the new site could not begin in less than four years. Meanwhile the cost of transfer had increased and seemed likely to exceed the sum which could be found; moreover, the number of students had risen faster than foreseen by the Commission, reaching 1,000 in the session 1953–4 instead of taking ten years to do so as anticipated, and in order to accommodate them much money had been spent on additional buildings which would have had to be abandoned if the move were made. Added to all this the medical faculty was never in favour of the move. Therefore in 1954 the decision was taken to abandon the Johore site and to make the best of the two sites in Singapore; at the same time it was agreed to prepare for the provision of university teaching at Kuala Lumpur, the capital of the Federation.

It was on the Raffles College site that the main development had to take place. The original buildings of that College which enclose two quadrangles have a massive and pleasing dignity; they crown a hill and are approached by a curving road; the sight of their white walls surmounting steep grass lawns is impressive. The difficulties in the way of development on this site have been somewhat lessened by the acquisition of more land bringing the area up to about 120 acres and by a project to drain the swampy area. In addition nearly 50 acres have been promised for the future use of the University, and it is hoped to purchase a similar area nearby. A development plan has been approved and is now being carried out; already the main buildings have been remodelled, and a library and a science block have been added to them; two new halls of residence have been finished. Under the plan a new arts block and several other new buildings, including student residences, are being erected. On the site of the Medical School much has also been done; the main building has been remodelled and enlarged, a new institute of health and a new pathology block have been built, and the old prison-like hostel has been demolished and a new residence for students has taken its place.

When the Federation of Malaya became independent in 1957, steps were taken to carry out the plan, agreed in principle in 1954, to provide teaching for degrees in Kuala Lumpur. Great energy was displayed; a site of 450 acres in the Pantai Valley, about three miles south-west of Kuala Lumpur, was acquired. A layout was prepared, and by the middle of 1960 buildings for arts, science, engineering and agriculture had been completed together with two halls of residence for students. The site offers good opportunities for landscaping; an artificial lake has been made round which the buildings are grouped. Judging from the first buildings this university in the making promises to be among the more attractive in the Commonwealth, and that is some compensation for the loss of the site at Johore Bahru. Teaching for degrees in engineering began in 1958, in arts and science in 1959 and in agriculture in 1960. This rapid and vigorous development of a university centre some 200 miles from Singapore made necessary a complete revision of the constitution of the University. In 1958 it was divided into two branches, one in Singapore and one in Kuala Lumpur, each having a large measure of autonomy with its own principal, council and senate, and power to appoint its own staff. The University survives as a degree-giving and co-ordinating body; there is a common court and a common guild of graduates, but the students' unions are separate. But this is a transitory arrangement; it is expected that the Kuala Lumpur branch will attain university status in 1961. Both branches have faculties of arts and science; Singapore has medicine and law, while Kuala Lumpur has agriculture and engineering, the latter having been moved from Singapore. The total number of students in 1960 was 2,356—654 in Kuala Lumpur and 1,702 in Singapore. In spite of the difficulties and uncertainties created by the site problem the University as a whole has made remarkable progress. Since it came into being in 1949 three new faculties of engineering, law and agriculture have been added, and a large number of new departments have been created as will be described in Chapter 9. Between 1949 and 1958 the staff increased from 58 to 195, and the students from 645 to 1,615. Of the students in 1958, 63 per cent were Chinese, 11 per cent Malay, 14 per cent Indian, 7 per cent Ceylonese, 2 per cent Eurasian and 3 per cent of other races. The proportion of Malays in the student body is very much below the proportion which they form of the total population (44 per cent), the chief explanation of which is that Malays live in rural areas where teaching in schools, particularly through the medium of English, is less advanced than in the towns. About 70 per cent of the students live in halls; the University has handed over an existing building which provides adequate premises for the students' union. The students have always impressed visitors as a keen and lively body of young people, actively interested in questions of the day. The annual report of the University for 1958–9 refers to the 'students' expressions of independent and fearless views on a wide variety of topics in their publications'.[4] Interest in games and sports is keen; the excitement roused at a cricket match contrasts strongly with the gravity with which that game is watched in the land of its birth.

It is a matter for speculation whether, if the Johore Bahru

plan had been carried out, a single university would have satisfied both governments, at least until such time as growth in student numbers demanded a second foundation. This is doubtful. The Commission of 1947 cast the University of Malaya for the role of helping to foster a common Malayan nationality. But the two territories have grown apart, and it hardly seems likely that either territory would be content with a university at Johore Bahru; to Singapore it would look like a university in the Federation; to the Federation it would look like a university under the shadow of Singapore. It may be that Singapore will have a university whose culture is predominantly Chinese, especially if some link is formed with Nanyang University, an institution described in Appendix 6, and that Kuala Lumpur's university, especially since it recognizes the Muslim College at Klang (22 miles from Kuala Lumpur) as a centre where teaching for degrees can be given and has as an adjoining neighbour the National Language Institute, will be influenced by Malay culture and religion.

THE UNIVERSITY OF KHARTOUM

To the Asquith Commission it was clear that in the Sudan there was no problem about the site of a university institution. Khartoum, where Gordon College and the Kitchener School of Medicine were situated, was the obvious place. The huge country of which Khartoum is the capital, twice as large as the Federation of Rhodesia and Nyasaland, has a population of over ten million. Just under three-quarters of the population live in the six northern provinces, and with few exceptions are Mohammedan and Arabic-speaking though a large proportion use a local language at home. Among them is a small number of Arabic-speaking Greeks, Syrians and others from outside Africa, domiciled in the Sudan, and the presence of a few of their children in the University gives a multi-racial aspect to the student body. The remaining quarter live in the three southern provinces where there are few Mohammedans and where Arabic is little known.

The cities of Khartoum and Omdurman together have a population of some 230,000. About half live in Omdurman; most of the other half live in the old part of Khartoum, but there is a growing city of Khartoum North on the right bank of the Blue Nile. The old city of Khartoum is situated at the tip of the triangle formed by the confluence of the Blue and White Niles, and its European appearance contrasts with the Sudanese aspect of Omdurman which is reached by a bridge over the White Nile. The original building of Gordon College stands on the bank of the Blue Nile about three miles from its junction with the White Nile and about a mile and a half from the city centre; it was designed by a Greek architect, living in Egypt and employed by the Khedive, and is built of red brick in an odd but not unsuccessful blend of the styles of east and west. Close to it are buildings, formerly occupied by the government higher schools mentioned in Chapter 1, and when the work of these schools passed to the College, so did their buildings. Thus the College acquired a compact area of some forty acres; an area of about the same size immediately to the east, on which there were disused army barracks, came into its possession in 1955. The buildings of the Kitchener School of Medicine (now the faculty of medicine) are in the city about a mile away from the main site. The College has also acquired some 600 acres of farm land at Shambat about five miles distant on the opposite side of the Blue Nile. Thus the College inherited a number of buildings and a convenient site with opportunity for further development. Full advantage has been taken of these possibilities; many new buildings have been put up which form interesting and pleasant groups. In the students' residences, designed by the late Mr W. G. Newton, the University possesses buildings of outstanding quality, admirably adapted to their purpose in a hot climate, most impressive, massive in outline, with elegant doorways and long vaulted passages, achieving grandeur with delicacy of detail.

This sketch of the development of the site and buildings runs up to 1956 when the College became a university. In 1942 the College was a small affair, and in that year its building was taken over by the military; the secondary school, which it was housing, was transferred to Omdurman whence it never returned. When the building was recovered, the government set about to follow the advice of the De La Warr Commission and acted with speed and vigour. In 1945 the government higher schools were brought together to form a reconstituted Gordon

College which was removed from government control and given an independent constitution. There was thus an element of discontinuity in the history of the College; what happened was that the higher schools, retaining their own buildings, jointly took over the main building of the College and also its name. At once there was a university college in embryo; in course of time the higher schools became faculties, and it says much for the foresight of the government that there was no need to found new faculties since the higher schools already covered the chief professional subjects.

Though the foundation had been laid the College had only some 200 students, few of whom had been prepared to work for degrees. The task was to raise the institution to university level. There are two ways in which a new university institution can arise; one is to start from the beginning on a university level, the other is to raise an existing institution to that level. Both encounter difficulties but of different kinds; the next chapter shows what they are in the first case. In the second case they are that the institution has a staff not chosen to teach in a university institution, that buildings and their equipment, including library provision, though suitable for teaching at a lower level, are not fitted for a university; that the need to raise standards of entrance and work may not be understood, and that in consequence action to that end may be resented. The task in the Sudan was made easier than it might have been by the attitude of the Sudanese people and the government who, inspired by the ambition to build up an institution of full university rank, were prepared to support whatever action was necessary. When the British government made a gift of £1,000,000 to the Sudan to be used as seemed best to the Sudanese government, the whole sum was handed to the College to form an endowment fund.

In 1946 when there were 188 students admitted on the basis of a school certificate, the College applied for, and was admitted into, special relationship with the University of London. The College was then offering a diploma; it was arranged that there should be a one-year preliminary course at the end of which there should be a separation between degree and diploma candidates, and that on the results of the intermediate examination there should be a further separation, those doing less well being

PLATE 1 University of Hong Kong: Chemistry Building. Architect: R. Gordon Brown. Consulting architects: Easton and Robertson, Cusdin, Preston and Smith

University of Malaya: Singapore branch. Faculty of Science building. Architects: Easton and Robertson, Cusdin, Preston and Smith. Associated architects: Palmer and Turner, Singapore

PLATE 2 University of Malaya: Kuala Lumpur branch. Aerial view. Two halls of residence (*top left*). Architects: Palmer and Turner, Singapore. Faculty of engineering (*top right*). Architect: Public Works Department, Kuala Lumpur. Faculty of arts, library and administration (*end of lake*). Architects: Palmer and Turner, Singapore. Faculty of Science (*left foreground*). Architects: Palmer and Turner, Singapore. Consulting architects for the lay-out: Easton and Robertson, Cusdin, Preston and Smith

University of Khartoum: Hall of Residence. Architect: W. G. Newton

PLATE 3 Makerere College: Main building (*left*). Public Works Department, Uganda. School of Agriculture (*right*). Architects: Cobb, Powell and Freeman

Makerere College: Library. Architects: Norman and Dawbarn

PLATE 4 Royal College, Nairobi: Main front. Architects: Government architect of Kenya and Bernard Webb

Fourah Bay College: Wilson Theatre and Students' Union. Architect: Frank Rutter

University College, Ibadan: Library.
Architects: Fry, Drew and Partners

PLATE 6 University College of Ghana.
Aerial view. Architects: Harrison,
Barnes and Hubbard

University College of Ghana: Balme
Library. Architects: Harrison, Barnes
and Hubbard

PLATE 7 University College of Rhodesia and Nyasaland: Kapnek Wing, Biological Sciences. Architects: Ayers, Wilson and Partners

University College of Rhodesia and Nyasaland: Library. Architects: Pallett, Price and Partners

PLATE 8 University College of the West Indies. Aerial view. Architects: Norman and Dawbarn

University College of the West Indies: Senate House (academic procession at the visit of HM The Queen). Architects: Norman and Dawburn

restricted to the diploma as their goal. Entrance standards have been progressively raised, and the minimum entrance qualification is now a school certificate with five credits. The diploma gradually disappeared; all students admitted since 1955 have studied for degrees and no diplomas have been awarded since 1958. To begin with the only degrees offered were general degrees in arts and science; in the last year of the special relationship degrees were offered in law, engineering and agriculture as well as in arts and science; in addition to these degrees the University of Khartoum now offers degrees in medicine, architecture, veterinary science, economics, social studies, and social anthropology. While there was from the beginning, as already noted, a wide coverage of the academic field, there was need to set up specialized departments; this need has been met and there are now forty departments, including anthropology, architecture, geology, philosophy, economics and arabic, grouped under eight faculties. In 1951 the Kitchener School of Medicine was fused with the College, becoming the faculty of medicine; at the same time the College acquired a new constitution and the title of the University College of Khartoum. In 1956, a few months after the establishment of the Republic of the Sudan, the University College became the University of Khartoum.

In 1946 there were 20 members of the teaching staff; in 1959–60 there were 158, of whom 54 were Sudanese, 56 British, 29 Egyptians and 19 others; the last category included representatives from over a dozen different countries. There were in the same year 1,216 students of whom only 40 came from the three southern provinces; the total included 17 non-Sudanese students and 52 women. In view of the still strong tradition of female seclusion even this number of women students points to changes in outlook. Hitherto all students have lived in university residences, but with the rapid increase in their number—it is expected that it will soon reach 2,000—it is inevitable that some will have to live at home or in lodgings. Teaching is in English, and there is no disposition to substitute Arabic for English as the medium of instruction; Arabic, however, is the medium for social intercourse between students. Thus while all students learn in a foreign language, the southern students must employ a second foreign language in out-of-teaching hours. The majority of students are very conscious that they have a share in the Arabic heritage, and they form a more compact body than is usually found in the other institutions with which this book deals. In consequence of this, and having regard to the dramatic events which their country has witnessed in recent years and to the habits of students in neighbouring Arab states, it is not surprising that they should on occasion have indulged in strikes and other political manifestations; but since independence these troubles have been less vigorous.

A number of facts stand out in the history of Gordon College, now the University of Khartoum. It was the first college among those entering into special relation with London University to achieve university status, and it was not eligible for grants under the Colonial Development and Welfare Acts. It has depended upon the Sudanese government for support; and from that government it has, at all periods in its history, received not only generous financial aid but also sympathetic understanding of its aims and objects; this is in contrast to the position of colleges in most British colonial territories when, even if financial support was adequate, the attitude of British officials and residents was often patronizing. The College has always worn the aspect of a national institution in which the hopes and trust of the Sudanese were placed; indeed most of the leaders of the country, with the exception of its present military rulers, have been educated there, and this was of great importance for the College since they understood it and believed in it. In other territories, from which many students went overseas for education, the difficulties of the colleges in their early days were increased because the returning graduates found it hard to believe that the new foundations could offer education of a standard comparable with that in established centres. Along with good relations between the College and the government, there has been remarkable harmony between the council and the senate, all the more striking because of the international composition of the teaching staff; as is proper now that more Sudanese graduates are available, Sudanese are coming to preponderate among the staff, but the staff still includes representatives of many countries—an outstanding example of successful academic co-operation.

NOTES

1. *Report of the Hong Kong University Advisory Committee*, 1946, p. 4.
2. *A Report on the University of Hong Kong*, 1953 (by Sir Ivor Jennings and Sir Douglas Logan).
3. *Report of the Commission on University Education in Malaya*, 1948.
4. *Tenth Annual Report of the University of Malaya*, 1958–9, p. 10.

CHAPTER 5

THE COLLEGES

The Asquith Commission had no hesitation in recommending that Makerere College at Kampala in Uganda should be developed as a university institution for East Africa, thus endorsing the opinion of the De La Warr Commission. If there had been no college with such promise anywhere in East Africa, there might have been some discussion of the claims of a number of towns to be the site of a future university; but even then the choice might well have fallen upon Kampala, the largest town in Buganda. Kampala is about twenty miles from Entebbe which lies on the northern shore of Lake Victoria and is the seat of the Uganda government; situated more than 4,000 ft. above sea level it is ringed by hills, all about equal in height, on one of which are the main buildings of the College; the hospital and medical school are situated on a neighbouring hill. Makerere Hill has steep sides and a long, narrow, level top running in a north-south direction with fine views to the east and west. The De La Warr Commission, which foresaw a great future for the College, expressed concern in 1937 about the site and suggested that the College might be moved to a 'larger site further from the centre of the town'.[1] The move was not made and was apparently never seriously contemplated. At that time the College owned some 200 acres on the southern side of the hill; the northern half was in the possession of numerous freeholders from whom the College tried to buy their plots one by one. The owners were unwilling to sell, and the government was unwilling to exercise its power of compulsory purchase; in the event only 30 more acres were bought on that side, but 45 acres to the east were acquired

68

bringing the total area of the main site to about 275 acres. The College also owns 40 acres on Mulago Hill, where the medical school is situated, separated only by a public road from the main site. The College has in addition bought some 300 acres for a farm at Kabanyolo, about eleven miles away, and owns 53 acres at Kabete near Nairobi where clinical teaching in veterinary science is carried on.

The planning of the main site, much of which slopes steeply, presents an awkward problem. On it must be found room for the buildings required for most teaching purposes and for housing students, as well as for playing fields. Originally also houses for the staff were placed on the site, but the College has acquired three plots of land outside the college precinct where further staff houses have been built. A two-mile journey uphill from the centre of Kampala brings a visitor, by way of a winding drive, to a straight level road stretching along the top of the hill. After passing the new arts block he reaches the original college building, behind which are the Anglican and Catholic chapels; this building is crowned by a tower which dominates the scene. Farther along the library comes into view and then the science blocks; these buildings, of which the library (architects Messrs Norman and Dawbarn) possesses real distinction, are in contrasting styles (they are the work of a number of different architects), but form a reasonably harmonious group. On either side of the ridge are staff houses and student residences at successive levels; if the whole hill had been acquired at the outset, it would have been possible to plan a more spacious lay-out and to avoid the overlooking of one building by another. But the general impression is very pleasing owing largely to the skilled attention given to the planting of trees and shrubs and to the making of lawns. Indeed a walk along the top road is an exhilarating experience.

The College was fortunate in that it was not occupied by the military during the war; it was thus able to continue its work and to develop along the lines suggested by the De La Warr Commission. In 1946 when an IUC delegation visited the College, the position was that candidates for admission sat for the college entrance examination; those who passed followed a two-year course in higher studies leading to a certificate, and could then be admitted to one of the four professional schools of medicine, agriculture, veterinary science and education. An interesting and valuable feature was the provision for the teaching of art and sculpture; this tradition has been carried on, and there is now a school of fine art with a record of which any institution could be proud. As in the case of Gordon College, so in the case of Makerere College the task was that of building up a university institution, and there was the further similarity in that the latter like the former had made provision for professional education. But equipment was less good than at Gordon College; the staff was small, twenty-two in 1946, including only one teacher for each of the following subjects: biology, chemistry, physics, geography and education. Also the College was hampered by the backwardness of secondary education in the territories. It was, however, full of promise; it had set out to create a collegiate atmosphere and had obviously succeeded. Nevertheless the College had a long way to go, and the IUC delegation reported that some time must elapse before it could offer degree courses.

The IUC delegation of 1946 strongly advised that the College should receive a constitution making it an autonomous body, but the governments held back and it was not until 1949 that it was given independence; its full title then became Makerere College, the University College of East Africa. This action, coupled with the raising of entrance standards to a school certificate with three credits, made it possible for the University of London to take the College into special relation in the same year. The higher studies course was transformed into a course for the intermediate examination, and post-intermediate courses in arts and science were added. Work began for general degrees in arts and science, and in 1953 the first London degrees were gained.

By 1954 student numbers had grown to 448, and there were 91 members of the staff. But the College was still hampered by the state of secondary education, and in 1954 out of 142 entrants there were 36 who, though reaching the minimum requirement of a school certificate with three credits, lacked a credit in English language. Nevertheless an IUC delegation of that year thought that plans should be made to introduce honours courses. From that time forward the College has made immense strides; entrance requirements were raised to a minimum of five credits in 1958, and the minimum requirement is now a higher school certificate. There are six faculties, an extra-mural department and a school of fine art; the College offers degree courses with honours in English, geography, history, economics and mathematics; the diploma in medicine was recognized by the General Medical Council in 1956. A transformation indeed as compared with 1946; the College is now a university in all but name.

The College was the only institution of university rank serving the three territories of Uganda, Kenya and Tanganyika and the island of Zanzibar, until 1960 when the Royal Technical College became Royal College, Nairobi. The mainland area is larger than that of the Federation of Rhodesia and Nyasaland but smaller than that of the Sudan, and has a population of over 22 million. Africans number 21·5 million, Asians about 330,000, Europeans under 100,000 and Arabs over 60,000. Africans account for over 95 per cent of the population of each territory; Europeans and Indians are relatively more numerous in Kenya than in the other two territories; over two-thirds of the former and over half of the latter are in Kenya. Among the Africans there is much tribal subdivision and diversity of language. There are said to be over 120 peoples in Tanganyika alone, and in 1956 over 60 peoples were represented among the students of the College. The Asians are also divided, the Ismaili sect forming a distinct and important group. Swaheli is used to some extent as a *lingua franca*; it is now less taught in the schools than at one time, but its use is nevertheless said to be spreading, and indeed into the neighbouring areas of the Congo and Nyasaland. But English is the only possible medium for teaching and is used in social intercourse between students though on occasions a small group of them may use their own vernacular. In 1958 33 per cent of the students came from Uganda, 38 per cent from Kenya, 26 per cent from Tanganyika and 3 per cent from Zanzibar and elsewhere. As to racial composition there were 797 Africans, 69 Asians, 9 Europeans and 6 Arabs in 1959. There are few towns in East Africa and those which exist are dominated by non-Africans; the home background of the African students is therefore rural, and usually primitive. The College was founded for Africans, but when its aim was acknowledged to be that of transformation into a university, it became properly

71

anxious that its door should be open to all irrespective of race. In theory it was so, but in fact it was not; the governments refused to make grants to non-Africans who, on the insistence of the governments, were required to pay the 'real cost' of their education (calculated by dividing total costs by the number of students) which in the case of medical students worked out at between £1,500 and £2,000 a year. The governments may have thought that they were safeguarding the interests of the Africans, but they were not acting in accordance with the wishes of the African students as the IUC delegation of 1946 found out, and they effectively prevented the College from becoming multi-racial until 1953 when non-Africans were given equal treatment with Africans in the matter of grants.

During the years since 1945 the governments of the territories have provided the College with an income sufficient to make possible the remarkable transformation from a small post-secondary institution to a university in all but name. Nevertheless it is regrettable that, though the coverage by faculties is wide, the College has not had the resources to increase the number of subjects offered; thus it has not been able to fulfil its reasonable ambition to provide teaching in any language, classical or modern, in philosophy, public administration and other subjects. It cannot be said that the governments have always readily exhibited an understanding of what is implied in the conception of a university institution, of the importance of a university centre for East Africa, or of the tradition of free discussion; as to the last matter, while they have refrained from overt action, they have exhibited on occasion an absurd degree of nervousness if not of panic. In other connections the position of the College has been difficult; unlike the situation in the Sudan, the College has not been, and could not have been, the focal point of nation building; wherever the political ambitions of the Africans lie, it is not in the construction of a unitary East African state. Moreover, the attitude of the Europeans has been, to say the least of it, lacking in sympathy; very few of them have troubled to find out anything about the College. The De La Warr Commission of 1936 said that the College 'had been the object of a certain amount of criticism from different sources'.[2] All delegations of the IUC have heard criticisms, mostly from

Kenya; that of 1949 was told that the College 'was a centre of African degeneration'. This accusation was not made by backwoodsmen, but by responsible and highly placed persons in Kenya. On that occasion definite statements were made about the conduct of certain Africans connected with the College; these statements were investigated by the delegation and were found to have no basis in fact. The delegation of 1954 heard similar accusations and reported that to the best of their knowledge the accusations were unfounded, adding that no college in Africa or elsewhere could be without a few undisciplined or degenerate students. The same delegation reported that they had attended a meeting of the Students' Guild Committee 'which was conducted in a most businesslike manner and at which the choice of subjects made by the Committee showed an intelligent concern for the sound development of the College'. 'We formed', they went on to say, 'a high opinion of the sense of responsibility, maturity, dignity and courtesy of the students'. Evidently some highly placed Europeans in East Africa, most of them in Kenya where these accusations usually originate, have something to learn from the African students of the College.

ROYAL COLLEGE, NAIROBI

In 1954 the Royal Technical College, Nairobi, was founded by an Act of the East African High Commission as an interterritorial college to serve all the East African territories. Its objects, as set out in the Act, were to provide facilities for higher technological professional and vocational training and research; no mention was made of degrees. The College came within the purview of the COCAST and has received £825,000 on its recommendation from CD and W funds. In the first year of its existence the College entered into an agreement with the Gandhi Memorial Academy Society under which the Gandhi Memorial Academy, founded by the Society, was incorporated in the College; the College accepted a large sum of money from the Society and undertook to provide courses in 'arts, science and commerce'. In 1955 a working party visited East Africa on the invitation of the East African High Commission to report on the development of higher education in the whole region. On its arrival in Nairobi the party learnt to their great surprise that the College had announced its intention of preparing students for the unmodified external London degree in economics. The party took the view that the College was running off the rails and recommended that it should confine itself to its objects as set out in the Act; at the same time, recognizing the need for a university college in Kenya, they recommended that such a college should be founded at a new site near Nairobi, adding that, in view of the urgency of the matter, the staff and students of the new college might be accommodated in the Royal Technical College while premises for the new college were under construction.

To the report of the working party published in 1956, the East Africa governments attached a foreword which, with reference to 'the accepted obligation' to the Gandhi Memorial Academy Society to provide courses in 'arts, science and commerce', said that it had been agreed 'that the obligation to the Society would be fully met if degree courses are provided as soon as practicable in Nairobi though not necessarily in the Royal Technical College'.[3] It would appear that this did not satisfy the Society which interpreted the undertaking as a promise that courses leading to degrees would be provided in the College, and the East African governments, having come to the conclusion that the undertaking to the Society, as interpreted by it, must be carried out, invited a second working party to visit East Africa in 1958 and to advise how best this could be done. This meant in effect to ask the working party to devise a plan for converting the College into a university college. This is an extraordinary story. When the College accepted a sum of money and gave an undertaking which bound it to exceed its functions as set out in the instrument which created it, it acted in a manner which cannot be defended. But it is understood that the East African governments urged the College to accept the money on these terms, and if this is so the blame must rest on them. Owing to this bungling entanglement with a body representing only a tiny fraction of the population (over 95 per cent are Africans and only 3 per cent are Indians and not all of the latter are Hindus) Kenya will have as its university college a converted technical college and not an institution designed for its purpose.

In 1960 the Royal Technical College became a university college with the title of Royal College, Nairobi. It is situated within the city of Nairobi, and its property consists of three portions divided from one another by main roads. The central portion is rather more than twenty acres in size and is irregular in shape; the western portion is reserved for residences, and to the east is a plot on which were workshops. The second working party were so impressed by the inadequacy of the site that they recommended the reservation of some 400 acres in the Karura forest region for additional buildings. The recommendation has been carried out, but it would be most unfortunate if the College were to be divided into two parts so far distant from one another. This may not be necessary; some more land adjacent to it has been acquired. Energetic steps have been taken to carry out the plan drawn up by the second working party, and already a fine engineering block has been built on the site formerly occupied by workshops. The transformation of the College into a university college has brought it within the purview of the IUC, and a further grant of £525,000 from CD and W funds has been made, bringing the total to £1,350,000. Thus a new start has been made, and the plan to be followed will ensure that the site will be used to the best advantage. But the College will not have the spaciousness which it was the intention to secure for all the university colleges, and for this the bungling of the East African authorities is to blame.

UNIVERSITY COLLEGE, IBADAN

The Asquith Commission made no proposal concerning the number and siting of university institutions in West Africa because, as already explained, the Elliot Commission was also at work; it was for the latter to recommend how to implement in West Africa the general principles outlined by the former Commission. The Elliot Commission presented two reports. The majority recommended that university colleges should be established at Ibadan for Nigeria, at Achimota for Ghana, and at a site in the Freetown peninsula for Sierra Leone and the Gambia to which Fourah Bay College would be moved; the last college would take students no further than the intermediate in science while offering an arts degree course for theology students. They added that there should be one medical school and one institute of education for all West Africa, the former to be at Ibadan and the latter at Achimota. The minority report recommended a single institution of university rank, to be called the West African University College and to be situated at Ibadan, which would serve all four territories, one reason being that they did not anticipate that there would be for some time enough qualified candidates to justify more than one college. They added the recommendation that there should be three territorial colleges; Achimota College would become one, Fourah Bay would become a second, while a new college of this kind would be set up east of the Niger. These colleges would provide courses up to intermediate level in arts and science. This last recommendation led to developments which were described in the third chapter.

In July 1946 the Secretary of State issued a despatch expressing preference for the plan set out by the minority. This provoked a strong reaction in Ghana where the Governor set up a committee whose report recalled Sir Gordon Guggisberg's plans and contained the following passage: 'There is an impelling sense of urgency and a demand that political progress shall be swift and that the extension of education, which must accompany sound political advance, shall be limited only by the ability of the country to finance it and the capacity of the young people to assimilate it. The country is determined to take full and immediate advantage of its present great economic, educational and political opportunities. In particular, the people consider it essential to provide themselves with a centre of higher education and learning for the training of their future leaders. They realize how much the possession of a University College, integrated with its way of life, will mean to a young country determined to build its own future on secure political foundations'. The report went on to indicate that the territory could find the necessary funds, both capital and recurrent, for a college which should 'evolve from Achimota' and in due course be removed to Legon Hill, an elevated ridge of land about two miles away.[4]

In December 1946 a delegation from the IUC led by Sir William Hamilton Fyfe visited West Africa and became convinced that Ghana would be right to set up its own college. In the spring of 1947 a letter was received in Ghana from the Secretary of State saying that, though he still preferred the minority plan, 'in view of the strong public demand in the Gold Coast for the establishment of a university college there and of the evident willingness and capacity of the people of the Gold Coast to provide the necessary financial support', he would agree in principle to the setting up of a college. Thus with the backing of the Fyfe delegation Ghana got its college.

The Elliot Commission, when recommending Ibadan as the site for the college, assumed that work there would not begin until permanent buildings were ready. But the Fyfe delegation were impressed by the urgent need to make a start at once; they visited Ibadan and, after pushing their way through the bush, Sir William planted his stick on a spot about five miles north of the city saying: 'Here shall be the University of Nigeria'. Four miles away were the abandoned buildings of a war-time military hospital which the delegation recommended as suitable for the temporary quarters of the college. It is not clear why Ibadan was recommended by the Elliot Commission as the site for the venture; to the Fyfe delegation the site made appeal because in their view an African university should be in an African environment behind which idea there seems to be some confusion of thought; for the growing points of Africa and what is most typical of modern Africa are to be found in those centres which have come under strongest outside influence. In any case no other possible sites were examined; Lagos was one obvious alternative, and if it could have been foreseen that it would become the capital of the Federation and that the College would become a federal institution, the claims of Lagos would have been strengthened.

Apart from this consideration Ibadan is a good site for a university. It is the largest city in tropical Africa with a population of about three-quarters of a million, ninety miles north of Lagos, and lies near the division between the forest and savannah areas; the climate is less humid than that of Lagos. The College set out to serve the whole of Nigeria which has a population of some thirty-five million, more than four times larger than that of the Federation of Rhodesia and Nyasaland, and an area which is about three-quarters of that of the Federation. Of the cultural groups the most important are the Hausas in the north, the Yorubas in the west and the Ibos in the east. The complexity of the linguistic pattern is said to be unequalled elsewhere in Africa; there is diversity of religion, nearly half of the population being Moslem.

The difficulties to be faced in the creation of a new university institution are quite unlike those met with when transforming a post-secondary college into a university college. The obvious procedure is to secure a site, to appoint a principal and the nucleus of a staff, and with their advice to erect and equip the buildings, and only when all is ready to open the doors. But in Nigeria there was urgency, and the Fyfe delegation proposed that the College should begin to teach as soon as might be possible in the buildings of the abandoned hospital which were four miles away from the ultimate site selected by the delegation. A principal was appointed in 1947, and he has published a most lively and readable account of the situation which faced him and how he coped with the problems.[5] When he arrived neither the permanent site nor the temporary buildings had been secured; he had no staff and only vague promises of money. The temporary buildings proved to be nearly derelict, and grass had grown up to roof level. They were acquired and reconditioned, and as the result of a great display of energy by the principal, the College opened in January 1948 with 104 students, many of whom came from Yaba Higher College and lacked the qualification to read for a degree. Until the College was incorporated in September 1948 the staff were government servants; it was given the title of University College, Ibadan, in compliance with African wishes, and not that of the University College of Nigeria which might have been more appropriate. In the same year the College entered into special relation with the University of London, and it became possible to design special syllabuses; meanwhile those students who had the necessary qualifications, worked for the unmodified London syllabuses. There proved to be no dearth of applicants for admission who had reached what was then the London entrance standard; the pessimistic forecast of the minority of the Elliot Commission had turned out to be ill-founded. The College concentrated its teaching at the outset on general courses in arts and science, but from the start it intended to have a medical school and among the first posts to be filled were chairs in that faculty; the story of the teaching hospital and medical school will be told in a later chapter. In 1950 the department of agriculture admitted its first students, and in 1958 the engineering department of the Nigerian College of Arts, Science and Technology, situated at Zaria in the Northern Region, was recognized as the faculty of engineering, an arrangement which while avoiding the duplication of engineering laboratories, was inconvenient since Zaria is 400 miles from Ibadan. There are now faculties of arts, science, medicine, engineering, and agriculture and veterinary science. In 1960 student numbers reached a total of 1,252 (1,173 men and 79 women), of whom only a small percentage came from the Northern Region, which contains over half the population of Nigeria but has relatively little provision for secondary education. Applications from qualified candidates to enter the College have always exceeded vacancies; of late years the excess of qualified candidates over vacancies has become embarrassing. The normal minimum entrance is the full London requirement, but the College has been willing to accept a few candidates with a lower qualification who come from areas where secondary education is little developed; this concessional entry will come to an end in 1962. The obstacle in the way of accepting more students is lack of residential accommodation; a proposal that students might live in lodgings in Ibadan has been examined but not approved since suitable quarters are not available. In the session 1959–60 120 students were living in the old huts four miles away where teaching began. To make its limited funds go as far as possible the College is now building a new type of residence with four wings for 600 first-year students who will live two in a room; each wing will serve as a feeder to a hall of residence which the students will enter in their second year.

While the College was getting going in its temporary quarters, negotiations were opened with the aim of acquiring the site designated by the Fyfe delegation for the permanent buildings; the aim was to acquire 3,230 acres; 1,600 acres were obtained in 1948, and in 1952 this was increased to a total of 2,850 acres or about four square miles (300 acres of which are now leased to the Nigerian Technical College). It was necessary to compensate the owners of the land and move them elsewhere, and all this took time. The firm of Fry, Drew and Partners were appointed architects. Difficulties arose over the lay-out; it was originally planned to make it more spacious, but the cost of the necessary roads and site works proved too expensive. To a visitor the present lay-out seems somewhat congested for a college with so much property. An avenue leads to the College at the end of which is Trenchard Hall; immediately behind and around are the halls of residence and the administration block dominated by a slender tower. Farther back on the right are the arts building and the library and, separated by a large open space, are the temporary science buildings on the left. When the latter are replaced by permanent buildings, the focus of the College will shift away from the group of buildings near the entrance and the whole complex will have a more spacious appearance. All these buildings are in the modern idiom, and those who accept it find that they form a group of very real distinction; indeed the usual verdict that they form the most attractive assembly of buildings which houses any of the new institutions. As a visitor passes along he is delighted by the changing vistas which catch his eye, by the quadrangles, lawns and gardens which knit the buildings together and by the achievement of harmony with variety—variety of colour and stylistic detail.

There are two chapels lying a little apart from the main group of buildings, one Anglican and one Catholic, erected mostly at the expense of the denominations but with contributions from the College. The staff houses are away to one side; they are very pleasant buildings, surrounded by trees and shrubs. The College also provides accommodation for its large staff of servants. The teaching and administrative staffs, the students and the servants, with their wives and children, probably number well over 10,000 all living on college property.

The College has throughout received generous and understanding support from the government and from officials, Nigerian and British alike. No one has suggested that it is a centre of 'degeneracy' as in East Africa; indeed it has attracted the loyalty and has embodied the aspirations of the people.

Apart from one incident in 1957 the relations between the authorities and the students have been harmonious. On that occasion a deliberate refusal by the students to obey instructions led to the closing of the College; when it was reopened, all students who applied for readmission were accepted. There is reason to believe that the incident, which has left no aftermath, was provoked from without the College.

THE UNIVERSITY COLLEGE OF GHANA

The circumstances under which the way was opened for Ghana to obtain the college for which there was so much local enthusiasm have already been described. Local opinion favoured Legon Hill, about six miles north of Accra, as the site; the Fyfe delegation were inclined towards Kumasi on the ground that the surroundings were more typical of Ghana by which they meant that Kumasi is less westernized—an argument which might seem to others to tell in the opposite direction. The region round Accra is indeed untypical of the rest of Ghana in respect of rainfall; it lies in a small sergment of the West African coast which has a low rainfall (under 30 inches) and in consequence bears an arid appearance at certain seasons of the year. This makes the climate less oppressive than elsewhere in the coastal belt. The population of Ghana is over five million; it is said that more than 100 peoples can be distinguished. There is great diversity of language; about a million speak one or other of the Akan group of languages; in the Accra region Ga is the chief speech; east of the Volta the languages used belong to the Ewe family while others are spoken especially in the north.

Local opinion won the day, and Legon Hill was chosen as the permanent site for the College. The first principal was appointed early in 1948; the difficulties to be overcome in order to set teaching going were far less formidable than at Ibadan. About two miles south-west of Legon Hill is Achimota College with its excellent buildings which had been occupied by the military during the war; the University College took over those of the buildings which had been used for post-secondary work together with some temporary structures put up by the military, and a little later also the quarters used by the teacher training depart-

F

ment when the latter was transferred elsewhere. Thus the University College came into possession of good accommodation from the start and, as needs dictated, erected additional temporary buildings while the work was in progress on the permanent site. It was taken into special relation by the University of London in 1949; ninety students, who had been in the postsecondary department of Achimota College, formed the nucleus of the student body, all of whom had the requirements necessary to work for a degree. The student body grew in size until 1954 when there was a pause because the College raised its entrance requirements to the full London standard; later the rise continued and there are now over 600 students.

With trifling exceptions the whole work of the College is now carried on in the new buildings on Legon Hill. The attention of a visitor approaching Accra by air is caught by a ridge rising out of the plain, sloping upwards gently at first and then more abruptly to a height of over 450 feet above sea level. This is Legon Hill which falls away abruptly to the north. The hill and a surrounding area, covering five square miles, was presented by the government to the College; the low-lying area to the west was designated for staff housing and the ridge for the college buildings. This striking site, which exposes the buildings to a welcome inshore breeze, has drawbacks: it imposes a longitudinal layout while erosion of the ridge makes difficult the establishment of shrubs and lawns. The architects are the firm of Harrison, Barnes and Hubbard, who designed Nuffield College; the first building to be completed was a hall of residence in 1953. An entrance gate admits to an avenue flanked by buildings; at the point where the ridge begins to rise more steeply there is another avenue at right angles. Further on a hall of residence has been built transversely to the main avenue; still higher up are the administration buildings and an assembly hall, while on the top of the hill is a tower, named Independence Tower. The distance from the entrance to the tower is a mile and a quarter, and though at such a site distances must be long, they have been made longer than necessary by keeping the buildings low and leaving very ample open spaces. Of the institutions described in this book this College alone has not been hampered in its building programme by shortage of funds;

through the generosity of the Ghanaian government eight million pounds have been made available for building and equipment to date. The style is conventional and uniform throughout; the white walls and red roofs give an impression of brightness and freshness. But the general effect is somewhat monotonous, that of a multiplication of similar units. The buildings do not form impressive groupings and the tower, not in itself remarkable, is too far away to dominate or to draw the assemblage of buildings together.

The College began with faculties of arts and science, and to them have been added faculties of agriculture and social studies, institutes of education and of extra-mural studies, and departments of law, theology and education. There is a research department of engineering, and a medical school is projected. In the faculty of social studies there is a department of archaeology, an interesting innovation not so far copied in any other of the institutions. The College has three agricultural research stations, one of 1,600 acres and an irrigation station of 900 acres, both on the Accra plain, and a forest region station of 2,000 acres seventy miles away. The generosity of the Ghanaian government has extended to recurrent finance, and the ratio of staff to students is higher than elsewhere. The College received a constitution by local legislation in 1948 which gave the council large powers to design the subsidiary constitutional organs. These powers were used to set up a system of government modelled on that of the University of Cambridge; it was very elaborate and departed widely from the form of internal government prevailing elsewhere. This unusual mode of government, coupled with the extensive introduction of ceremonies copied from the practices of colleges in the older British universities, gave the impression that the College was a somewhat exotic institution withdrawn from, if not opposed to, normal Ghanaian life. This impression was unhelpful to the College; but certain of its activities, notably the extra-mural work, have brought it as closely into touch with the people of the country and their needs as has been the case in any of the other colleges.

The government takes great interest in the College; it regards it as an institution of the first importance upon which the future of the country must in considerable measure depend.

Ghana became independent in 1957, but the government has shown no undue haste in wishing to raise it to the rank of a university; the students still work for London degrees. It seems that it will become a university shortly, and that at the same time it will receive a new constitution which will probably take a form which is more normal than that of the present constitution. This is not likely to be unacceptable to the College. But the unusual constitutional features extend beyond the government of the College as a whole to the position occupied by the halls of residence. Just as the government is modelled on that of the University of Cambridge, so the halls are modelled on colleges of that University each having a measure of autonomy. All members of the teaching staff are members of a hall and possess dining rights; some rooms are reserved for tutorial purposes. Each of the men's halls, built so far, has its chapel (though future halls are planned without chapels). These arrangements for worship leave no provision for Muslims and Catholics; of the former there were only five in 1959, and for the latter, who are more numerous, a separate chapel is projected. A new form of government for the College as a whole could leave the position of the halls unchanged. That is what, it seems, the College would wish. The system has advantages; it incorporates all members of the staff and has a beneficial influence on tuition. The disadvantage is the consequential fragmentation; as at the older English universities the students as a body have no influential organ to represent them. Nevertheless this unusual feature of the College might well be retained as an interesting variant from the familiar pattern. The most notable facts about the College are that, four years after independence, it is not regarded as a relic of colonialism, that high standards are appreciated as is evident from the continuance of London degrees and that its importance as a national institution has been steadily enhanced in the eyes of the government and the people.

FOURAY BAY COLLEGE,
THE UNIVERSITY COLLEGE OF SIERRA LEONE

An outline of the long history of Fourah Bay College up to 1945 was given in the first chapter. In that year the majority report of the Elliot Commission recommended that the College should become a university college in embryo, while the minority report recommended that it should continue as a purely missionary enterprise and that an independent college of arts, science and technology should be set up. As in the case of Ghana the Secretary of State favoured the minority recommendation, and again met with strong local opposition. In 1950 a compromise solution was found under which the College became a composite body including a university department, strictly limited in its range of studies, and a section providing teaching in the subjects falling within the purview of the COCAST; in respect of this section the College became eligible for grants from CD and W funds. In 1954 on the recommendation of a commission, the limitations on the work of the university department were removed, and arrangements were made to offer degree courses in science. Another commission appointed in 1958 found that the university department had grown in importance and had come to dominate the College; the commission approved this development and recommended that the College should become a university college, thus passing from the purview of the COCAST to that of the IUC. This recommendation was accepted, and the College became the University College of Sierra Leone by virtue of a royal charter in 1960.

After 1876, when affiliation with the University of Durham enabled students of the College to work for Durham degrees, the College became the focus of the ambitions of West Africans who wanted university education, and this missionary foundation, subsisting on a minute income, attracted enterprising West Africans decade after decade who manifested warm loyalty to it. When it became possible after 1945 to foster these ambitions and to assist the College financially, is so happened that the Secretary of State had been a member of the Elliot Commission and had signed the minority report. He was a sincere advocate of the Asquith plan in general and took more personal interest in its advancement than any other holder of that office, but he held the view of the minority of the Commission, a mistaken view as it turned out, that a single university college would suffice for British West Africa, at least for the time being. In respect of Ghana, as already related, he gave way to local opposition, and permitted the foundation of a university college, but only on condition that Ghana found the finance. Sierra Leone could not provide the money for the college which it wanted, and the arrangement described above was made. But this did not turn out badly in the long run; to the technical education section of the College a grant was made from C D and W funds; this grant was used to build science laboratories which the authorities of the College, who throughout did what they could to meet local aspirations, were eventually able to employ in connection with degree courses in science.

It is now appropriate to turn to events on the ground. After unhappy experiences during the war the College found accommodation in temporary war-time buildings on Mount Aureol overlooking Freetown, with a population of 80,000, which has a lovely situation on the foreshore whence promontories extend into the sea; behind rise steep hills up to a height of 3,000 ft. Mount Aureol is the name given to the level end of a very sharp ridge projecting some 900 ft. above Freetown; to this property were added two higher areas on the ridge which are reached by a steep and winding road. The topmost of these areas is the most extensive, some 1,200 ft. above sea level, and it was at first proposed to erect the academic buildings on it; but available funds were insufficient for the purpose and the plan was abandoned with regret. The academic buildings are being erected on Mount Aureol, and staff houses on the next area, while part of the top area will be used for playing fields, the rest remaining available for an extension of the College at some future date. The whole site has the advantages of beautiful views and is exposed to welcome breezes, but access is by a laborious climb. It is unfortunate that the plan to build on the top area could not be carried out because it is large enough to make possible a satisfactory layout. That is not the case with Mount Aureol, the level edge of which is short and narrow; it is necessary to place many buildings on terraces below the ridge on ground so steep that the roads running up to the ridge have an inclination of about one in four. The College shares with the University of Hong Kong the difficulties of an awkward and restricted site.

The College serves the territory of Sierra Leone with some

two and a half million inhabitants, and has long attracted students from other territories, especially from Nigeria whence came nearly half of the 330 students in the session 1959–60. The creoles, descended from Africans returning from the New World, have occupied a commanding social and economic position in the population and contribute most of the local students. There is the diversity of tribal groupings and languages always found in Africa; creole patois is used fairly widely, but English seems likely to remain the medium for higher education. The hinterland is little developed and secondary education has not advanced far; nearly all students enter by concession at a lower level than is required in Great Britain by the University of Durham, with which this late recruit to the rank of a university college continues its cherished affiliation. The University has allowed modifications to be made in certain syllabuses to suit local needs, in geography for instance, but has only recently made arrangements under which college teachers can take some part in setting and marking papers.

During the period when the College obtained grants through the COCAST it was able, as already related, to build up its scientific departments; in 1959 it instituted a general B.Sc course, in which honours are available, alongside the traditional BA course. Honours degree courses are now planned in a number of subjects. In the sphere of technological training, which it was the function of the COCAST to encourage, a course for a general diploma in engineering was introduced. The College is in fact now at long last in process of fulfilling its ambition to become a normal university institution. The first chair was filled in 1959.

THE UNIVERSITY COLLEGE OF RHODESIA AND NYASALAND

In 1949 two members of an Inter-University Council delegation to East Africa were invited to visit Salisbury and meet a committee, set up by the Central African Council, of which Sir Harold Cartmel-Robinson was chairman; this committee was studying post-secondary education for Africans in the light of an announcement by the South African government that it would not accept more African students from outside its territory for degree courses. This was the first contact which the Inter-University Council made with the problem of higher education in the territory now included in the Federation; during their stay in Salisbury the visitors met Mr L. M. N. Hodson who had been mainly responsible for founding the Rhodesia University Association the object of which was to establish a university for Rhodesia, and learnt that the City of Salisbury had made a generous offer of 250 acres in the northern residential suburbs for this purpose. In accordance with a recommendation of the Cartmel-Robinson Committee a commission was appointed to report on the need for the higher education of Africans in Central Africa; it visited the three territories in 1952 and found that Mr Hodson's plans had made further progress during the three preceding years, since a bill, promoted by the Association, had been passed by the Southern Rhodesian Legislative Assembly setting up an Inaugural Board for the proposed university. The Commission recommended the establishment of a university college on an inter-racial basis, either in Salisbury if their proposal could be appropriately associated with the plans of the Inaugural Board, or, if not, in Lusaka in Northern Rhodesia.[6] In 1953 the Inaugural Board decided that the sole test for admission to their proposed college should be one based on educational attainments and character; this made it possible to implement the Commission's preference for an inter-racial college in Salisbury. In the same year Her Majesty Queen Elizabeth, the Queen Mother, laid the foundation stone. Shortly afterwards representatives of the three Central African governments and of the Inaugural Board visited London for discussions with the British government, the Inter-University Council and London University. As a result of these discussions the British government agreed to contribute £1,250,000 towards the capital cost of the College provided that the three governments met the recurrent costs—a condition subsequently fulfilled by a grant of £150,000 per annum for five years.

There were no buildings on or near the site which could be used for teaching while the permanent buildings were under construction, and therefore, in contrast to events in Nigeria, Ghana and the West Indies, the opening of the College had to wait until new buildings were ready. This meant delay which was regrettable in one sense, but there was compensation in that the difficulties of improvisation and makeshift in temporary (and usually unsuitable) quarters with only a skeleton staff were avoided. Moreover, good use was made of the interval; a principal was appointed, staff were chosen, equipment was carefully selected and the nucleus of a library was assembled. Thus it was possible to form an academic board ahead of the beginning of teaching; the board was able to discuss with the University of London, which took the College into special relation, the arrangements relating to entrance requirements and appropriate syllabuses. In this fashion all was made ready for the opening of the College in March 1957. Meanwhile a royal charter was granted, the City of Salisbury increased its gift of land to a total of 474 acres, and the government allotted 1,200 acres in the Mazoe Valley about twenty miles to the north of Salisbury for development as a farm for the department of agriculture.

The Mount Pleasant site of 474 acres is between three and four miles from the centre of Salisbury. The property forms a compact area sloping downwards from north to south; it offers excellent opportunities for landscaping of which full advantage is being taken. The layout was prepared by Sir William Holford, and three local firms of architects have been employed. On the northern boundary is a plateau on which the library is situated; more buildings, such as the great hall, are to be placed there later. To the south-west are other academic buildings and to the south-east the halls of residence; below are the recreation grounds. To the north-west is a quarry which is to be converted into an open-air amphitheatre for ceremonies and dramatic performances. Portions of the slope are being developed as terraced gardens and rockeries; thousands of trees and shrubs have been planted. The buildings, pleasing in themselves, form harmonious groups and the library attains real distinction. Although the total area is considerably less than that of the property of other new colleges, it is sufficient because no room has to be found to house the staff since they can live in the city. As building goes on, the College will certainly come into the first rank for the overall merits of the site as developed.

All the universities and colleges described in this book are multi-racial in the sense that they are open to all races on equal terms. The multi-racial aspect of this College is remarkable only for the fact that it is situated in a region where multi-racial institutions are the exception. It was laid down by the college authorities from the start that students of all colours should be treated alike; following a recommendation of the Commission of 1952 the College stated that it was prepared to offer separate residential accommodation for Europeans and non-Europeans. Had it not done so there might have been few European applicants. But separate accommodation by colour and sex implies four halls, and there are still only three. What the college authorities foresaw from the start was that the available accommodation would hardly make it possible for all students to live in a residence inhabited solely by students of their colour, and that the students could only be accommodated if some were willing to live with those not of their colour. This willingness was manifested, and there is now no question of reservation of a hall of residence for students of one race. Nevertheless an accusation was levelled at the College by certain members of the House of Commons alleging that the College practised racial segregation; in fact they were attacking the most successful and most prominent example of multi-racialism in the Federation.

The College serves a population of over eight million of whom 96 per cent are Africans and less than 4 per cent Europeans—the remainder, including Indians, forming less than half of 1 per cent; the Europeans, 223,000 out of 308,000, are concentrated in Southern Rhodesia. The full-time students numbered 74 in the session 1957–8 (including 8 Africans), 125 in 1958–9 (including 19 Africans), 166 in 1959–60 (including 32 Africans), and 209 in 1960–1 (including 49 Africans). The College demands the full London entrance qualifications and is the only new foundation which has done so from the start. The College adopted this policy because, if it had set a lower level, London University would have required four years attendance in college before sitting for a degree, and in consequence Rhodesian students coming to the college would have been at a disadvantage compared with those going to South African universities who, after entering at a lower level than the London level, could have sat for a degree after three years. At the same time the policy of a high entrance requirement coincided with the intention that the College should be distinguished for high standards in all respects. There is ample provision of good secondary schools for Europeans in the Federation and hence no lack of opportunity to work for the higher school certificate. When the College opened there were sixth forms in only two schools for Africans (at Goromonzi in Southern Rhodesia and at Munali in Northern Rhodesia where sixth form work began in 1954 and 1956 respectively); they drew pupils from all three territories. Now there are two other schools for Africans with sixth forms at Gwelo in Southern Rhodesia and at Dedza in Nyasaland. But the opportunities for Africans to gain the required entrance qualification are still limited, and this creates a problem to which the College is giving attention.

The College opened with faculties of arts and science (including agriculture). Agriculture was the first professional course to be offered; the next two professional courses to be initiated will be medicine and engineering in that order of priority. Until more professional education can be provided in Salisbury, a large number of students must go outside the territory for their education; it was estimated that in 1959 over 200 students were studying engineering elsewhere. Alongside these major developments it will soon be possible to make provision for specialized (honours) degree courses in certain subjects in arts and science; that was not possible in the first quinquennium, but the grant made by the Federation for the second quinquennium will enable it to be done. The College expects that total student numbers will rise to 600 by 1965.

THE UNIVERSITY COLLEGE OF THE WEST INDIES

The Irvine Committee, which went out to the West Indies on behalf of the Asquith Commission while the latter body was sitting, had a most difficult task. Its main duty was to select a site for the college which was to serve a population then amounting to over three million. About half the total live in Jamaica; the remainder inhabit the two mainland territories, British Guiana and British Honduras, and the numerous islands of which Trinidad is the most populous. But these territories are widely separated; if British Honduras is placed at London, Jamaica is as far away as Danzig, Trinidad as Odessa, British Guiana as Asia Minor, while the Windwards and the Leewards are to the east of Moscow. There were many possible sites for a college; broadly speaking, they fell into one or other of two groups, a small island or one of the larger territories. A small island, like Grenada, would afford a charming setting for a college, but would have the disadvantages of isolation, of a too small hospital population for teaching purposes and of lack of contact with any active centre of business and administration. On the other hand to put the college in one of the larger territories would disappoint the others who had a claim for consideration. The Irvine Committee favoured the second solution and, having decided that Jamaica would be the best location for a college, succeeded in obtaining the agreement of all the territories to place it there.

A most suitable and beautiful site, about 600 feet above sea level, was found in the upper end of a valley about seven miles from Kingston the capital of Jamaica. To the north is the magnificent range of the Blue Mountains rising to over 7,000 feet, and to the south a limestone ridge of some 2,000 feet. It must be among the most lovely sites occupied by any university institution in the world, vying with Paradynia to which the University of Ceylon is being moved. An area of about a square mile, presented by the government of Jamaica, offered one great additional advantage; on it were hutments, with storehouses, offices and canteens, which had been built to accommodate refugees during the war and could be used as temporary buildings for the College. Thus the story of the College follows the pattern in West Africa, the temporary buildings presenting less of a problem than the derelict hospital at Ibadan, but not offering such good quarters as the buildings of Achimota College.

The first principal was appointed in 1946; the College was taken into special relation with London University in 1947. There was much to be done in order to convert the hutments into temporary class-rooms and laboratories and to make other necessary preparations for the reception of students. The first students, thirty-four in number of whom ten were women, were admitted in October 1948; they read in the pre-medical subjects. Priority was given to medical training for which there was pressing need in the West Indies. The Irvine Committee recommended that medical students should work for the medical qualification of McGill University while other students aimed at London degrees; this was the one recommendation of the Committee with which the Asquith Commission did not agree, on the grounds that the McGill degree was not registrable in Great Britain and that in any case there would be difficulties if two universities had a hand in the teaching arrangements at the College; therefore it was arranged that medical students should aim at the London medical degree. The later story of the medical school, which has involved building a hospital within the area of the College, will be told in the chapter dealing with professional education. In 1949 students were admitted to the faculty of science and in 1950 to the faculty of arts. New departments have been added to these faculties, in both of which honour degree courses are available in certain subjects. But the priority given to medicine had important consequences; the demands of a medical faculty are large and difficult to resist; the territories served by the College are not rich, and the diversion of its limited financial resources towards medicine tended to restrict the development of other aspects of its work.

While the hutments were being used as temporary teaching accommodation a layout was prepared for the permanent buildings. Construction began in 1949; by October 1950, a hall of residence and some staff houses had been completed and were in use, and in 1951 the library and some laboratories were finished. By 1954 the hutments were used only to serve ancillary purposes. The College was fortunate in that the hutments were close to the permanent buildings, and not miles away as at Ibadan and Achimota, with the result that the College escaped a frustrating period when the temporary and permanent buildings were widely separated. The architects were the firm of Norman and Dawbarn who, in spite of the limited sum available for construction, have planned a spacious and attractive lay-out for the buildings which form most pleasing groups; white walls, balconies and covered passages showing against the wooded background of the surrounding hills.

From the beginning it was intended that agriculture should figure in the programme, but it was recognized this involved co-operation in some form with the Imperial College of Tropical Agriculture in Trinidad. The Imperial College was founded in 1921 as a centre for graduate training in tropical agriculture of all those recruited to serve as agricultural officers in the various tropical dependencies of the Commonwealth; it also offered a diploma for non-graduates who were mostly West Indians. In addition to its main site of some 200 acres it owned three farms some distance away, of 430, 300 and 100 acres respectively. Various forms of co-operation were proposed, but after years of discussion none was found acceptable to both bodies. At length in 1957 the Imperial College offered to transfer all its property to the University College to serve as the latter's school of agriculture. This generous and welcome offer was accepted and opens the prospect that the University College will at last be able to undertake teaching and research in a subject which, more than any other, bears directly on the welfare of the territories. But Trinidad is more than 1,000 miles distant from Jamaica, and to meet the difficulty which would be created by the isolation of a single faculty, the college authorities have decided to expand and diversify the teaching in Trinidad. The plan is to have one campus in Jamaica and another in Trinidad. At both centres there will be basic teaching in arts and science, but so far as possible duplication will be avoided. Jamaica will provide facilities for medicine, the social sciences and education, and will offer special (honour) degree courses in arts and science, while Trinidad will offer courses in agriculture and engineering and general (pass) courses in arts and science. To the substantial buildings of the Imperial College must therefore be added new accommodation for teaching in arts, science and engineering. Under a unified direction it is hoped to develop two institutions, each well balanced in itself and each complementary to the other, as parts of a single organization.

Up to 1958 the College was supported by contributions from the governments of the territories in proportions as agreed at a conference of their representatives; in 1958 it became a charge on the federal government, the two mainland territories, which did not join the federation, making separate grants. The College was the first federal institution of the new state. This fact is of great importance for the future of the College and of the West Indies. The population is scattered and in consequence there is not the same degree of ardent nationalism as in the territories served by the other colleges. Though scattered the people are not isolated as are the African peoples; the proximity of the North American continent has made possible a constant flood or visitors from the United States and Canada, who take a great interest in the West Indies; indeed from these countries the College has received much valuable help. Nevertheless, though the mainland territories stand somewhat apart, it is correct to speak of a common culture and a common loyalty shared by West Indians for which the College as a federal institution can now form a focus.

Except for certain groups in the mainland territories the home language is English, and therefore the use of vernaculars does not complicate the education problem. Secondary education has had a relatively long history in the West Indies, but until recently provision was limited. In 1940 there were 3,000 pupils in secondary schools in Jamaica; in 1959 there were 17,000; the number of those with qualifications to pursue higher education is thus increasing rapidly. In the absence of facilities for higher education there grew up the practice of frequenting universities overseas; in 1945 there were some 250 West Indian students in North American universities and 100 in British universities. By 1956–7 the total had grown to 2,362 (625 in the universities of the United Kingdom and Eire, 837 in those of Canada and 1,170 in institutions of higher education in the United States). It was not for want of residential accommodation in the College that numbers were not higher since in 1957 there were 656 places in the halls of residence but only 566 students. In part the reason for seeking university education overseas was the lack of provision for professional education, except in medicine where the intake of students was perforce limited, and in part it was that the governments spent substantial sums on grants to students going overseas—grants not confined to those who could not follow their chosen courses at the College. But the most important reason emerged from an enquiry made in 1957; in that year only just over a third of the qualified applicants for admission entered the College, the remainder not having sufficient means to pursue their application and not being able to get help from the limited provision of government bursaries. Of these qualified applicants it seems likely that a number went to North America paying their way by vacation work.

This situation produced some doubt and questioning about the College and its policies and led to the appointment by the Standing Federation Committee of the West Indies in 1957 of a Committee of enquiry. This Committee, which apart from a British vice-chancellor was local in its membership, produced a most comprehensive and thorough report.[7] It can be said that in general the College came well out of the review; there were no fundamental criticisms of its policy or of its performance though there were numerous recommendations on special points. The report has done much to improve the position of the College in public esteem and to make known to West Indians that they have their own centre of university study which can stand comparison with centres overseas. Moreover the preparations now being made to offer degree courses in agriculture and engineering will make it unnecessary to go abroad in order to study these subjects. With a second centre in Trinidad the whole outlook is changing, and the college authorities now expect 5,000 students in 1970.

NOTES

1. *Report of the Commission on Higher Education in East Africa*, 1937, p. 85.
2. *Ibid.*, p. 76.
3. *Higher Education in East Africa*, Entebbe, 1957, p. 10.
4. *Report of the Committee on Higher Education, Accra*, 1946, p. 3.
5. Kenneth Mellanby, *The Birth of Nigeria's University*, 1958.
6. *Report of the Commission on Higher Education for Africans in Central Africa*, 1953, Central African Council.
7. *Report of the Committee appointed to review the policy of the University College of the West Indies*, 1958.

CHAPTER 6

FINANCE

In the first chapter some account was given of the source and extent of the financial provision before 1945 for those institutions which were in existence at that date; this chapter is concerned with the finance of all the institutions since 1945. No more than a general picture can be given here; what follows relates to the grants for capital purposes received by each institution, the benefactions which have come to them, their present recurrent income, the sources of this income, and the procedure and conditions under which their funds are obtained.

The Asquith Commission foresaw that their plans could only be carried out if 'very substantial financial sums' were made available from Great Britain, and suggested that part of the funds provided under CD and W Acts should be used for that purpose; they added that, if this were done, the expenditure to be met might be for both recurrent and capital purposes.[1] Their main recommendation has been carried out; allocations for higher education have been made by the Secretary of State out of the funds provided by successive CD and W Acts. Before 1959 the IUC were invited to draw up estimates of the needs of each institution, based on figures supplied by the latter, and to transmit the estimates to the Colonial University Grants Advisory Committee for presentation to the Secretary of State; but in 1959 the allocation was made by him without affording the IUC or the Grants Committee an opportunity to present estimates of needs. When the allocations are announced, the Grants Committee, after consulting the IUC, divide the sum made available between the institutions. With one or two trifling exceptions in early days the sums so made available to the institutions have been for capital purposes only; grants for recurrent purposes were ruled out by government policy, and in this particular matter the intentions of the Asquith Commission were not fulfilled. Until 1956 the grants were made without attaching any conditions that the territorial governments, within which the institutions are situated, must make a matching grant; in that year, however, the United Kingdom government began to insert such conditions. The conditions vary from place to place and from scheme to scheme; for example, no matching grant is demanded from Malta, but from Sierra Leone the matching grant must in general be one-tenth, from Rhodesia one-eighth, and from Hong Kong a substantial percentage of the United Kingdom grant. In principle these conditions are arbitrary and in practice harassing; it is doubtful whether, by insisting on them, more support is acquired for the institutions.

The total grant for capital purposes from United Kingdom through the CD and W higher education allocation to each institution up to date is as follows:

	£
Royal University of Malta	539,000
University of Hong Kong	650,000
University of Malaya	1,410,380
University College of the West Indies	3,645,000
University College of Ibadan	2,225,000
University College of Ghana	400,000
Fourah Bay University College	450,000
Makerere College, the University College of East Africa	3,462,000
University College of Rhodesia and Nyasaland	2,875,000
Royal College, Nairobi	525,000
	16,181,380

The University of Malaya has received from United Kingdom funds outside the higher education allocation an additional sum of £308,620. The figures are for sums allocated; in some cases not all the money has yet been spent. When examining the figures certain facts need to be recalled. The University of

Khartoum was never eligible for assistance from CD and W funds because the Sudan was not a colony; but a grant of a million pounds, made to the Sudan by the United Kingdom after the war, was handed over to Gordon College which later became the University of Khartoum. A territory ceases to be eligible for this help when it attains independence; Ghana and the Federation of Malaya became independent in 1957 amd Nigeria in 1960. When the Secretary of State agreed to the foundation of a university college in Ghana, he made it a condition that the cost should be borne locally; hence the University College of Ghana has received no more than a token grant. It should be added that before the university colleges in Sierra Leone and Kenya attained their present status, they came within the sphere of the COCAST and were eligible for grants out of the allocation for colleges of technology from CD and W funds.

The contributions made by the territorial governments, apart from grants for recurrent expenses which will be mentioned later, have been in the form of gifts of land, of grants for capital purposes and endowment funds. The new foundations in Nigeria, Ghana, Rhodesia and the West Indies and the new branch of the University of Malaya have received valuable gifts of land (in Rhodesia from the city of Salisbury). The Ghanaian government has given £M.8 for capital expenditure, the Hong Kong government about £700,000, the Nigerian government £M.2·6, the governments of Singapore and the Federation of Malaya £M.1·9, and the East African governments £783,106, to their respective universities and colleges. Governments and semi-governmental bodies have also given sums as endowments: the government of Ghana £M.2, the government of Nigeria £M.1, the government of Hong Kong £M.1, the Ghana Cacao Marketing Board £M.2. It is also appropriate to record the large sums spent by governments on hospitals (£M.4½ in Nigeria, £M.2½ in Uganda) which, though not paid to the colleges, provided teaching facilities without which there could have been no medical schools.

All the universities and colleges have received a very large number of gifts from corporations, firms, trusts and private benefactors. It would be pleasing to be able to list them in full as an acknowledgment of such munificence, but the record would take up many pages. As an indication of the extent and variety of help from private sources it must suffice to take the case of the most recently founded college, that in Rhodesia. The gifts can be classified under ten heads according to the object in view: (1) buildings, three including one of £200,000 for the library; (2) equipment, seven; (3) teaching and research, ten; (4) research fellowships, ten; (5) agriculture, three including £74,000 from various sources for the needs of the department of agriculture; (6) development, one of £40,000; (7) scholarships, nine; (8) prizes, five; (9) library, numerous gifts of books; (10) general funds, many gifts, including one of £50,000, another of £20,000 and a third of £10,000. Also, beginning with their earliest days, the institutions have received numerous gifts from the United States, and in more recent times from the older Commonwealth countries. The University of Malaya and the University College of the West Indies have raised large sums by public appeals to which many people of small means have contributed.

The decision of the United Kingdom government that its grants to overseas universities and colleges must be used only for capital purposes threw the whole burden of recurrent expenditure on to the territorial governments. When submitting estimates of recurrent expenses, the universities and colleges deal directly with the governments; thus their grants do not figure in the budgets of any one department of government such as that of education. In all cases the grant made by a government is a block grant for a period of three or five years. This procedure is modelled on that used in Great Britain except for the fact that in Great Britain the universities communicate with the University Grants Committee, a standing committee appointed by the Treasury, which conducts negotiations with the government. In Great Britain, where there are twenty-one universities looking to the government for support, there is need for a standing committee; but where there is only one university the need does not arise, and in none of the territories concerned has a standing committee, corresponding to the University Grants Committee, been set up. Nevertheless it has been found useful in some territories, when the estimates are received by the government, to appoint an *ad hoc* committee, to which the government can refer them for scrutiny. These *ad hoc* committees always include one or more members of wide academic experience, usually from the United Kingdom and usually nominated by the IUC, along with territorial government officials of standing and perhaps one or more local residents of influence. A committee of this kind, after scrutinizing the estimates, comments on the desirability and urgency of any proposed enlargement of the programme of the institution, and indicates that the carrying on or the extension of its activities ought not to cost more than a certain sum and cannot cost less than a given amount if proper standards are to prevail. This protects governments against over-ambitious programmes and the inflation of estimates; at the same time it protects the institutions because it makes plain to the governments that a particular programme cannot be carried out, as it should be carried out, with less than a certain amount of support. *Ad hoc* committees, appointed before the end of the grant period, to scrutinize the estimates for the next period, have served a useful purpose in Ghana, East and Central Africa, Sierra Leone and the West Indies.

Table 1 sets out the sources whence the institutions derive their recurrent incomes. It should be noted that the institutions usually include in their incomes the payments made by students for board and lodgings in halls of residence; these receipts may figure under the headings of fees or under the heading of other sources. This means that the figures under these headings are not comparable; it also means that the total income is increased by payments which do not appear in the figures for the income for English universities. This latter fact must be borne in mind when comparing the proportion which government help forms of the total income in England and overseas. Taking the available figures as they are it appears that in England the average proportion is just under 70 per cent, varying from 61 per cent to 80 per cent. Overseas, where for the reason given the proportions should be somewhat raised (though not for Malta where there is no hall of residence and therefore no receipts from that source) the percentage varies from 90 in the case of Malta to 54 in the case of Hong Kong. Hong Kong is in the fortunate position of having large endowments, in part presented by the government. But the

TABLE 1
SOURCES OF RECURRENT INCOME OF UNIVERSITIES AND COLLEGES

University or College	Year	Government Grant	Fees	Interest on Endowment	Other Sources	Total
		£	£	£	£	£
University of Malta	1959–60	60,000	6,274	—	268	66,542
University of Hong Kong	1958–9	350,781	115,766	170,284	15,139	651,970
University of Malaya	1959	953,647	136,288	11,353	55,086	1,156,374
University College of the West Indies	1959–60	617,940	22,480	16,980	183,367	840,776
University College, Ibadan	1958–9	484,880	155,330	363,660(1)	35,841	1,039,711
University College of Ghana	1958–9	900,000	52,781	(2)	109,813	1,062,549
Fourah Bay College, the University College of Sierra Leone	1959–60	247,000	44,624	996	2,900	295,520
Makerere College, the University College of East Africa	1959–60	562,137	118,921	20,802	8,934	710,794
University College of Rhodesia and Nyasaland	1959	164,700	7,621	1,550	28,874	202,745

(1) including government endowment allocation.　(2) interest re-invested to increase capital.

usual percentage is between 70 and 80 (73 for the West Indies and 79 for Makerere College). The percentage for Ibadan looks low, but is not so in fact because it draws year by year on an expendible government endowment. Broadly speaking the position is as in England; the institutions depend upon government grants for the greater part of their incomes.

The Asquith Commission hoped for 'substantial' financial assistance to the universities and colleges from the British government. £M.16·2 is certainly a substantial sum. But the hopes of the Commission were not fulfilled in respect of contributions for recurrent expenses, and the amount allocated for capital purposes by the British government has met only part of the needs of the institutions for capital as estimated by the IUC and presented to the Secretary of State. If we look at the total amount (capital and recurrent expenditure) devoted to the colleges since their foundation we find that only a small part has been supplied by the British government; thus University College, Ibadan, has received £M.2·25 from the British government and £M.12·6 from the Nigerian government, including in the last figure the cost of the teaching hospital without which there could have been no medical school.

The Commission foresaw that 'the cost of educating each student' in the colleges would be 'substantially higher than the cost of the education of an English student in most English universities'[2]. If 'the cost of educating each student' is found by dividing the total expenditure of a university or college by the total number of its students, this forecast has come true. In 1959 the cost so calculated of educating a student was £400 at Birmingham, £345 at Bristol and £250 at Exeter, whereas it was £934 at Ibadan, £770 at Makerere College and £514 at Hong Kong. But these figures are subject to an important correction; in the figures for the overseas institutions the cost of providing board and lodging in halls of residence is included while it is excluded from the English figures; therefore a sum above £100 should be deducted from the figures for the former. This still leaves the overseas costs higher than the English costs. Various factors account for this situation. The overseas institutions are smaller than the English (Makerere and Ibadan being between a quarter and a third of the size of Birmingham and

Bristol), and in consequence overhead costs are higher for each student. More important is the fact that the overseas colleges have a wide range of professional faculties (medical, agricultural, veterinary, engineering) which are very expensive; this is why the cost at Exeter, a small university with 1,232 students, which spends little on professional education, is so much less than overseas. Added to all this is the relatively big area of most of the overseas colleges and the consequential large cost of maintenance on roads and open spaces; this factor is of much importance at Ibadan where well over 10,000 persons (men, women and children) live within the college precinct.

NOTES

1. *Report of the Commission on Higher Education in the Colonies*, 1945, p. 54.
2. *Ibid.*, p. 56.

CHAPTER 7

THE GOVERNING AUTHORITIES

The constitutions of the University Colleges of the West Indies, Rhodesia and Fourah Bay are embodied in royal charters; in all other cases they are found in an act of the local legislature. The constitution of the University of Hong Kong, drawn up in 1911 on the lines of those then in force in the new English universities, was amended in 1957, while the University of Malta received an entirely new constitution in 1947. The pre-war constitutions of Gordon and Makerere Colleges were revised after the war as mentioned in Chapter 5; the constitutions of the other foundations date from after 1945. The constitutional machinery to be described in this chapter is that which now functions; in all cases it has been constructed or amended with the recommendations of the Asquith Commission in mind. 'In our view', the Commission said, 'it is essential that colonial universities should be autonomous in the sense in which the universities of Great Britain are autonomous'.[1] So far as written constitutions can secure autonomy, this has been achieved; the universities and colleges are corporations whose actions need no confirmation by a minister or by the legislature. But autonomy means more than that; what it implies, especially in regard to the relation between governments and universities, is discussed in Chapter 17, where the experience of the universities and colleges in the realm of these relations is also reviewed.

Under the form of government recommended by the Commission there are two chief officers, a chancellor and a vice-chancellor in the case of a university, a visitor and a principal in the case of a university college, and two chief organs of government, a supreme governing body, here called the council, and a body of purely academic composition, here called the senate. In the new English universities the supreme governing body is the court which alone can make or amend statutes. It is usually a large body; it may have over 300 members including all members of the council and senate together with representatives of bodies and organizations of all kinds, national and local. Attendance is usually very small and the proceedings formal; it meets once a year to give its necessary consent to recommendations submitted by the council. It also elects representatives to the council, in practice those nominated by the council; election by the court is in fact a concealed form of co-option by the council. It seems to be a superfluous piece of mechanism, and it was not recommended by the Commission as suitable for the new colleges. The type of constitution recommended was that which prevails in fact but not on paper in the new English universities. Alone among the institutions under review the Universities of Hong Kong and Malaya have a body called a court, but in neither case is it, as in England, the ultimate governing body. To it are assigned only advisory powers and the right to elect representatives to the council. Experience shows that, if the territory served is not too large and if professional, industrial, commercial and research organizations are represented in the court, the university can use the court as a bridge between itself and the community at large. In Africa and the West Indies the size of the territories served makes this impossible, and in addition there is a paucity of organizations suitable for representation.

The Commission emphasized that the members of the council nominated or elected by any one outside organization should not be in a majority; 'otherwise the university may become a mere creature of that organization'.[2] They recommended that the council should have about twenty members of whom not less than a third should belong to the academic staff, not less than two should be representatives of the graduates, and either one or two should represent the IUC, while the rest should be nominated by the legislature, the executive government, the chancellor or some other authority. These recommendations have guided the size and constitutions of the councils; the average size is a little over twenty, and between a quarter and a third of the seats are held by senior members of the academic staff. There are one or more representatives of the IUC on the councils of all the colleges where their presence is more appropriate than in the case of universities. While these representatives can seldom attend more than one meeting a year, their membership is useful; they can bring to bear on the deliberation of the council their experience of British university practice; moreover they receive agenda and documents, and in consequence there are always among the members of the IUC persons who possess full and up-to-date knowledge of the affairs of the colleges. Where the constitution provides for an organization of graduates, generally called convocation, as in the cases of Malta, Hong Kong, Malaya, Ibadan, Fourah Bay and the West Indies, this body usually has power to express its opinions on university matters and to submit them to the university authorities. This arrangement helps to secure the continuing interest of the graduates and to keep the university informed about outside opinion. It is also usual to find that convocation has, as recommended by the Commission, the right to appoint representatives to the council, but the value to the council of such representatives is doubtful. Graduates have knowledge of university matters only as seen from one angle; this experience, which is often much out-of-date, is of little use and may be a positive disadvantage when dealing with current problems. The Commission made no mention of co-option by the council to its membership; Ibadan and Fourah Bay have made provision for such co-option which might be more extensively permitted since an effective council is in a good position to know whose help would be valuable.

Most seats on the councils are held by persons nominated by various authorities; only in Malta and Ghana does the legislature elect representatives. The nominated members, except in East and Central Africa, are mostly of local birth and are drawn from a large variety of occupations, and in consequence seldom adopt a common policy and seldom act together. But in Singapore things have so worked out that at times over half the members of the council have been graduates thus giving undue weight to an element in the community which tends to act as a group. Such a situation, however, is an exception. In general the lay members have not represented outside interests, but have set themselves to forward the welfare of the institutions. Thus in respect of relations with the outside world the lay members have served the institutions well.

The relations between council and senate are equally important. 'The senate', said the Commission, 'must possess full authority in purely academic matters'.[3] To it should be assigned responsibility for questions relating to curricula, examinations and the discipline of students, while the framing of statutes and ordinances would need the co-operation of both bodies. The constitutions do assign such functions to the senate. But the council is the supreme governing body; it controls and must control finance, and no matter what the constitution may say about the power of the senate over academic matters, those who hold the purse strings can, if so minded, control everything. The English convention is that in academic matters the council does not take the initiative. Orders do not come down from the council; policy originates in the senate and the faculties, and comes before the council as recommendations for approval. The council, however, is not a rubber stamp; its duty is to examine recommendations in the light of the financial situation and to be on the outlook for anomalies, inconsistencies and unobserved implications; if it has doubt about proposals its practice is to refer them back rather than to reject them. This English convention has been followed in the overseas institutions, and this fact is as remarkable as it is welcome, since it must have been unfamiliar to most lay members of councils whose self-abnegation of their powers is evidence that they acknowledge the value of an unusual procedure which best suits university needs. The relations between councils and senates have been as a rule remarkably harmonious, but in Singapore this has not always been so. As already noted, graduates may form a majority of the council in Singapore and tend to act together. The graduates were foremost to welcome the foundation of the University in 1949; their interest in it and their genuine concern for its welfare have led them to press their own point of view which has not always coincided with that of the senate. Into these controversies, when the right was not always on one side, it is not necessary to go. It should be added that in important issues, such as the autonomy of the University in relation to the government, the University has received strong support from the graduates.

In addition to participation in the work of a council lay members can render valuable service in other ways. When they are persons of high standing in the community, their connection with the university helps to secure for it the confidence of the community at large; moreover they can do much to make known its aims and ambitions and to explain its policy. Such services are of special value in countries where universities are a novelty and where in consequence much ignorance prevails about their functions. If any criticism is to be made of the lay members it is not that they seek to impose their own policies or that they serve outside interests, but that they listen too often to personal grievances of staff and students and to unfounded rumours circulated by the press or otherwise.

The overseas institutions possess the usual subsidiary organs of government such as faculties, but there is nothing which needs special mention. Reflection on this way of solving the constitutional problem suggests certain comments. A supreme governing body with lay and academic members, the former being in a majority, is a British practice; the alternatives are a wholly lay governing body on the American and Canadian models, or the absence of lay members, coupled with the subjection of the university to a government department, on the European continental model. The British system works well in Great Britain, and in the overseas territories it has special advantages. Subjection to a government department, which in the British view is objectionable in principle, would be far more open to objection in countries where universities are novelties and where there is no university tradition to guide officials, while in the absence of this tradition a wholly lay governing body would not be able to appreciate academic aims and needs.

On the other hand certain features of the organization of the newer English universities, which are less to be recommended, have been translated to the territories. In these English universities academic policy is effectively in the hands of teachers because the conventions described above are observed. But relatively few teachers have any knowledge, except by hearsay, of the major problems facing the university; most of them may know nothing about these issues, and if they do, they have no formal means of expressing their opinions. In other words the teachers as a whole are not fully incorporated in academic society. This situation has been carried overseas and is the more to be regretted because problems are novel, because conditions are rapidly changing, because traditional solutions may not be appropriate, and because in consequence all who have ideas should be heard. One motive behind the constitutional experiments made by the University College of Ghana was a laudable desire to find a remedy for this situation; unfortunately the arrangements proved to be too cumbersome and were abandoned. Again the rigid departmental system which characterizes the newer English universities has been translated overseas; this system creates artificial boundaries between what are no more than centres of interest, leads to undue specialization and results in the neglect of general education because it is the business of no one since all are within some limited academic territory. So ingrained is the system that most English teachers cannot picture a university without it; but it is not a necessary feature of university organization; departments do not figure in the constitution of one college of the University of London, the London School of Economics, to its great advantage. The translation of the system overseas is especially inappropriate in view of the need for flexibility and experiment.[4]

In order to ensure the smooth working of the organs of government continuity of administration is important; otherwise appropriate procedures and conventions do not easily become established, understood and accepted. But continuity has not always been easy to secure; in eight years the University of Malaya had three successive vice-chancellors, five acting vice-chancellors, three registrars and two bursars. This, however, is an exceptional case. Failure to secure continuity in the tenure of office is, more often than not, due to ill-luck; on the other hand certain impediments to the rapid and efficient conduct of business arise out of the tendency to make procedure over-elaborate. The Commission of Enquiry on the University of Malaya, reporting in 1957, found that agenda paper had 'grown to unmanageable bulk', and that verbatim reports of discussions in the council, senate and committees were circulated for correction and incorporation in the minutes.[5] It seems to be a fact, not easy to explain, that young academic organizations readily tie themselves up in time-wasting devices; on the whole it appears that mature academic organizations succeed best in making machinery the servant rather than the master.

It is an ancient and honourable tradition of universities that they do not close their doors to would-be students on account of race, religion, class or nationality, though there have been notable lapses in its observance. Most overseas university institutions have clauses in their constitutions similar to that obtaining for the University of Malaya which lays down that 'membership of the University . . . shall be open to all persons of either sex and of whatever race, religion, nationality or class; and no test of religious belief or profession shall be adopted or imposed in order to entitle any person to be admitted to such membership or to be awarded any degree or diploma of the University'. It is not to be inferred that, because their constitutions are silent on the matter, the University of Hong Kong and Makerere College do not follow the same policy. Among overseas institutions the position of the University of Malta is peculiar though it cannot be held to be in contradiction to the fundamental principle. The Roman Catholic religion is the basis of instruction and no teaching inconsistent with its principles is permitted. But persons not professing that religion are admitted to any course and may obtain any degree or award other than those offered in the faculty of theology, and they are not to be subjected to any religious examination or test.[6]

There remains the question of unitary as against federal organization. Federation is regarded in British university circles as a device which may be suitable under certain conditions but is not in general to be recommended. When the constituent colleges of a federal university are near one another as in London or when they have close cultural links as in Wales, the federal system works well enough; but when the colleges are geographically separated and have little in common, the constituent colleges resent central control and seek independence as happened in the case of the Victoria University of Manchester. The Asquith Commission assumed that the new institutions would become unitary universities. But a situation has arisen in East African which may best be met by a temporary federal arrangement. The working party of 1958 recognized the immediate

111

need for a university college in Kenya and also at a later date for a university college in Tanganyika. They also recognized that before long it will be appropriate for Makerere College to become a university. Thus in order to avoid difficulties arising from the presence of a university in Uganda conferring its own degrees while colleges in the two other territories worked for London degrees, and in order to ensure co-ordination of effort and the best use of the limited financial resources of East Africa, they suggested that a federal university of East Africa might be created with three constituent colleges, each of which would in due course become a university.

By federation in this context is meant the bringing of colleges, which lack degree-granting powers, under a central organization which has such powers. If a university is divided into two geographically separated and semi-autonomous branches, it does not comply with this definition of a federal university. Nevertheless the end product may be indistinguishable from a federal university. The University of Malaya and the University College of the West Indies have each been divided into two such branches. It is clearly the intention of the latter to maintain unity, and this is likely to be possible owing to the cultural similarity between the constituent elements of the Caribbean area; hence a university, federal except by origin, may come to serve the West Indies. In Malaya, on the other hand, there are cultural and political differences between the Federation and Singapore, and it is likely that the Kuala Lumpur branch will become a separate university.

NOTES

1. *Report of the Commission on Higher Education in the Colonies*, 1945, p. 34.
2. *Ibid.*, p. 35.
3. *Ibid.*, p. 35.
4. The situation in the Universities of Oxford and Cambridge is different. Every university teacher is a member of a body (congregation at Oxford and the regent house at Cambridge) whose consent must be given before the University acts. Thus all teachers

know what is going on and can have their say about it if they wish; in addition the majority are fellows of a college, and as such have full voting rights in the governing body. Broadly speaking it is correct to say that in neither university are there departments with establishments on a hierarchical basis; departments exist only where there are laboratories and consequential need for control.

5. *Report of the Commission of Enquiry on the University of Malaya*, 1957, p. 25.

6. The Rector of the University of Malta is not a priest, and in that respect the University appears to be unique among Catholic universities.

CHAPTER 8

SITE, BUILDINGS, CLIMATE

Twelve new universities have come into existence in England since 1880. They grew out of small colleges founded by public-spirited citizens in the great provincial cities. Whatever ambitions the founders may have had about the future transformation of the colleges into universities, it was out of question for them to ask what kind of site would best suit their future status and functions. The amount of money available for the purchase of land and for the construction of buildings was very limited, and the donors gave their contributions to found a civic institution. Thus there was no option; the earlier colleges had to be placed on small sites within the city boundaries and the consequences are familiar: desirable extensions are only possible at great cost, if possible at all; hence a cramped and inconvenient layout offering little opportunity for creating the atmosphere of dignity which should characterise a university. As time went on and colleges were founded in less populous centres, more spacious sites, not so much encircled by built-up areas, were acquired. Nevertheless the situation has not yet been such in England as to permit the uninhibited choice of a site for a new university.

Of all this those in Great Britain and overseas who had a hand in carrying out the Asquith programme were aware. In those cases where there was freedom of choice the aim was to secure an ample area of natural beauty, offering the opportunity for dignified planning, near a city, preferably the capital. The size of the area must be enough to accommodate the academic buildings, student residences and playing fields up to the requirements of the ultimate student population; depending on local circumstances, it may have to house the teaching, administrative and servant staff. In the latter case experience shows that where there are 1,000 students the total population, counting wives and children, may exceed 10,000. So much depends on the nature and lie of the land that no figure can be provided for the size of area needed for a given number of students. But it can be said that one square mile is seldom likely to be excessive, and that four times this size may be justified in circumstances such as exist at Ibadan and at Legon Hill in Ghana. The sites chosen for the University Colleges of Ghana and the West Indies and for University College, Ibadan, were described in Chapter 5 and no more need be said about them; they are all of sufficient size and near capital cities though Ibadan is the capital of a region and not of the country. The University College of Rhodesia is an exception in that it is within the built-up area of the city of Salisbury, but the site had already been chosen before there was any question of a development in Southern Rhodesia under the Asquith programme.

In cases where existing universities and colleges were to be developed there could only be question of a new site if the defects of the existing site were very serious, and then not unless a more suitable site and the necessary finance were in prospect. Difficult as is the site in Hong Kong there was never a prospect of a move. In Khartoum the acquisition of a large adjacent area remedied the one defect of an otherwise very suitable site. The situation of Makerere College on one of the hills ringing the city of Kampala is very appropriate, but the failure to acquire the whole hill has led to some congestion of the buildings. There were two cases where the defects seemed serious enough to justify a move, those of Malta and Malaya. The transfer of the University of Malta was delayed for lack of finance; but money is now in sight and the University will be moved to a very suitable situation two miles outside Valetta. How it came about that the attractive site purchased for the University of Malaya at Johore Bahru was abandoned has been explained in Chapter 4; the Singapore branch therefore remains where it was with its two precincts separated by some three miles. It is interesting to note that for the new branch of the University the government of the Federation of Malaya has chosen a site of ample size in the Pantai Valley, some three miles from the capital, Kuala

115

Lumpur, showing that the government is of one mind with those who have selected sites under the Asquith programme.

There can be no doubt that there is much to recommend the type of site which has been sought for the new foundations—away from the stir and bustle of a city but in touch with vigorous urban life. Proximity to a city, and especially to the capital, is of great advantage to universities in these territories whose remoteness from other intellectual centres can be to some extent offset by easy access to the capital which attracts visitors from foreign countries. Whatever benefits these territories may inherit from colonial times, site planning and architecture of merit will hardly be numbered among them. It was in the minds of those who helped to carry out the Asquith programme that the construction of the colleges would afford one of the last opportunities to build with British government funds, and that the chance to build worthily should not be missed. How well the chance was taken informed opinion will presently decide; but it can hardly be doubted that particular buildings, such as Mr Newton's hall of residence at Khartoum, and certain groups of buildings, such as Messrs Fry, Drew and Partners' creations at Ibadan, will bring credit to their designers.

Building for these colleges raises aesthetic questions as to the style appropriate for each region; it also produces technical problems related to climate. All the colleges are situated in regions which are warmer than western Europe; most of them are in regions with a hot wet or a hot dry climate. The question of the influence of climate upon history opens the way to fascinating speculation, but one thing at least is certain: great civilizations have risen and flourished both in the extreme hot wet and hot dry climates. A high level of physical and mental activity is possible in such climates, but this does not mean that all types of climate are equally favourable to these activities. A European who goes to live in a hot wet or a hot dry climate finds, even after many years of acclimatization, that he is less disposed to be active than at home, at least at certain times of the day or seasons of the year. He also finds that the locally born, whose ancestors have lived in such a climate for generations, feel just as he does; they too 'suffer' from the climate. This is a very remarkable fact since it might be expected that the descendants of

116

dwellers in hot climates would in time become adapted to the conditions in the sense that they would not find them as oppressive as do immigrants from temperate climates. But this has not happened and, whatever the explanation may be, those who design buildings in these climates must do what is possible to mitigate their oppressive effects in the interests of the locally born as much as of visitors. That this is so is supported by careful scientific work; it has been shown that, as the temperature rises, a critical point is reached above which members of all races feel discomfort and begin to work less effectively.

Attention to layout of the site and to the construction of buildings can help appreciably to overcome the effects of climate. There must be much coming and going between the main university buildings; and if they are placed fairly close together, much unnecessary effort is avoided; the planning of the buildings at Ibadan may seem congested when there is so much space available, but anyone who, after spending some time there, goes to Legon Hill and is faced with a mile and a quarter between the entrance and the tower, will appreciate the Ibadan layout. Buildings can be protected against sunlight on their main walls by placing their long axes east and west and by deep eaves and louvres over the windows; through ventilation can be encouraged by careful planning of entrances, windows and corridors. But all this amounts only to alleviation; air conditioning amounts much more nearly to a cure. When the first buildings of the colleges were designed, air-conditioning was in its infancy, and no provision was made for it. It is not easy to introduce it with effect into buildings designed for through ventilation; the practice is increasingly to provide it in new buildings, and those who work in air-conditioned rooms are unanimous in saying that their comfort and efficiency are greatly enhanced. But books and instruments benefit as much as men from air-conditioning; electrical apparatus in particular suffers from humidity and dust. There can be no doubt that air-conditioning will spread and will create something like a revolution in working conditions in these universities; but the cost of cooling, which seems to equal that of heating, will come in as a new expense though it is said that, since with air conditioning rooms can be small, building costs may be less.

The manner in which the problem of climate presents itself and the steps taken to overcome it can be illustrated from the experience of the University of Hong Kong where the summer months are hot and humid. The old plan produced large, well-ventilated buildings without road access; the new plan, which has gained the day, is for more compact and largely air-conditioned buildings with road access and parking places. The new library will be wholly air-conditioned, but in other new buildings rooms, which are large and not in continual use, will not be air-conditioned. The dissecting room in the new pre-clinical building was regarded as a marginal case, but it has finally been decided to air-condition it. Air-conditioning is being introduced into old buildings for heavily used rooms and wherever it is advantageous for the maintenance of apparatus.

It is easy to disparage bricks and mortar and to point to the scholar in his attic and to the experimentalist with his home-made apparatus, and it is indeed possible to attribute undue importance to the material background as promoting or hindering intellectual effort. But no one can say that the overseas universities and colleges have failed to set their intellectual aims high; the most insistent criticism to which they are subjected is that their academic standards are too advanced, and this criticism will be considered in Chapter 18. Their attitude to the material background of university life is in line with that now dominant in most western universities where its influence as a factor in the social and cultural education of students is increasingly understood. To students everywhere the university is a great experience; to students in the overseas universities it is an experience making a far greater impression than in countries where the kind of influence associated with universities is also felt outside them. While all universities can offer much more to students than intellectual training if they make provision for a dignified way of life in surroundings of spaciousness and beauty, the overseas universities can exert most influence in this manner. It is the duty of the overseas universities to serve the students in this respect so far as it lies in their power, and those who are acquainted with them will not say that they have failed to do so.

CHAPTER 9

DEVELOPMENT AND RANGE OF STUDIES

(1) THE UNIVERSITIES

The last three chapters have dealt with the organization which enables the universities and colleges to do their work. We now pass on to consider the growth in the number of students and of the range of studies. All the universities select for admission from among those who reach minimum entrance standards. The University of Malta sets its own matriculation examination; the Universities of Malaya and Hong Kong require the Cambridge School Certificate or other equivalent qualification up to a pre-scribed level while in addition they require candidates to sit for their entrance examinations unless specially exempted. The total student population since 1946 (in the case of Malaya since 1949) is shown year by year in the accompanying graph. The fluctuations in the Maltese figures in the first part of the period are due to the triennial system of entry, while the decline in the second part is due to the attraction into the emergency teacher training scheme of some of those who would otherwise have entered the University. In Hong Kong where the University was closed during the war, the number of students, who had registered by 1946, has increased thirteenfold; at Khartoum, where there was no interruption, there has been a sevenfold increase, while in Malaya the student population has more than trebled since 1949 when the University was formed by an amal-gamation of two colleges. Before the recent decline in numbers the ratio of students to population in Malta was about the same as that in Great Britain where it is about one to every 500 persons; this is the only case among the universities and colleges where the ratio approached the British level. In Hong Kong the

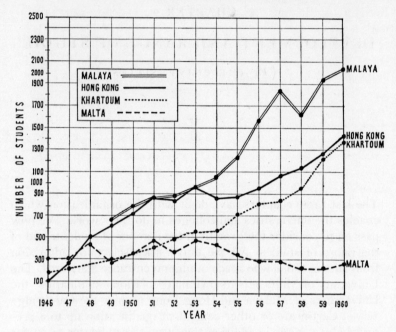

ratio is one to well over 2,000, in Malaya one to over 3,000 and in the Sudan one to over 6,000.[1]

TABLE 2

UNIVERSITIES: PERCENTAGE OF STUDENTS BY FACULTIES

Faculty	Universities of Malta, Hong Kong, Malaya and Khartoum	
	1950	1959
Arts	27·1	38·1
Science	13·4	17·1
Medicine	36·7	20·8
Other Professions	22·8	24·0

Table 2 shows the students classified by faculties in 1950 and 1959. All students, whether whole-time or part-time, whether seeking degrees or diplomas, are included; part-time students are few in number (fifty-four in Malaya and forty-eight in Hong

Kong in 1959); diplomas, with one or two exceptions, are open only to graduates. The most notable change in the distribution of students between faculties in the overseas universities during these nine years is the sharp decline in the proportion of medical students whose absolute number has however increased. The growth in the proportion of arts students is due in large measure to the institution or the development of departments of economics and commerce; in this period advance was made in the provision of professional faculties other than medicine which accounts for the increased proportion of students found in them. Table 3 sets out in greater detail the position in 1959. All the universities make provision for medicine and engineering, and three do so for law and architecture. To the existing provision for dentistry in Malaya and Malta facilities may soon be added in Hong Kong. There is no local demand for agricultural and veterinary teaching in Hong Kong and Malta. The most obvious gap was the lack of teaching in agriculture in Malaya, but teaching in this subject began in 1960 in Kuala Lumpur; in Malaya there may be a case for veterinary education and in Hong Kong for law. But the coverage of professional education is already large, and the criticism sometimes made of the overseas universities that they neglect professional training is clearly very wide of the mark.

Some account has been given in Chapter 4 of the chief events in each of these four universities since 1946 to which some further facts may be added. For the matriculation examination of the University of Malta candidates must offer six subjects: English, Maltese, mathematics, another language, ancient or modern, and a science subject are compulsory, an unusual concentration on the tools of learning. The courses for the BA and the BSc are general, and take four years; no special courses are offered, but students who do well at the intermediate examination for the BA can read for honours. The content of the course for the BA with its considerable linguistic requirements and its emphasis on Mediterranean history reflects the island's position. Alone among these universities Malta offers a degree in theology; in 1959 there were thirty-one students and six professors (part-time) of that subject.

The University of Hong Kong had faculties of arts, science,

TABLE 3

THE UNIVERSITIES: NUMBER OF STUDENTS AND SUBJECTS OF STUDY: 1959

Subject	University					Total
	Malta	Hong Kong	Malaya		Khartoum	
			Singapore	Kuala Lumpur		
Arts	85	568	560	163	418	1,794
Science	29	163	218	31	352	793
Medicine	69	298	462		141	970
Dentistry	12		99			111
Pharmacy	7		27			34
Engineering	4	83		129	71	287
Architecture	7	57			13	77
Law	14		147		112	273
Agriculture					67	67
Veterinary Science					42	42
Education		99	87			186
Total	231¹	1,268	1,600	323	1,216	4,620¹

¹ Total adjusted for double entries.

medicine and engineering before the war; the major innovation since the war has been teaching in architecture, included in the faculty of engineering. While the energy of the University has been largely expended on re-establishing itself, there have been considerable additions to the subjects studied in the faculties; thus in the faculty of arts, in addition to the basic subjects, there is provision for economics, commerce and business administration, and for philosophy and modern languages including French, German, Spanish, Portuguese and Italian. Under the original ordinance of 1911 the University was required to provide teaching in Chinese, and this has always been carried out in the faculty of arts. The work of the Chinese department was augmented in 1952 by the foundation of an Institute of Oriental Studies which provides facilities for research and sets out to act as a focus for students of all countries who are interested in that field. The course for the BA lasts three years and is general in content; successful candidates are classed as having gained honours or as having passed. The arrangements for the BSc are different; the course, which is general, lasts three years, and those who gain the degree, which does not carry honours, may study for honours in one of five subjects during a further year. The failure rate is low which is the result of severe competition for entrance and of the habit of assiduous study which is characteristic of the students. Candidates for higher degrees are increasing (fourteen in 1958–9).

Of the two institutions which were fused in 1949 to form the University of Malaya, the College of Medicine was relatively well developed, whereas Raffles College, though its standards were high, could provide teaching only in the basic subjects of arts and science; it has therefore been outside the medical field that developments have taken place. Three new faculties have been added, of engineering (1955), of law (1957, faculty status in 1959), and of agriculture (1960); new departments have been introduced as follows: in arts, education (1950) now a separate school of education, philosophy (1952), Chinese language and literature, Malay studies (now in Kuala Lumpur), social studies (1953), an art museum with subsidiary teaching in the history of art (1955), and Indian studies (now in Kuala Lumpur) (1956); in science, zoology (1950) and geology

(1956); in medicine, parasitology (1950), and clinical medicine and orthopaedics (1952). It was not, as in the case of Hong Kong, an original requirement for Raffles Colleges to provide facilities for oriental studies; they were introduced somewhat late in Malaya to fill a gap in the scope of teaching rather than as part of a comprehensive plan to facilitate study and research into Asian problems. Now that the University has been divided into two branches, that at Kuala Lumpur is proposing to develop south-east Asian studies. A statement issued by the branch states that 'the Federation of Malaya is ideally situated' for this purpose; 'it has been the meeting point and path of dispersal of south-east Asian cultures, having absorbed aspects of all cultures, and could now become the local centre of learning for students who have inherited these traditions as well as for research workers from non-Asian countries'. At present each branch has faculties of arts and science, and there is an agreed distribution of the professional faculties, Singapore retaining medicine and law, Kuala Lumpur housing engineering and agriculture. In time most faculties are likely to be duplicated, and as already noted, each branch, when it becomes a separate university, is likely to go its own way and develop its own special interests and traditions. The arrangements for the BSc course are much like those in Hong Kong; those who have gained the pass degree of BSc can work for honours during a fourth year of study in a special subject. But in regard to the BA there is this difference: only those students who show enough promise at the end of the first year can seek honours. In 1959 75 candidates graduated with BA honours, 115 with BA pass, 14 with BSc honours and 36 with BSc pass. In the session 1958–9 there were 53 students working for higher degrees. Both in Hong Kong and Malaya external examiners are employed and standards are at the British level.

Alone among the four universities the University of Khartoum was at one time in special relation with the University of London (1946 to 1956). Gordon College, as it then was, suffered no interruption of studies through enemy occupation; it was transformed after the war as described in Chapter 4 where an account is given of the raising of an already wide range of studies to university level. The courses of study are oriented towards the local situation and local problems. There is a department of Arabic in the faculty of arts and a department of Islamic law in the faculty of law, while special attention is given to Islamic philosophy in the department of philosophy. In the faculty of economics and social studies students can work for one of three degrees, in economics, in social studies or social anthropology; opportunities are given to study Sudanese ethnology and the problems of peasant society. The course for the BA degree lasts for a minimum of four years; this arrangement is carried over from the period of special relation with London under which students entering with less than London admission requirements had to take not less than this period over the course. At the end of the third year students who seek honours undertake more specialized work which they complete in two more years—making five years in all. The course for the BSc also lasts four years; students who have gained the degree may specialize for another year and are then eligible for honours. As in the Far Eastern universities this system permits some specialization and gives scope for academic ability, but does not demand that high degree of specialization which characterizes most honours courses in British universities. A regulation provides that external examiners, 'one or more in each subject', shall take part in 'the intermediate examination and every examination for a degree, diploma or certificate of the University'. In this way the standards required by London University during the period of special relation continue to be exacted.

NOTE

1. Appendix 9 shows the number of students in the universities and colleges in October 1960.

CHAPTER 10

DEVELOPMENT AND RANGE OF STUDIES

(2) THE COLLEGES

The colleges form a more homogeneous group than the universities; all but one are in Africa, all but Fourah Bay College are in special relation with the University of London, and all but two have been founded since 1946. The accompanying graph shows the growth in the number of students from the dates when the colleges came within the Asquith plan. The decline in the number of students in Ghana between 1953 and 1956 was due to the introduction of sixth forms into the schools; otherwise growth in numbers has been steady.

Those concerned with carrying out the Asquith plan took the view that it was urgent to begin teaching for degrees in order to hasten the emergence of graduates whose services were so much needed in territories advancing towards independence. But in the early days of the scheme teaching in the secondary schools seldom reached a level which enabled pupils to satisfy the minimum entrance requirements of London University with which the colleges were in special relation. It was evident that, unless special measures were taken, few pupils would matriculate and that a long period would elapse before the number of students working for degrees at some of the colleges would be substantial. To meet this situation the University agreed to accept lower qualifications for entry to the University Colleges of Khartoum and of East Africa in the knowledge that students would spend four years in residence. The situation became more difficult in 1949 when the University raised its entry requirements from the level of school certificate to that of higher school certificate and abolished the intermediate examination. To meet this new difficulty the University agreed to continue to accept

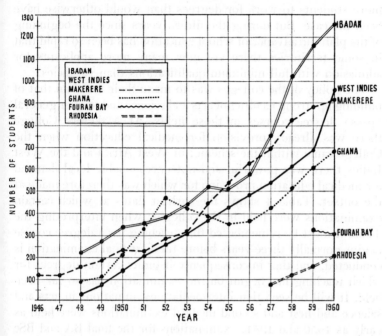

for intermediate courses students in colleges in special relation who had been qualified to matriculate under the old regulations on the condition that such students spent four years in residence in a college. The University has also, where necessary in each case, made modifications in the detailed requirements for entry without imposing further conditions.

With the exception of Rhodesia, which demanded full London entry requirements from the start, all the colleges have taken advantage of these arrangements for a time; at Makerere College, for example, the requirements up to 1957 were a school certificate with three credits. The requirements have been steadily raised following the introduction of sixth forms in schools: Ghana demanded full London qualifications in 1955; in Nigeria and the West Indies full London qualifications are normally required but candidates coming from regions where the standard of school education is still low may matriculate at concessional level; Makerere College will demand full London qualifications in 1961. By these means it was made possible for more students to work for degrees than would otherwise have been the case. But during the fifteen years since the beginning of the plan the advance of school education has been so rapid that in some territories there are now many more applicants for admission with full minimum qualifications than vacancies.

The policy of the colleges was to make their first aim that of building up strong faculties of arts and science and to offer general (pass) degree courses in those fields. At Makerere College there was already provision for medical education when the College came within the scheme; in West Africa and the West Indies there was powerful and not unreasonable local demand for medical education provision for which was therefore made at the outset. Table 4 shows the earliest dates at which certain examinations were held in the colleges; when interpreting the Table it must be remembered that teaching for a degree course begins normally three years before the first final examination is conducted, and that in consequence it omits certain degrees for which teaching has begun but no examination has so far been held. It will be seen that intermediate examinations in arts and science and first and second medical examinations were held as early as 1950 and 1951; examinations for the final BA and BSc soon followed. The next step was the holding of examinations for special (honours) degrees in arts and science, the first of which were held in 1952 in Ghana. Other examinations for special degrees followed in rapid succession; examinations for professional degrees, other than in medicine, came somewhat later. Dates for medical examinations at Makerere College do not appear in the Table because the College offers its own medical diploma which is recognized by the General Medical Council.

A very important feature of the scheme of special relations with London University is that, if the colleges so wish, the University is prepared to modify syllabuses to meet local needs. In response to requests from the colleges for modification London University has adopted a most liberal attitude. In such subjects as history and geography there is most occasion for special papers relating to the territories, and an inspection of the syllabuses shows that local history and local geography figure prominently. The modifications have extended beyond the replacement of papers suitable for British students by others suited to the locally born; London University has agreed to the inclusion of papers which do not figure in the London syllabus, for example of sociology at Makerere College and of government at Ibadan among those which can be taken for the BA general. The study of languages presents a special problem; except in the

TABLE 4

EXAMINATIONS IN COLLEGES IN SPECIAL RELATION
WITH LONDON UNIVERSITY

Dates when examinations were held for the first time.

Examination	College					
	Khartoum	Makerere	Ibadan	Ghana	West Indies	Rhodesia
Intermediate Arts	1948	1951	1950	1950	1951	
BA General (P)	1950	1953	1951	1952	1953	1959
BA Special. English		1960	1957	1953	1955	
BA Special. French				1956	1957	
BA Special. Latin			1954		1957	
BA Special. Classics			1954	1953		
BA Special. History		1960	1955	1952	1955	
BA Special. Geography		1960	1956	1952		
BA Special. Sociology				1954		
BA Special. Mathematics		1961				
BA Special. Philosophy				1954		
BSc Economics		1961	1961	1958		
LLB	1953					
BD				1952		
Intermediate Science	1948	1951	1950	1950	1950	
BSc General	1950	1953	1952	1951	1952	1959
BSc Special. Chemistry			1955	1952	1961	
BSc Special. Physics			1954	1953	1961	
BSc Special. Mathematics		1961	1961	1960	1960	
BSc Special. Botany			1954	1953		
BSc Special. Zoology			1954	1953		
BSc Special. Geography			1958			
BSc Special. Geology				1955		
First Medical					1949	
Second Medical			1950		1951	
MB, BS			1960		1954	
BSc Engineering	1956		1960			
BSc Agriculture (P)	1952	1961	1953	1956		
BSc Agriculture			1960			1960

All final examinations carry honours except when marked P (equal pass)

West Indies students are learning in a language which they do not speak at home.[1] Therefore in order to permit concentration upon the study of English (a second language for most students) London University has not demanded the inclusion of a classical or modern foreign language in the entrance requirements and has left it for the colleges to decide how far they will make provision for languages other than English in degree courses. But knowledge of modern foreign languages is of value for these students, French in Africa for example, and special degree courses in French are available in Ghana, and in both French and Spanish in the West Indies. But Table 4 does not bring out by any means the full extent to which modern foreign languages can be studied since they may be subjects for the BA general, French and Portuguese in Rhodesia for example. That there should be provision for the classical languages of Europe may cause surprise; but this is not to be interpreted as an attempt to foist on to African students what is relevant primarily for European students; it has been made in response to a local demand for opportunity to study these classical languages for which some African and West Indian students exhibit marked aptitude.

It may be asked whether, after taking account of the modification of the syllabuses for courses such as those in history and geography, enough opportunity is provided for the study of local society, local organization and local conditions. In answer it is relevant to say that provision is made for these studies whether it passes under the name of African studies (Rhodesia), sociology (Makerere, Ghana and the West Indies), or social studies (Ibadan). Sociology, to use that term as a comprehensive title for these studies, may figure in three different degree courses; it may form the subject of a special degree course as in Ghana, it may be an option in the BA general course, or, if the course for the BSc economics is available as at Makerere, Ghana and Ibadan, it may appear as one of the subjects since that course is broadly based and is not confined to economics. Turning to science little modification is called for in chemistry and physics, though modifications have been introduced to suit the special interests of teachers; but some adaptation is called for and has been approved in zoology and botany to take account of local fauna and flora and conditions of life in the tropics. The kind of changes in professional degree courses, which are needed and have been approved, do not need illustration. Looking at the whole situation it can fairly be claimed that the courses are not courses for British students to which a local twist or slant has been given; so far as content goes, they are such as would be designed for the needs of the students of each territory if the colleges had a free hand. That this is so receives support from the fact that the University of Khartoum, which became independent in 1956, has left almost intact the syllabus designed during the period of special relationship with London University.

TABLE 5

The Colleges: Percentage of Students by Faculties, 1959
(University College, Ibadan, Fourah Bay College, the University Colleges of East Africa, Ghana, Rhodesia and the West Indies)

Faculty	Percentage
Arts	46·4
Science	25·5
Medicine	14·3
Other Professional	13·8

The distribution of students between faculties is shown in Table 5 and may be compared with Table 2 which gives a similar distribution for the students in overseas universities. The distribution in respect of arts and science is much as in Great Britain, but medicine is relatively more important and other professions less so. It has always been the intention of the colleges to offer as soon as possible professional courses in law, education, veterinary science, engineering, architecture and agriculture, but various factors have caused delay. In some cases, agriculture in the West Indies for example, there were special local difficulties. Everywhere lack of finance has been a factor; education is the least expensive professional faculty and this is the faculty in which professional teaching, other than in medicine, has been most expanded; indeed, if education students were excluded from those in other professional faculties, the percentage in the remaining other faculties would drop from nearly 14 to under 9. But there have been additional factors tending to inhibit or to delay the provision of professional

131

TABLE 6

THE COLLEGES: NUMBER OF STUDENTS AND SUBJECTS OF STUDY, 1959

Subject	Makerere	Ibadan	Ghana	West Indies	Rhodesia	Fourah Bay	Total
				College			
Arts	345	448	383	279	77	214	1,746
Science	267	267	124	186	51	88	962
Medicine	121	206		211			538
Agriculture	49	69	43		6		167
Veterinary Science	32						32
Engineering		90				15	105
Education	66	32	33	20	25	13	189
Law			27				27
Total	880	1,112	610	675	159	330	3,766

teaching which will be described in the following chapter.

The number of students and their subjects of study are set out in Table 6. It includes all students, whether whole- or part-time; part-time students are rare except in Rhodesia where there are twenty-six. Students seeking diplomas and certificates are mostly graduates, but in some colleges the education diploma is open to non-graduates, and at Fourah Bay College the engineering course is for non-graduates and leads to a certificate. All the colleges offer courses in arts, science and education; three offer medicine, and two colleges, Ghana and Rhodesia, have plans for medical faculties. Teaching in agriculture is beginning in the West Indies and that will leave only one college without provision for that subject. The present gaps are in law, veterinary science and engineering; in making provision for teaching in these subjects colleges have encountered special difficulties to be mentioned in Chapter 11.

At the colleges in special relation with London University the British degree system is in use which in respect of one aspect has been subject to some criticism in British academic circles. It is the ambition of the head of each department in the newer English universities to have his own special (honours) degree course; the more promising students are encouraged to enter such courses which are narrow in range. In consequence general degree courses lack prestige; moreover, since they are not the responsibility of any one department, the teachers tend to lose interest in them. It may be asked whether the multiplication of special (honours) degree courses best suits the needs of overseas students, and indeed whether the needs of many British students would not be met better by general degree courses carrying honours than by the highly specialized courses which most of them follow. It is difficult for those brought up and educated in western society to realize how scarce are the opportunities for learning anything outside school and college, and how feeble and limited are the intellectual stimuli, in the environment from which many overseas students come. Hence if their intellectual training is narrowly concentrated, their intellectual horizon and grasp are likely to be more restricted than in the case of western students, many of whom, however, might profit from a wider education. The arrangements for degree courses in the Universities of Hong Kong and Malaya, described in the last chapter, do not provide for the same degree of specialization as do those in England, and it is interesting to note that the University of Khartoum, which had no degree courses carrying honours while in special relation with the University of London, has now instituted such courses on the model of Hong Kong and Malaya. It may be that this model, rather than the English model, suits overseas students best.

Table 7 shows for 1956 and 1960 the number of candidates from four university colleges in special relation with London University who passed or failed when sitting for certain examinations. The percentage of candidates who passed is also given, and can be compared with the percentage of internal and other external candidates who passed at equivalent examinations. Internal candidates are students of London University who have attended a college of the University or an institution in London with teachers recognized by the University; other external candidates are all students in that category except students in colleges in special relation with the University. It will be seen that the performance of the students of the university colleges is on a level with that of the internal students and better than that of other external students. During the nine years 1952 to 1960 forty-four candidates gained first class honours; honours are not awarded for the BA general but candidates are placed in divisions, and twelve candidates were in the first division. Moreover performance improved between 1956 and 1960; in the former year 72 per cent of candidates for all degrees passed, and in the latter year 85 per cent.

The number of students sitting for final examinations is still small though rapidly increasing; it was 226 in 1956 and 452 in 1960. In consequence the number of those who have so far graduated is small; the number who have graduated from the University of Khartoum (between 1950 and 1959 while in special relation with London University) is 137, from the University College of East Africa (1953 to 1960) 223, from the University College of Ghana (1951 to 1960) 538, from University College, Ibadan (1951 to 1960) 578, from the University College of the West Indies (1952 to 1960) 571, from the University College of Rhodesia (1960) 23, making a

TABLE 7
EXAMINATION RESULTS

| Year | Degree | Candidates from the University College of the West Indies, University College, Ibadan, University College of Ghana, and the University College of East Africa | | | Other candidates Per cent Passes | |
		Number Passes	Number Failures	Per cent Passes	Internal	External
1956[1]	BA General	72	27	72	71	68
	Honours	38	1	97	93	86
	BSc General	41	32	56	60	49
	Special	12	3	80	86	46[2]
1960	BA General	144	31	62	57	54
	Honours	143	17	88	95	77
	BSc General	45	15	75	74	51[2]
	Special	55	2	96	87	67

[1] No examinations were taken at the University College of East Africa between November 1955 and March 1957. The figures used for 1956 were those for the examinations held in November, 1955.

[2] The BSc Special Examination under Old Regulations was held for the last time for External Students in 1956, and the BSc General Examination under Old Regulations was held for the last time in 1960. The proportion of successful candidates in both examinations was abnormally low owing to the inclusion of a substantial number of 'last chance' entries.

total of 2,070. No figures are available showing the number of those coming from these territories who have graduated abroad in the same period, but it must certainly be larger. In Appendix 7 there are figures, gathered from various sources, relating to the number of students, coming from all the territories with which this book is concerned, who were studying at universities abroad at the dates then shown. These figures must be treated with reserve; it is possible that some students are included who should not have been counted; on the other hand it is likely that the figures omit many students who should have been included.

These figures show how far the present situation falls short of the aim of the Asquith Commissioners. 'The whole tenour of our report', they wrote, 'has pointed to the conclusion that the undergraduate education of colonial students should, wherever practicable, be carried on in colonial universities'.[2] This conclusion is founded on a principle of world-wide application; before young people can profit from the experience of living in another country they require knowledge of their own country, its people and institutions, and also a firm social and emotional background which they can acquire only if they are educated in their own country up to first degree stage. It is the graduate who profits from experience abroad. This is not to say that, if a student cannot follow his chosen course at home, it is not right for him to go abroad; by so doing he can acquire intellectual training, but it would be better for him to obtain it at home along with all else that an education at home can give. But to achieve the aim of the Commissioners far more time is needed than that which has elapsed since their programme was launched.

NOTES

1. An interesting modification has been made in the regulations for the BA general at the University College of the West Indies; students may take both 'English' and 'English Language with special reference to the Caribbean.'
2. *Report of the Commission on Higher Education in the Colonies*, 1945, p. 49.

CHAPTER 11

PROFESSIONAL EDUCATION

It is a dominating ambition of the locally born in colonial territories to enter the higher ranks of professional practice, and it is broadly true to say that, in order to do so, they must possess the qualifications which serve that purpose in Great Britain. Therefore it is important that, for those students who cannot come to Great Britain, there should be awards obtainable locally, which are recognized in Great Britain as passports to the higher ranks. This fact has hitherto governed the policy of the universities and colleges when they contemplated setting up professional schools. When colonial rule comes to an end, an independent government can lay down what conditions it pleases relating to professional practice, and the governments of Ghana and Nigeria have taken advantage of their freedom to do so in relation to the practice of law.

LAW

In Great Britain the right to plead in the courts is confined to barristers while solicitors alone can perform certain functions such as drawing up legal documents for a fee. Apart from Malta where special conditions have long prevailed, and apart from Ghana, Nigeria and Malaya where changes, described later, have recently been introduced, the position is as follows. In a few territories, notably some of the West Indies, there is no substantial departure from British practice; the right to plead in the courts is confined to those who have been called to one of the three bars of the United Kingdom while solicitors perform functions similar to those falling to solicitors in Great Britain. In most of the territories, however, the right to plead in the courts is extended to those admitted as solicitors by the English Law Society or by one of the corresponding bodies in Scotland and Northern Ireland, and when this is so, the profession may be said to be 'fused' and the term 'advocate' may be used for the fully qualified lawyer. Therefore interest centres on the procedure through which a call to a bar of the United Kingdom and admission as a solicitor in the United Kingdom can be obtained. As it happens, it is not necessary to describe the procedure for admission as a solicitor because very few advocates have attained that rank by virtue of a qualification as a solicitor; a survey carried out in Nigeria in 1959 revealed only one advocate who had qualified in that way. To obtain a call to a bar a student from these territories must come to the United Kingdom, must keep eight terms (there are four terms in a year, and this is a concession since students resident in the United Kingdom must keep twelve terms), and must pass two examinations. To do so a student must have the financial resources needed for the journey and for prolonged residence in the United Kingdom; in spite of this serious financial obstacle a number of colonial students have been called to a bar and, together with expatriate lawyers, form the nucleus of a legal profession which is less inadequate in size to the needs of the territories than is the case in respect of most other professions. Though relatively adequate in size, in some territories the composition of the profession is preponderantly ex-patriate (in East Africa out of 520 lawyers only 31 are Africans, the rest being British or Indian), while in all territories where the profession is fused, the training is defective because it is directed to advocacy and not to the work undertaken by a solicitor. To this state of things conditions in Malta have always been an exception; to become an advocate in Malta it is necessary to hold a degree in law of the University of Malta or a degree recognized by it.

It is remarkable that this system, which favours the locally rich, should have lasted so long; it seems that advocates of local and expatriate origin were strongly entrenched and used their influence to delay the recognition of a local qualification which would make access to their ranks more easy. It was in Ghana in 1958 that a change was first made, that is a year after independence. In that year the Legal Practitioners Act was passed; it set up a General Legal Council with power to define the qualifications for admission as advocate, and also a Board of Legal Education which supervises legal training. The Council has established a School of Law and has laid down that a degree in law, gained at the University College of Ghana after a four-year course and followed by a fifth year of practical work at the School, is essential for admission, except in the case of holders of foreign law degrees of approved universities who may also be admitted if they pass an examination held by the University College. The College played its part by establishing a faculty of law and a four-years' course for a degree; the School of Law has a link with the College because the professor of law is also head of the School. In order to increase the number of advocates (in 1958 there were 120 in private practice and 60 in government service) the School of Law will grant a diploma admitting to practice during the first five years of its existence.

A committee set up in 1959 to consider the legal profession in Nigeria recommended a programme very similar to that adopted in Ghana; the recommendation has been accepted by the government, and University College, Ibadan, is making preparations to found a department of law. In the same year the Bar Council of Malaya and the Bar Committee of Singapore approved the recognition of the LLB degree of the University of Malaya for practice in Malaya and Singapore. It has been suggested that the proposed university college in Tanganyika should offer a course leading to a legal degree and thus fill a gap in the provision for higher education in East Africa; presumably, if this comes about, the degree in law will become a recognized qualification for local practice. A school of law is a relatively inexpensive professional school, but it is easy to see why the colleges held back from instituting such schools; there was a greater lack of practitioners in the other professions than in law, and until the system of entry into the legal profession was changed, a legal degree was no passport to practice. The University of Malaya, however, did set up a legal degree in advance of such a change, and this step proved to be justified because the change was made before the first students of law had completed their degree course.

MEDICINE

Legal schools were the last, whereas medical schools were the first professional schools to be instituted; in origin the latter often antedated all other teaching facilities. The General Medical Council of Great Britain recognizes certain medical qualifications whose holders are entitled to place their names on the register which it maintains. The medical degrees of the Universities of Malta and Hong Kong and the medical diploma of the King Edward VII Medical School in Singapore (now the degree of the University of Malaya) have been recognized by the Council. Since 1940 holders of the medical diploma of Gordon College, Khartoum (now the medical degree of the University of Khartoum), the examination for which is supervised by the Royal College of Physicians and the Royal College of Surgeons, have been entitled to come to Great Britain and sit for the examination held jointly by them which leads to a qualification registrable by the General Medical Council. This is in effect making a local qualification registrable at one remove. In all these cases a government hospital was available for clinical teaching; they lack a hospital board of management on the model found in Great Britain whereas there are such boards in the new hospitals mentioned below which were built as teaching hospitals.

To the Asquith Commission the need for a greatly enlarged medical profession in Africa was very obvious; it was estimated that the ratio of doctors to population was one for every 100,000 of the population in Nigeria. The Commission recognized that a grade of medical assistant, with qualifications inferior to those of registered practitioners but superior to those of a nurse, could be of great service in the diagnosis and treatment of the commoner diseases, but they held that training for such a grade should be given in special institutions for which the universities would not be responsible. The Commission were emphatic in their view that in some of the new universities from the outset, and in all of them in due course, there should be courses in medicine leading to a registrable qualification. It was obvious to them that there was strong local demand for facilities leading to a registrable qualification which arose, in their opinion, from

140

ambition to demonstrate capacity to achieve the same standard of professional competence as that reached by Europeans rather than from desire to acquire the privileges of practice in Great Britain which registration confers. Moreover, medical schools, which aimed at the highest standards of training, would become centres for much-needed research into local medical problems.

In 1945 elementary medical training was being provided by Makerere College in conjunction with the hospital of the Uganda government situated on the adjoining Mulago Hill. Facilities were greatly improved and standards were rapidly raised in the following years. In 1950 the College applied to the General Medical Council for the recognition of its medical diploma. The Council made a preliminary inspection in that year and a more thorough inspection in the following year; as a result it was learnt what it was necessary to do in order to bring facilities up to a standard which would justify registration. Energetic steps to fill the gaps were taken by the College and the Uganda government; the latter undertook to modernize the hospital at a cost of £2¼ million. A further inspection led to the recognition of the medical diploma in 1957. Since this diploma is awarded by the College medical education falls without the scheme of special relation with London University; in due course, when the College becomes a university, the diploma will be converted into a degree. Thus in East Africa the aims of the Asquith Commission have been fully achieved. Medical education is at the same standard as in Great Britain, and there is an active centre of medical research. There is an interesting and valuable arrangement with Great Ormond Street Hospital which seconds a registrar and two sisters for a period of two years and arranges for an annual visit of four weeks by a senior consultant.

In the West Indies there was no provision for medical education before the war. The Irvine Committee recommended that the college proposed by them should have a medical school from the outset and that medical students should work for the medical degree of McGill University. With the latter recommendation the Asquith Commission did not agree on the grounds that the McGill degree was not registrable with the General Medical

Council and that complications would arise if some students of the college were aiming at the degree of one universty while others were seeking the degrees of another university. It was common ground that a medical degree should be offered in the college, and therefore no consideration was given to the plan, adopted at Makerere, under which recognition is sought from the General Medical Council for a college award. The obvious solution was adopted; it was arranged that the medical course should come within the scheme of special relations with the University of London whose medical degree is registrable. It was always recognized that the hospital in Kingston could not be converted into a teaching hospital and that a new hospital would have to be built; it was erected on land belonging to the College, from whose main academic buildings it is only a few minutes walk, and was opened in 1952, the money coming directly or indirectly from CD and W funds.

The West Indian plan was adopted in Nigeria, but the events leading to that end constitute a long and chequered story. For some time there was considerable doubt about the medical qualification for which it would be best to aim; eventually it was decided that it should be the London medical degree. The attempts to find an answer to the problem of how to provide clinical teaching cannot be recounted here; it must suffice to say that use was first made of facilities in Lagos, that clinical teaching was moved to Ibadan where conditions in the local hospitals were most unsatisfactory, that various schemes to rebuild and extend these hospitals fell through and that it was ultimately decided to build a new hospital. Meanwhile students had çome forward who had passed the second medical examination; since for them there was no local centre for clinical teaching which could be approved, places had to be sought in British medical schools which, at a time of great pressure on them, offered the necessary accommodation. The new hospital was built about three miles from the College at a cost of £4·6 M provided by the government of Nigeria. It is a palatial building; it was worth waiting for, since to a layman at least, revisiting the scene, who remembers the successive but unavailing attempts to produce something tolerable out of the local hospitals with the few thousands of pounds then available, the appearance of this palace is reminiscent of the unveiling of Valhalla. Under a scheme recently adopted by the Royal Free Hospital School of Medicine there are to be joint appointments on the temporary lecturer scale tenable at the School and the College. The holders of these appointments will spend a period in Great Britain, a period in Ibadan and will return for a year to the Royal Free to complete their appointments.

Thus three new medical schools have come into existence, aiming at the highest standards and actively engaged in investigations of local problems. The University Colleges of Ghana and Rhodesia have plans for medical schools; the former has appointed a professor of medicine who will have charge of the plans. It is proposed that students of the Rhodesian College shall work for the medical degree of the University of Birmingham. Under colonial conditions it was essential to aim at a registrable qualification which was the sole passport to medical practice, but it has sometimes been asked whether it was wise to aim at a London medical degree in Nigeria and the West Indies. A medical school, proposing to train for London degrees, must comply with the requirements of London University in respect of staffing, buildings, syllabus and equipment, and must be recommended by the University to the Privy Council as fit for recognition as a centre of medical education. The standards of the University are high, and it has not been easy for the colleges to reach them; the University has not been able to recommend more than temporary recognition, in the case of the West Indies for example, from 1951 to 1954, from 1955 to 1957, for the year 1958 and from 1959 to 1961. Temporary recognition is a device intended to hasten compliance with the requirements of the University, but it leaves a college in a state of uncertainty about the future of its medical school. This is unlike the procedure of the General Medical Council which recognized Makerere College in 1957 without a time limit, with the result that it will remain recognized unless some future inspection reveals defects demanding the withdrawal of recognition. Added to this the London medical degree is by general repute more difficult to obtain than most other British medical qualifications, and the University has not seen its way to permit certain modifications in the syllabus such as the Colleges would like to see.[1] The University of London was not happy about the situation. A conference on medical education, attended by representatives of University College, Ibadan, was held in 1952; the report of the conference stated that the University had always been of opinion that arrangements for alternative qualifications should be made. In 1953 the University expressed the opinion that the University College of the West Indies should as a matter of urgency explore alternative means of obtaining a registrable qualification. Therefore it cannot be said that such difficulties as may have arisen from the high standards and procedure of the University were inescapable for colleges in special relation with the University. It can be added that so far as the anxieties of the University related to the difficulty of the course, they have proved to be unfounded. The performance of candidates at examinations has been remarkably good; performance has not been below that of internal candidates, and has sometimes exceeded it.

DENTISTRY

The registration of dentists is compulsory in nearly all the territories; to be eligible for registration it is necessary to hold a qualification recognized by the government. A degree which is registrable by the General Dental Council of the United Kingdom is everywhere recognized; the Universities of Malta and Malaya offer dental degrees which are registrable, and it is only in those countries that a dental qualification, recognized by the government, is obtainable locally. The University of Hong Kong proposes to institute a dental school; elsewhere there are no dental schools, and local residents must seek dental qualifications abroad. The policy of giving priority to medical schools was justified, not only by the greater need for medical than for dental services, but also by the fact that, when a medical school has been firmly established, a dental school can be set up without much difficulty since the first two or three years of the dental course are largely common with medicine. The time has now arrived when consideration could be given in East and West Africa and in the West Indies to the provision of courses for dental degrees.

VETERINARY SCIENCE

In British colonial territories veterinary practice is confined to those who possess the degrees of certain British universities which are registrable with the Royal College of Veterinary Surgeons. Over a period of years Makerere College built up a veterinary department with facilities for clinical teaching at Kabete near Nairobi; when it was ready to offer courses leading to the veterinary degree of London University, difficulties arose. Counsel advised that the holder of a London external degree of Bachelor of Veterinary Medicine would automatically be able to claim registration as a member of the Royal College of Veterinary Surgeons and so would be entitled to practice in Great Britain. The Royal College of Veterinary Surgeons objected to this result of the award of external degrees in veterinary medicine to students of Makerere College. Later the College agreed with the University to nominate members to a joint delegation which visited East Africa and inspected the facilities provided for veterinary education by the University College of East Africa at Makerere and at Kabete. The report of the delegation recommended that there should be a substantial improvement in those facilities. It suggested that, when work of degree standard became possible in the department of veterinary medicine, if Makerere College had not then become an independent institution awarding its own degrees the University of London might consider instituting a special degree of BVetMed (Tropical), a proposal to which there are a number of serious objections.

At that point the matter now rests. There is no prospect that students of Makerere College, or of Ibadan University College which also has a veterinary department, will be able to work for the London veterinary degree. This is a most unfortunate situation for which no responsibility falls on the colleges or on London University; it is deplorable because the need for veterinary services in Africa is immense. It seems that there can be no solution until the territories become independent when the successor governments will be at liberty to lay down by legislation the qualifications needed for professional practice; these qualifications will presumably be the veterinary degrees of their

universities if the colleges have attained that rank; if they have
not, veterinary diplomas could be recognized.

AGRICULTURE

Though agriculture does not come under the accepted definition
of a profession, it calls for discussion in this chapter for two
reasons. Appointment to the post of agricultural officer in the
service of colonial governments is normally limited to those
with degrees in agriculture or to those with a special degree in
science or economics who after graduation have taken a course
in an agricultural faculty. Therefore, in the interests of local
students, there is a good case for faculties of agriculture in the
universities. Added to this is the fact that, even more than in
medicine, agricultural problems assume special forms in each
territory, and in consequence there is need in each territory for a
centre of agricultural research such as a faculty of agriculture can
provide. This was recognized by the Asquith Commission which
advocated provision for the teaching of agriculture at degree
level.

With the exception of the Universities of Malta and Hong
Kong in whose areas agriculture is not important and Fourah
Bay College which has as yet no professional faculties, all the
institutions have set up, or are in process of setting up, faculties
of agriculture. But progress has been slower than in the case of
medicine as is shown by Table 6. For this there are various
reasons. In the West Indies it was clearly the right policy for
the College to seek an arrangement under which the Imperial
College of Tropical Agriculture in Trinidad would participate in
teaching and so avoid wasteful duplication of facilities; but, as
was described in Chapter 5, the negotiations occupied a regret-
tably long time with the result that the institution of a faculty
of agriculture has been delayed. In Malaya the institution of a
faculty of agriculture waited on the transfer of the University to
Johore Bahru; when it was decided not to transfer, it became
evident that agricultural facilities would be best provided near
Kuala Lumpur, but it was not until 1960 that courses in agriculture at that branch of the University became available. In Africa
the University College of Rhodesia made agriculture the subject

of its first professional faculty. In 1945 Gordon and Makerere Colleges were already providing elementary courses in agriculture; in both centres degrees have been instituted though advance at Makerere College was delayed until the necessary money was provided by a special grant from the territorial governments. In West Africa both the new colleges have been fortunate in acquiring large special funds for agricultural teaching; but there as elsewhere staffing has presented unusual difficulty. If progress has been slow, it is not due to lack of interest by the authorities of the institutions who have always recognized the importance of the subject; it has been due to a variety of obstacles which have been overcome. A visitor cannot fail to be impressed by the flourishing state of the agricultural faculties with their farms and the large amount of investigation, research and demonstration which is in progress. They do, however, not recruit as many students as they would like to do; prospects of other careers, in medicine, for instance, form superior attractions.

ENGINEERING

Unlike the position in medicine, dentistry and veterinary science, the practice of engineering is not regulated by statute in Great Britain, but at the higher levels it is confined in effect to those with corporate membership of one of the professional engineering institutions or to those with a degree or diploma in engineering which is recognized by the institutions as exempting from Parts I and II of the examinations held by them. In the colonial territories practice at these levels is more or less limited to those with these qualifications or others gained outside Great Britain which are regarded as being of a comparable standard. The Asquith Commission found that in 1944 890 engineering officers were employed by the colonial governments of whom 580 were classified as civil engineers, and were anxious that the universities and colleges should undertake to equip students for the important and expanding field of employment in engineering; they recognized that there were difficulties which arose from lack of local opportunities for gaining good

147

practical experience, especially in mechanical and electrical engineering.

The University of Malta was first in the field; it instituted courses in engineering in 1907 and now offers a degree of bachelor of engineering. But it is hampered by inadequate buildings and equipment, and the degree is not recognized as exempting from the examinations of the Institution of Civil Engineers; a scheme has been suggested under which certain facilities of a proposed polytechnic would be made available to the University. The University of Hong Kong taught engineering before the second world war, but experienced much difficulty in re-establishing the department which suffered devastation during the war. It now offers a degree of BSc in engineering which is recognized by the Institution of Civil Engineers; the Hong Kong technical college offers courses in engineering in preparation for the examinations of the Institutions of Mechanical and Electrical Engineers. The Malayan Commission of 1947 recommended that 'the University should set up a department of engineering forthwith', but it was not until 1955 that this step was taken in Singapore; the department has now been moved to Kuala Lumpur. The delay is not easy to explain though the failure to come to an early decision about the site played a part.

The Irvine Committee recognized the importance of engineering as a subject in the University College of the West Indies, but did not recommend the immediate institution of a department. Lack of resources held back this development until 1960 when it was decided to found a department in the new branch of the College in Trinidad. The University of Khartoum, in this as in other spheres, has a remarkable record, having built up its engineering courses from small beginnings until it was able in 1952, when still a university college in special relation with London University, to offer an engineering degree of that University. Elsewhere in Africa the story is not so happy. Before the war the engineering course, provided in the university department of Achimota College, was recognized by the University of London as preparing for the London external engineering degree. After the war the University College of Ghana became the sole centre for university studies in the country, but made no provision for engineering. University College, Ibadan, which assumed responsibility for medical education given formerly at Yaba Medical School, did not do likewise in respect of the engineering training provided at Yaba Higher College, which, however, was at an intermediate level. There were some technical courses at Makerere College in its earliest days; but they had long been abandoned, and there was no tradition of engineering on which to build.

These three university colleges were very fully occupied until after 1950 with the task of building up strong departments of arts and science; in addition University College, Ibadan, was developing medical education while Makerere College included agriculture as well as medicine in its programme. By the time when the university colleges could consider the introduction of engineering, the colleges of arts, science and technology had come into existence. These colleges offered courses in engineering; it was hoped that they would be recognized by the British engineering institutions as offering preparation for corporate membership. This being the prospect, the university colleges left engineering to the colleges falling within the purview of the COCAST, since duplication of facilities would have imposed an unnecessary burden on the territories. But difficulties arose; the institutions took the view that the most suitable road to membership lay through obtaining a degree. This meant that in East and West Africa there were no local facilities for gaining full professional qualifications. This led the colleges of arts, science and technology to look for a way out by seeking recognition of their courses as preparing for the London external degree in engineering. The sequel was described in Chapter 3. The engineering course at the Kumasi College of Technology has been recognized by London University, and the engineering department of the Zaria branch of the Nigerian College has become the faculty of engineering of University College, Ibadan. But these arrangements are not entirely satisfactory; Kumasi is more than 100 miles from Legon Hill, and Zaria nearly 400 miles from Ibadan; moreover the Kumasi College has no connection with the University College of Ghana. The outcome in East Africa is different; the Royal Technical College in Nairobi has become a university college and will offer an engineering degree. It should be added that, when Fourah Bay College came within the purview of the COCAST, it instituted a course leading to a diploma in engineering; this course, which continues at the College (now a university college), does not lead to a professional qualification, but does cover a preliminary stage of the Durham degree course in applied science.

In view of the importance of engineering in these territories, this is a disappointing story. But there is at length provision in East and West Africa for engineering education at degree level; in Central Africa the University College of Rhodesia proposes to institute a department of engineering as soon as it can find the necessary funds. The problem of bringing the engineering courses in Ghana and Nigeria into closer touch with other university work is now being studied as will be mentioned in the last chapter.

ARCHITECTURE

The Asquith Commission made no reference to education for the profession of architecture which in Great Britain takes the form of following courses leading to associate membership of the Royal Institute of British Architects; membership is obtained either by passing the examinations held by the Institute or by the possession of a degree or a diploma recognized by the Institute as exempting from its examinations. The silence of the Commission can be understood having regard to the obviously greater need for doctors, engineers and others than for architects; but work for architects and planners is growing rapidly, and it is most desirable that the locally born should have a hand in the developments which are changing the face of their countries; moreover, education for architecture varies and enriches the range of university studies by directing attention to aesthetic questions. The Universities of Malta, Hong Kong and Khartoum have been pioneers in the field and all offer degrees in architecture; it is proposed that Royal College Nairobi shall offer a course leading to a diploma in architecture which, it is hoped, will be recognized by the Royal Institute of British Architects. But there are as yet no plans for teaching architecture in Ghana or the West Indies.

EDUCATION

In England it has long been the practice for universities to offer in their departments of education courses, open only to graduates, leading to a diploma in education which secures certain advantages for those entering the teaching profession. In recent times English universities have assumed a measure of responsibility for the education provided in teacher training colleges and for the certificates giving holders the status of qualified teacher, which it is the aim of students in these colleges to secure. This has come about by setting up institutes of education of which their own departments of education and the teacher training colleges within their regions are members; the functions of an institute are to exercise oversight over the content of the courses and on the award of certificates. At the same time the universities have sought to become centres where educational problems are investigated and discussed; conferences are organized and courses are arranged for teachers in schools.

The universities and colleges overseas have endeavoured to make progress along similar lines. With the exception of the University of Khartoum they all offer courses leading to a recognized diploma in education, usually but not always confined to graduates. Tables 3 and 6 show the number of students studying for a diploma or a certificate in education; the figure for Makerere College includes students who have not graduated, and that for Rhodesia includes British graduates who are under contract, after acquiring a diploma, to teach for a period in Rhodesia. With this in mind and in view of the serious shortage of teachers in secondary schools the number of local graduates seeking an educational qualification is disappointing; as in Great Britain, but even more so, other careers are more attractive, and vacancies for graduates in other forms of employment greatly exceed the supply. As centres for the investigation and discussion of educational problems the universities and colleges are active and influential, but they have met with difficulties when attempting to establish institutes of education. Unlike the English universities which have relatively small parishes, they serve vast areas where the training colleges are of very varying standards; furthermore it has not been easy to fit institutes into the arrangements made by territorial directors of education who have the training colleges under their wing. A brief survey will illustrate the situation.

The University College of Ghana was early in the field having set up an institute in 1949. There is also a separate National Teacher Training Council of Ghana which is concerned with syllabuses and certificates; with this Council the institute co-operates; the secretary of the latter is also the secretary of the former. Development came later in Nigeria; the University College of Ibadan opened an institute in 1956 which also acts as its department of education though it is proposed to make the latter separate. It is hoped that the major training colleges will become affiliated to the institute, each major college undertaking to supervise other colleges in its area. As in Nigeria, so in Rhodesia, the vast extent of the territory makes co-ordination very difficult; it has been proposed that there should be five central colleges, each responsible for teacher training in its region, and that these central colleges should be linked with the institute. At Makerere College there is a faculty of education; it has not been possible for it to play a direct part in the supervision of training colleges since each of the three East African territories has developed its own method of co-ordinating their work, but it is hoped that the faculty will become associated with each territorial organization. In the West Indies an education centre was set up within the department of education in 1954; it is associated with the Jamaica Board of Teacher Training of which the professor of education is chairman; if other boards came into existence and were associated with the centre, the latter would begin to assume the functions of an institute. The University of Malaya has converted its department of education into a school of education; there is an advisory board, including representatives of the school and of the government education department, which attends to problems of teacher training.

While progress is being made towards building up institutes of education and thus assuming a measure of direct responsibility for teacher training, the universities and colleges have, by providing centres for the investigation and discussion of educational problems, come to exercise much indirect influence over school questions. The faculty of education at Makerere College possesses an excellent building with a library, conference hall, child-study centre, laboratory and workshops; nearby is a demonstration school. The institute in Rhodesia has promoted discussions relating to teacher training in Africa as a whole, and has organized a conference on this subject which was held in Salisbury in 1956. But these are only examples; in all the institutions activity within this range is vigorous.

NOTE

1. The syllabus for the London medical degree allows a wide range of emphasis on different aspects of the curriculum, and in the London medical schools there are considerable differences in teaching. There are no special papers in paediatrics and preventive medicine, but questions in these subjects are asked in the general medicine papers. No restrictions have been placed on the teaching of any subject, and it has been open to colonial medical schools to set a special internal examination in any subject if they thought that it would be helpful.

CHAPTER 12

ADULT EDUCATION

Adult education is an extra-mural activity of universities which, as understood in Great Britain, sets out to provide education for adults which is not undertaken for vocational purposes. In late years doubts have been expressed in British universities as to whether they should continue to include it in their programmes. There are various reasons for doubt; chief among them seems to be the belief that in origin adult education was in part at least a remedial activity in the sense that it aimed at helping those who had not been to a university, and that remedial action is now less needed because opportunities for university education have been greatly expanded and many new facilities for the pursuit of liberal interests by adults have been created. However things may stand in Great Britain, no one with knowledge of the overseas territories has ever questioned the great importance for them of adult education and the obligation which falls upon the universities and colleges to provide it. In the absence of extra-mural work the influence of the new colleges is limited to the younger generation and to a very small proportion of that generation. There is the older generation which never had educational opportunities and the younger generation for which such opportunities are scarce. There are other reasons for extra-mural work. 'The fostering of extra-mural studies would in particular do much to guard against a danger, of which we are fully conscious, that the university graduates might become a separate community . . ., divorced from the concerns and aspirations of their fellow-citizens. The development of a self-contained group of this kind is certainly no part of our purpose. The universities as we conceive them have on the contrary a vital contribution to make to the development of the community as a whole'.[1] This was said by the Asquith Commissioners in 1945. They were far more aware of forthcoming independence and of the problems it would bring than was common at that time, but they could not foresee how soon independence would arrive. This means that subsequent events have magnified the importance of adult education which, by fostering the habit of free discussion, can help to bring into existence a community capable of self direction.

There is provision for many other forms of education for adults among which are literacy campaigns, extension work, recreational activities and community development. Under extension work come the efforts of government departments, such as those of health and agriculture, to inform people about new and improved practices and to persuade people to adopt them; under recreational activities comes the work of the British Council in the fields of art, literature and drama; under community development come many schemes the purpose of which is to develop a sense of common citizenship. They are not adult education as universities understand it; nor are they vocational education, provision for which is notably lacking when understood to mean preparation for public examinations leading to a certificate or other award which is a guarantee of competence in some line of work, or at least has, like a school certificate, vocational relevance. The lack of facilities for vocational education affects the problem of adult education because it presents a difficulty to those who seek to promote it; many who frequent adult education classes do so, not because they want to study for the sake of study, but because they hope to improve their knowledge of English, or pick up something which may be of use to them in an examination. This is not to suggest that vocational education is inferior to adult education; the urge to acquire useful knowledge should be encouraged in every possible way, and the evidence of the widespread existence of this urge is one of the most encouraging aspects of the whole situation.

This is only one among many difficulties which face those who attempt to provide adult education. The territories are vast in extent, communications are poor, travel is expensive and at times impossible, the supply and cartage of the necessary books is a formidable problem; tribal jealousies may create trouble; suitable premises are scarce; only a small proportion of the population knows English, and it is not easy to assemble and keep together classes, members of which are able and willing to attend week after week. Added to all this, following the pattern in England, adult education is aided by special government grants in most of the territories, and this practice adds another difficulty since it encourages governments to believe that they have a greater concern with the content of courses in adult education than with that of intra-mural courses. They may take fright if they hear that there are courses in political science, and they may suspect the worst if they learn that a tutor has discussed marxism. Policemen may be deputed to attend. Of these policemen an adult education tutor in Kenya has said that they are

'so stolidly obvious. They know nothing of the subject and show no interest in it; but they sit on, hoping, no doubt, to be able to pounce on some "subversive" catch-phrase. At one course an askari joined the course, rather late, signing himself "trades-man". As the discussion went on uneventfully the askari began to doze. Without warning the tutor rapped out: "Is there a policeman in the class?" Automatically the askari's hand shot up.'[2]

With this as a background we may now briefly survey the work of adult education departments in the various territories. The University College of the West Indies was early in the field; in that area the scattering of the population over a great arc of islands and part of the mainland enhances the importance of one object of any extra-mural department, namely that of making the college known to the population which it serves. The Vice-Principal of the College was for many years the Director of the department and under his energetic guidance a remarkable range of activities was developed. There are seven resident tutors and three staff tutors. The staff tutors look after specific subjects, drama for instance, and may extend their responsibilities over the whole region served by the College. The resident tutors are each responsible for an area and, to help them, advisory committees have been appointed the members of which are drawn from the area; the tutors represent the College in their areas, and to them fall duties which come under the head of public relations in addition to their teaching work. In the absence of technical institutes and other centres of which the function is to provide vocational education, the department has organized many courses which meet the needs of those seeking to pass public examinations; by so doing the department has performed a valuable public service, but it may be hoped that vocational education will soon be available elsewhere and that the department may be able to concentrate on its primary task of non-vocational education. The department has organized residential and other full-time courses, mostly for particular occupational groups, such as nurses, welfare workers, civil servants and trade unionists; the success of such courses has been great. The vigorous shouldering by the College of its responsibilities in this field has made a powerful and invigorating impact upon the people of its region. But this is only a beginning. Reviewing the situation Mr Andrew Pearse has said:

'The habits of free enquiry, of objective disputation, of judging values, have not deeply penetrated the West Indies. They are seldom fostered by colonial status. Yet the territories are moving towards responsible democratic government, which is unthinkable unless such habits are to be found in different degrees at various levels in society. It is true that many West Indians have studied at universities in the Old and New Worlds, but their training has been carried out in situations quite remote from West Indian "facts of life" and on their return they have seldom found institutions in which the scholarly outlook has been embodied. They have therefore contributed little more than technical and professional skill to the community in which they have frequently felt themselves aliens. Our University has therefore unique obligations, which no other institution can be expected to fulfil: that of fostering and propagating free enquiry, objective discussion of ideas, and not merely the right of the individual to his opinions, but his duty, his obligation to make judgements.'[3]

In West Africa, pending the time when the two new colleges could assume responsibility for adult education, the Oxford University Delegacy for Extra-Mural Studies undertook to

157

prepare the way by sending out tutors; in 1949 the colleges took over the work for their respective territories. Developments in Ghana have been outstanding. At a conference organized by the College in 1949 it was decided to promote the establishment of a People's Educational Association. The promoters had in mind the Workers Educational Association of Great Britain; the new body was to be a voluntary, democratically constituted, non-sectarian and non-party-political organization wholly concerned with education. Its success has been remarkable; it is a nation-wide body on a strictly democratic basis, which has attracted a large membership, and has incidentally provided valuable opportunities of learning how to conduct important business. The Association stimulates and canalizes student demand for tutorial classes and bears the main burden of their local administration all over the country. The institute of adult education of the College supplies tutors and takes responsibility for the academic standard of tutorial classes which must enrol a minimum of students and extend over a period of months. In recent years over a hundred tutorial classes lasting twenty weeks or more have been held; the institute has a director, an assistant director and six resident tutors, employs about a hundred part-time tutors, and possesses a library with some 12,000 books. The institute also organizes residential courses for extra-mural students using for that purpose the halls of residence at Legon Hill during vacations, suitable accommodation at other centres or its own Awudome Residential College in the Trans-Volta Togoland region—the latter being an interesting venture which owes much to the welcome help it has received from the inhabitants of the locality. The theme for a residential course held at Legon Hill in 1957 was 'knowledge and independence'. It attracted an attendance of 240; a cabinet minister gave an address; basic political issues, including party organization and the role of an opposition, were discussed. The Association, in addition to stimulating demand for tutorial classes, has a wide range of activities of its own; it organizes short courses, brains trusts, debates, public lectures and social service projects.

The People's Educational Association of Ghana has no parallel elsewhere. There is no similar voluntary association in the West Indies or in Central Africa; an association does exist in Sierra Leone but is not very active. A beginning has been made in East Africa by the establishment in 1958 of the Makerere Extra-Mural Association, a voluntary society the purpose of which is to further extra-mural studies in the three East African territories, and a people's association on the Ghana model is projected in Tanganyika. In Nigeria the formation of a Nigerian Extra-Mural Association was considered in 1953; the problem was taken up again at a conference in 1955, and it was agreed that two organizations were desirable, an extra-mural association on Ghanaian lines and a Nigerian Council for Adult Education, a small body which would survey the situation and attempt to co-ordinate the various activities.

Though there is but one flourishing people's association, this does not mean that the colleges elsewhere than in Ghana have been inactive. The striking achievements of the University College of the West Indies have been described. The efforts made by the department of extra-mural studies at Ibadan are hardly less remarkable; the department has a director and an establishment for twelve tutors, five in the Northern Region, two in the Eastern Region and five in the Western Region. The department organizes weekly tutorial classes with at least twenty meetings and also vacation and refresher courses, usually arranged for occupational groups such as teachers, civil servants, and trade unionists. The size of the country, the diversity of its peoples and the facilities for communication set the department a harder task than that which is faced in Ghana. Though the programme of the department is now limited to the functions generally understood to be those falling under the head of adult education, it began with a very comprehensive programme. It set out to provide facilities not only for those prepared to take up serious study, but also for the illiterate and the semi-literate; for the latter it employed the film and the radio. The attempt to use visual aid material yielded interesting experience of the capacities of the medium but proved to be too ambitious; for a time a weekly programme called 'The Voice of the University College' was broadcast, but this service came to an end when Nigerian broadcasting was reorganized. Another experiment took the form of organizing courses in public administration for officers in the service of the governments of the Eastern and Western Regions; it was hoped that this would lead to the setting up of an institute of public administration. But owing to the pressure of public business and the consequent inability of the governments to spare officers from their duties this experiment came to an end; the governments subsequently set up courses for officers under their own auspices. Hence the contraction of the functions of the department to their present dimensions; recently its efforts have been concentrated on raising standards of work in the tutorial classes.[4]

The department of extra-mural studies of Makerere College began work in Uganda in 1953, in Kenya in 1956 and in Tanganyika in 1960; and the department has been so fortunate as to have had the services as part-time tutors of people so eminent as Sir E. Vasey and Dr L. S. B. Leakey. But it has been hampered by lack of government support for the work; the government of Uganda alone made a grant which supported two resident tutors; in Kenya the Carnegie Corporation supported one tutor and the Ford Foundation made a tutorship possible in Tanganyika. The government of Uganda has now agreed to support four tutors, and it is possible that the government of Tanganyika will contribute to the support of tutorships. The government of Kenya offered to finance two posts for the first half of 1961 provided that the posts were financed from other sources for the following five years, and the Carnegie Corporation has agreed to shoulder this additional burden. All this makes possible an advance in the much-needed expansion of the work, and is an example of the valuable help which all the universities and colleges have received from American sources. The University College of Rhodesia has recently set up an institute of adult education which will not itself provide facilities for adult education; it will be prepared to advise such organizations as may be working in the field. This self-imposed limitation of functions may fit in with local conditions; but it is not easy to understand why the direct provision of adult education, so successfully carried out by other colleges, would not be equally valuable in the Federation. Fourah Bay College took the first steps in adult education in 1951, but it was not until 1956 that extra-mural work got into its stride. In the Far East the University of Hong Kong organized courses after the war under the supervision of the registrar. In 1956 a department of extra-mural studies was set up, a director was appointed and in 1959–60 there were over 40 courses, some aiming at particular professional examinations, but most being non-vocational. The University of Malaya has done nothing in this field in spite of the facts that an entire chapter of the report of 1947 which led to the foundation of the University was devoted to the importance of adult education, and that, having regard to the relatively good provision of secondary schools and to the widespread interest in affairs, there must be a harvest ready for reaping.

Colonial governments and officials are suspicious of discussion which may bear upon current issues, while to local people non-political bodies, such as people's associations, appear to ask for a diversion of their energy from the struggle in which they are engaged. Conditions change as colonial rule recedes, and an interesting prospect opens out. Governments of an authoritarian nature are not likely to favour the adult education movement with its tradition of free discussion of all subjects, and one of the tests of the independent governments will be their attitude to the movement and to people's associations.

NOTES

1. *Report of the Commission on Higher Education in the Colonies*, 1954, p. 19.
2. A. M. Healy, 'University Extra-Mural Classes in Kenya', *Overseas Education*, Vol. XXX. No. 1. April 1958.
3. Andrew Pearse, 'Outside the Walls', *Caribbean Quarterly*, Vol. II. No. 4.
4. See S. G. Raybould, *Adult Education at a Tropical University*, 1957.

CHAPTER 13

LIBRARIES

A visitor who wants to find out about a university will examine
its library. To any university the importance of its library is
central, but to overseas universities and colleges their libraries
are of even greater importance than to western universities. In
all subjects members of the staff must depend almost wholly on
the library provision made by their institution. Such public
libraries as exist are very seldom of any use to them, and few
even serve the needs of students. There are some exceptions;
the Raffles Library in Singapore, from which books can be bor-
rowed, is used by students of the University of Malaya; in
Bulawayo there is a library with a postal service which has been
used by Africans working for the degrees of the University of
South Africa; the public library in Accra has six regional
branches and a lending service, and seems to be the most useful
library for students in these territories. Apart from the handling
of school literature it is largely true to say that for many students the university library offers them their first opportunity of
acquaintance with books. The bookshops maintained by most
colleges are very valuable adjuncts to the university libraries.
One of the most encouraging sights for a visitor is to observe
the frequenting of the attractive and well-stocked bookshops at
Makerere College, University College, Ibadan, and the University College of Ghana. It is often said that university education
in Great Britain is handicapped because many students come
from backgrounds where books are little in evidence. But in
comparison with Great Britain these countries are bookless, and
hence the overwhelming importance of the university libraries
and bookshops.

In pre-war days, when no money was available from C D and

W funds, the Universities of Hong Kong and Malta and the two colleges in Singapore were unable to provide adequate accommodation for their books. The University of Malaya, formed by the fusion of the two Singapore colleges, has built an excellent new library, but the Universities of Hong Kong and Malta have not yet been able to carry out their plans for new library buildings. The new colleges put library provision in the forefront of their programmes. Among the first members of the staff to be appointed was the librarian who has professional status. It was usual to give him facilities to visit libraries in Europe and America and thus to make it possible for him to study the latest arrangements and equipment; thus he was in a position to advise the architect about the construction and furnishing of his library. In all cases a central site has been allocated to the library; they are all impressive buildings of distinct architectural merit; they possess the most modern equipment though they were built just before the advantages of air-conditioning became generally appreciated and the necessary apparatus easy to procure.

Table 8 sets out certain particulars about the libraries. When it is remembered that the earliest of the new colleges have only been in existence for just over ten years and occupy sites which were a jungle or a wilderness, their achievement in building up their stock of books is remarkable; so is that of the University College of Rhodesia and the Kuala Lumpur branch of the University of Malaya which have been in existence less than five years. As regards book capacity the library of the University of Hong Kong is overflowing; the Kuala Lumpur branch of the University of Malaya is engaged in building its library which will have a capacity for 500,000 books and 300 readers places; Makerere College is planning an extension of its library; the University College of Rhodesia has completed its library building in which up to 500 readers places can be provided as need arises. Eight libraries have their own binderies. The arrangements usually include access to stacks and generous borrowing facilities. The policy adopted is to centralize the collections since the need for departmental libraries is not so great as in institutions whose departments are more scattered; to this there are one or two exceptions such as the housing of medical books

163

TABLE 8

LIBRARIES: BOOK STOCK, CAPACITY, READERS PLACES, STAFF AND CLASSIFICATION

University or College	Book Stock	Book Capacity	Readers Places	Staff Senior	Staff Others	Ancillary Staff Bindary	Ancillary Staff Others	Classification
University of Malta	38,000	51,000 almost full	95	3	3	–	–	Bliss
University of Hong Kong	General 113,380 Chinese 118,215	almost full	216	10	29	2	–	Dewey Decimal
University of Malaya in Singapore	300,000	320,000	445	14	30	1	2 photographers	Library of Congress
University of Malaya in Kuala Lumpur	48,628	45,000	126	9	20	1	1 photographer	Bliss
University of Khartoum	71,800	168,000	315	10	33	–	–	Bliss
Makerere College	60,000+30,000 unbound serial parts	120,000	220	5	29	9	4 printers 3 photographers	Dewey Decimal
University College of Ghana	140,000+3,000 current periodicals	250,000	338	6	17	9	1 photographer 14 messenger-cleaners	Library of Congress
University College, Ibadan	125,000+2,100 current periodicals	250,000	320	14	39	9	20 printers 3 photographers	Bliss
Fourah Bay College	28,000	180,000	190	3	8	–	–	Dewey Decimal
University College of Rhodesia and Nyasaland	48,000	350,000	186 actual 500 potential	7	8	3	–	Library of Congress
University College of the West Indies	90,000	200,000	300+	10	17	11	–	Library of Congress

of the libraries of the University of Malaya and Makerere College at their medical schools.

To their libraries the universities and colleges have devoted a considerable fraction of their resources. When building up their collections the assistance of the IUC library adviser has been available. He has procured for them bibliographical assistance and he operates a microfilm service which is valued by teachers and research workers. He has endeavoured to make the needs of the libraries widely known, and through him numerous gifts have been made by libraries in Great Britain; the help received from the British National Book Centre, which is part of the National Central Library, has been most valuable. Gifts have also been made locally; though the territories were described as bookless, there have been local residents who have made collections, usually relating to local history, customs and antiquities; some of these collections have been presented to the local university. The libraries of the University of Malaya and of Makerere College, University College, Ibadan, and the University Colleges of Ghana and the West Indies have privileges of copyright deposit for their territories. Many Commonwealth and foreign countries have made gifts of their publications, but requests to the British government to extend to the universities and colleges the arrangements under which universities in Great Britain acquire British government publications at reduced rates have been refused. All the libraries have built up special collections; the Universities of Hong Kong and Malaya have acquired large Chinese collections which are reported to be among the most notable of such collections outside China. University College, Ibadan, Fourah Bay College and the University College of Ghana are especially fortunate in that extensive collections of local archives have been deposited with them which are housed in separate buildings.

Hitherto it has been necessary to make arrangements under which local people, who wish to take up librarianship as a career, can be sent abroad for training. University College, Ibadan, has recently set up a scheme which, under the direction of the librarian, will provide training for entrants to the profession of librarianship; this will help to staff the libraries with fully trained African librarians.

CHAPTER 14

RESEARCH

The aim of the Asquith Commission was to foster the rise of universities whose conception of their functions and whose standards of work would be similar to those prevailing in Great Britain. This led the Commission to place strong emphasis on the place of research; the reasons for doing so need not be recapitulated since they are familiar, compelling and universally accepted as valid. All that needs saying is that the overseas universities and colleges have regarded research as a duty no less incumbent upon them than teaching; a visitor to any of them soon becomes aware that he is in touch with an academic society in which the spirit of active inquiry is fully as alive as in Europe.

It is convenient to make a distinction between opportunities and facilities for research. By opportunities is meant access to material calling for investigation, and by facilities the apparatus and the time necessary for investigation. The universities and colleges are so situated that rich and tempting opportunities abound for students of social data, of political science, applied economics, and of languages, and for anthropologists, archaeologists, educationalists, geographers, and others; the same is true for medicine, veterinary science and agriculture. In geology and meterology the opportunities are obvious, and there are aspects of the biological sciences, ecology for instance, where the same holds. In the physical science the prospects are not as limited as is sometimes supposed, as the work done during the geophysical year has shown. As to history the field is largely unexplored in the Far East and the West Indies while in Africa it is becoming apparent that, in addition to the period of colonial rule, there is material for earlier times which is more extensive than was formerly believed.

Among the facilities which must be available if research is to flourish libraries take the first place, and the last chapter records the emphasis which has been placed on library provision by all the institutions. It is here that the microfilm service of the IUC is at its greatest usefulness. Laboratory equipment and apparatus are of the utmost importance for the natural sciences; of this the institutions are well aware and they have exerted themselves to furnish their laboratories as adequately as their resources permit. Some modern apparatus is so expensive as to be beyond their present means, and there are in consequence lines of investigation which cannot be pursued. It is the case however that, for most of those fields of research where local opportunities are especially favourable, no very costly apparatus is needed. What does create difficulty is the shortage of technicians which means that in some lines of work investigators spend time on tasks which would be performed for them elsewhere. Likewise there is a shortage of demonstrators and assistants which throws more work on the established teaching staff than would fall to them in other centres. But facilities in the shape of libraries and laboratories are not enough; the staff must not be overburdened with teaching and administrative duties. Numerical estimates of the time which these duties occupy are always unsatisfactory; no one can say when they end. The ratio of staff to students is more informative. In Great Britain the ratio is one full-time member of the staff to nine full-time students; the corresponding figures are for Malaya nine, for Hong Kong and Khartoum eight, for Ibadan six, for the West Indies and Makerere College five and for Ghana four. But when the universities of Great Britain are compared with overseas universities these figures must be used with caution since like is not being strictly compared with like; teachers overseas may have to do more teaching and may need more time for their investigations. When overseas institutions are compared with others it must be remembered that, the smaller a college, the smaller is the number of students to a teacher; furthermore some subjects need more teachers in relation to students than others, and therefore account should be taken of the faculties in existence. But in general it is probably correct to say that teachers in these institutions are not seriously overburdened with teaching and administrative duties.

In the overseas institutions additional facilities are needed; it is often necessary to travel in order to make observations and collect material, and this is not easy since distances are huge and communications bad. To assist its staff Makerere College has a scheme of allowances for local staff duty travel, and other colleges have somewhat similar arrangements. But schemes for these purposes are required of a kind more generous than most colleges can afford if advantage is to be taken of many attractive opportunities for investigation. There is another aspect of the whole matter. In Europe and America it is largely through contact with others in the same field that ideas for research are prompted and methods for carrying it out are suggested, and such contacts are easy and frequent; the universities are relatively near one another, there are meetings of learned societies, there are associations of workers engaged in the same subject and there are conferences. If it had been possible so to arrange matters that the universities and colleges were situated side by side with government research stations, this would have done something to reduce isolation. But most government research stations had been set up before the colleges came into existence, and placed at sites which were not appropriate for the colleges. Thus the main government research stations in East Africa are in the region of Nairobi, and the medical and veterinary research stations for Nigeria are on the Jos plateau. It is rare to find, as in the case of the Moor Plantation agricultural research station for Nigeria which adjoins University College, Ibadan, a station in the proximity of a college.

There is, however, an increasing amount of contact between the African colleges. With the financial support of the Leverhulme Trustees annual conferences are being arranged at the University College of Rhodesia and Nyasaland so that heads of departments and others can meet and pool their experiences, exchange ideas and co-ordinate research programmes. The first of this series of conferences was held in September 1958, for heads of departments of education. Other similar, if smaller, meetings of an informal nature take place periodically in London when staff are on leave—for example, professors of chemistry in the overseas colleges met in London in 1960, and members of theology departments have held joint discussions regularly for several years. The West African Institute of Social and Economic Research has organized annual conferences which are international in character. Little contact in research projects has as yet been established with universities in French West Africa or the Congo, but it is hoped that, as a result of recent discussions, closer contacts will be developed.

The presence of holders of visiting professorships, that is of senior academic people coming from other universities, who share the life of the staff, conducting their own investigations but not assuming the duties attached to a particular teaching post as in the case of secondment, is most valuable, and such professorships are made available by certain American and other foundations. During the last five years the University of Hong Kong has had the advantage of the presence of eight visiting professors who stayed three months or longer. But the most effective remedy for isolation is to provide generous terms for study leave which can be spent in making or renewing contact with academic circles in other countries; the terms of leave now granted are mentioned in the next chapter, and it is to be hoped that university authorities will continue to be wise enough to understand that, if the universities are to remain lively centres of research, ample study leave facilities are essential. It may be added that during the first half of the period since 1945 the overseas institutions excited little interest; apart from academic people visitors were few. Now they have become centres of attraction, especially those in Africa, for itinerant commissions, politicians, journalists, enquirers and novelty seekers to an extent which is embarrassing. No doubt it is to the good that the institutions should be more widely known, but this kind of contact is no solution for academic isolation.

It would be tedious and unrewarding to enumerate books and papers published by the staffs of the universities and colleges; but two examples may be given. In the session 1958–9 the University of Hong Kong recorded the publication of nine books and ninety-five papers, and the University of Khartoum reported that 130 papers had been published, accepted for publication or were being prepared for publication. Evidence of two kinds may be mentioned which points to activity in investigation. By 1960 sixty-six members of the staffs of the colleges had gained the

London PhD degree and in that year eighty-five were registered for the degree. In the next chapter figures will be given relating to staff mobility, that is to say to members of the staffs who have resigned to take up other appointments. Mobility has been on a large scale, and in general those who have passed on to other appointments have done so because they have provided evidence of their standing in their subjects by publishing work carried out when at a college. This is impressive evidence both of promise when appointed and of accomplishment since appointment.

It is not only the members of the staffs who are engaged in investigation. There are the young graduates. Not many local graduates take up research; attractive opportunities for employment await almost every graduate. Among those who take up research some wish to study in a foreign university and so widen their experience, and are encouraged to do so by their teachers who, much as they would like to have more research students, know that it is in the interest of a young graduate to study abroad. Thus, if the colleges are to have young research students in sufficient numbers, they must attract them from abroad; they cannot offer scholarships from their own funds and therefore only those young graduates can come who win awards granted abroad. In the autumn of 1959 there were at Makerere College, nineteen research students from abroad supported by such bodies as the Nuffield Foundation, the Leverhulme Trust, the Ford Foundation, the Goldsmith Company, the Fulbright organization and the Norwegian Research Council, studying problems varying from the chemistry of decomposition processes in Uganda swamps to the formation of capital in East Africa. Apart from work carried out by individual members of the staff and by graduate students, there is much other investigation organized and supported in different ways. There are research units financed from outside and engaged on specific problems, such as those supported by the Medical Research Council at the University College of the West Indies and at the University of Malaya (the Tropical Research Unit), and that supported by the Department of Scientific and Industrial Research in Malaya (the Ionosphere Research Unit); there are collective research projects organized and carried out by the staff but financed by some foundation or other source of funds; there are organizations directing attention to problems of local importance for which the university and the government are jointly responsible, such as the Hydrobiological Research Unit at Khartoum; there are senior scholars who, with the help of a special grant, come to spend some time at a college in furtherance of some special investigation in which they are interested.

To this picture of wide ranging and active prosecution of investigation in the universities and colleges it remains to add some account of the institutes of social research. It was decided by the British government to allocate a sum out of C D and W funds for the furtherance of research in the colonies; of this sum a proportion was set aside for social research. A Colonial Social Science Research Council was set up to advise on the expenditure of money available for this object. The policy of the Council was to devote part of the available money to research conducted under its auspices and part to the foundation of social research institutes, one for East Africa at Makerere College, one for West Africa at Ibadan, and one for the West Indies at the University College. Each institute was placed within the grounds of a college by agreement with the College, and came under a director who, while responsible to the principal of the college for compliance with general college regulations, had control over the research programme. The cost of the buildings erected for the institutes and of the salaries of the staff were borne wholly by the social research allocation and not by the colleges. By 1959 nearly £90,000 had been spent on buildings and over £450,000 on salaries and expenses. The Council adopted this policy because a director of research on the spot would be in the best position to judge what problems most needed attention and because they wished to associate research activities with the colleges. All three institutes were at work by 1950; their resources have been supplemented by grants from governments and outside bodies to help finance special projects. The institutes have been most active. The West Indian Institute publishes a journal, *Social and Economic Studies*, containing the results of investigation undertaken by its staff; nine volumes have appeared, each containing four numbers. Between 1950 and 1955 the East African Institute published seven studies, two linguistic reports and four books; four more books and other studies were in preparation while members of the staff had published thirty papers.

At the outset it was realized by the Colonial Social Science Research Council that, since C D and W funds would not be available after independence, it was desirable that the institutes should be integrated by stages with the relevant teaching departments of the colleges. This process has begun. The West African Institute has been renamed the Nigerian Institute of Social and Economic Research, of which the professor of economics acts as director, and receives a direct grant from the federal government. The East African Institute is now the joint responsibility of the professor of economics and the professor of sociology; it has received substantial support from the Ford Foundation. The funds of the Institute are now available to teaching members of the staff for their own research work, thus bringing to an end the situation under which only full-time research workers had access to them.

CHAPTER 15

STAFF

The colleges are as free as the universities to make such appointments as they please. With the exceptions of the University of Hong Kong, which has continued its pre-war practice of using the services of the Association of Universities of the British Commonwealth for recruitment, and of the Kuala Lumpur branch of the University of Malaya, they have taken full advantage of the offer of the IUC to assist in staff recruitment. The IUC is fortunate to be able to enlist as members of selection committees those in British universities with expert knowledge of any subject in which there is a vacancy; this has had the incidental advantage of spreading knowledge of the overseas institutions and their needs widely in British university circles. The views of the selection committees are transmitted to the institutions which decide what action to take. Since the object of the programme is to build up universities of a standing not inferior to that which prevails in Great Britain, the recommendations of the committees are framed with this criterion in mind.

Owing to the foundation of new university colleges and the growth of existing institutions the number of vacancies has steadily increased; it was ten in 1946 and 296 in 1959, and in the latter year the IUC put forward 240 names. Since 1945 there has been a large increase in the number of teachers in British universities, and it is surprising as well as pleasing that candidates of high standing have come forward in response to advertisements of vacancies overseas. In the last year or so the response has not been as large as before, especially for vacancies in senior posts; for this the changing political scene may be responsible. The vacancies have been widely advertised and the composition of the staffs by country of origin is shown on Table

173

9. The figures in the Table are not strictly comparable; they include full-time members of the teaching and senior library staffs and in addition, except in the case of Makerere College, of the senior administrative staff. The figures for the University of Hong Kong also include demonstrators, and those for the University

TABLE 9

DISTRIBUTION OF STAFF BY COUNTRY OF ORIGIN: 1960

	Origin				
University or College	Locally born	United Kingdom	Rest of Commonwealth	Other	Total
Royal University of Malta (1958–9)	62	3	—	1	66
University of Hong Kong	53	57	18	90	218
University of Malaya (Singapore)	74	44	29	17	164
University of Malaya (Kuala Lumpur)	29	19	20	7	75
University of Khartoum	60	54	7	44	165
Makerere College, the University College of East Africa	14	91	28	3	136
University College, Ibadan	57	118	23	7	205
University College of Ghana	34	109	14	18	175
University College of the West Indies	61	90	6	10	167
University College of Rhodesia & Nyasaland	5	43	21	1	70
University College of Sierra Leone	16	40	5	4	65
Royal Technical College, Nairobi	4	46	10	—	60
Total	469	714	181	202	1,566

College of Rhodesia include research fellows. The total under the head of 'Other' for the University of Hong Kong is large and needs explanation; it is accounted for by the inclusion of many who were born in China.

All those concerned with overseas institutions hoped that, year by year, a growing proportion of vacancies would be filled by local candidates leading to the time when the great majority of the staff would be locally born. And this has happened; the number of appointments of locally born rose from 26 in 1957 (14·5 per cent of the total) to 41 in 1958 (20·4 per cent of the total) and to 49 in 1959 (23·2 per cent of the total). The number of appointments from the United Kingdom was 114 in 1957 (63·7 per cent of the total), 96 in 1958 (47·7 per cent of the total) and 107 in 1959 (50·7 per cent of the total). During these years more appointments were made of candidates from other countries.

The principle followed when making appointments has always been that the best candidates should be appointed irrespective of race origin. It is natural and inevitable that each appointment should arouse interest within and without the university or college, and that note should be taken of the nationality of successful candidates. Whenever an expatriate is appointed it can always be asked whether there was not a local candidate with adequate qualifications; this must be so wherever national sentiment is strong; such a state of things is familiar in the Principality of Wales where the appointment to a chair of an Englishman whose wife was Welsh was announced by the local press with the consoling comment that the better half was Welsh. To the principle that the best candidate should be appointed, careful attention was given by the Committee, of which the chairman and the majority of the members were West Indians, appointed by the Standing Federation Committee of the West Indies to report on the policy of the University College of the West Indies. This Committee devoted a chapter to the appointment of West Indians to the staff. After expressing sympathy with those who wished to increase the proportion of West Indians on the staff, they examined proposals made to them for speeding the process. One proposal was that being a West Indian should in itself be a qualification to be taken into account; on this the Committee commented as follows: 'We fully acknowledge that in making its appointments a university or a university college must take account not only of the intellectual qualities of applicants; it must also take into account a number of imponderable personal qualities which are rightly judged to fit a man or a woman for an academic career. But it remains true that an appointing committee must look first and foremost to the vitality of the intellectual and scholarly gifts of applicants and to their power to provide intellectual stimulus to the students they teach. The academic name and standing of the College is paramount; to depart from those criterion would be dangerous to its life and reputation'.[1] Another proposal was designed to overcome the disadvantage under which young West Indian graduates suffer by lack of opportunity to undertake post-graduate study; for this reason they cannot compete for university appointments on an equal footing with overseas candidates. As a remedy post-graduate awards, tenable in the West Indies or overseas, were proposed, and this proposal was warmly supported by the Committee. The Committee also expressed themselves as strongly in favour of study leave and travel fellowships for members of the teaching staff; for it is not enough to ensure that young local graduates will have opportunities, equal to those available to young graduates in other countries, to prepare themselves for an academic post by a period of postgraduate study; it is necessary in addition that, if appointed, they should have opportunities of keeping in direct touch with work in progress in their own fields in other countries if they are to compete with chance of success for vacant chairs and readerships.

The importance of providing opportunities for local graduates to undertake postgraduate study is being increasingly recognized. The Universities of Khartoum and Malaya make awards to promising young graduates enabling them to study overseas in the expectation that they will thereby become fitted to compete successfully for vacancies on the staff. Through the generosity of the Carnegie Corporation of New York the IUC is able to award about six fellowships annually to locally born residents in the territories who have the firm intention of seeking appointments in a university or in a university college in their country. In Ghana a scheme of another kind is in operation with the aim of speeding up the appointment of Ghanaians to posts in the University College. Eight associate lectureships, open only to Ghanaian graduates who have completed satisfactorily periods of postgraduate study, have been established; these posts are supernumerary to establishment and are intended only for those for whom, at the time of the completion of post-graduate work, suitable vacancies in departmental establish-ments do not exist. The usual machinery for making appoint-ments to the establishment will continue to operate, but it is obvious that, if during the tenure of an associate lectureship (three years) a suitable vacancy occurred, the holder would have a good chance of securing an appointment.

It is not only lack of locally born who have the necessary qualifications for university appointments which makes it necessary still to rely partly on those born elsewhere; for those among them with these qualifications there are other attractive openings, especially in government service where the desire to see the replacement of expatriates is stronger than in the uni-versities. And that is not all; to locally born members of the academic staff offers are made of administrative posts in the service of governments and commercial organizations, and these offers are sometimes accepted, thus depleting the teaching staff of members who promised to go far in an academic career.

As regards terms and conditions of appointment, the Univer-sity of Hong Kong has always paid an expatriate allowance as an addition to the basic salary of those recruited from overseas; the University of Malaya follows this practice. The Asquith Commission recommended that the practice should be extended to the new colleges in Africa and the West Indies; their argu-ment was that for a period a considerable proportion of the staff must be recruited from overseas to attract whom high rates must be paid, that to attract local candidates it was not necessary to offer the same rates, and that, if the high rates prevailed for the whole staff, the resources of the territorial governments would be burdened beyond necessity, and increasingly so as the pro-portion of local recruits rose. Anticipating that discrimination between expatriates and locally born in the matter of salary would not be acceptable to local opinion, the Commission suggested that to a uniform basic rate of salary a supplement might be added to expatriate salaries taken out of the allocation of C D and W funds for higher education; this would have relieved local finances but would have left discrimination, though in a form perhaps easier to accept. Nothing came of the suggestion because, under official ruling, the use of C D and W funds was limited to capital expenses. Expatriate allowances were never paid in the West Indies; they were paid for a time at Ibadan but were given up in 1950. Salaries in the colleges are now on a uniform basis, corresponding closely grade by grade to those paid in Great Britain; following each salary revision in Great Britain there has generally been a like revision of college salaries. Superannuation schemes are universal; family, car and outfit allowances are common.

As in regard to salary, so in regard to duration of appointment the terms usually correspond to those in Great Britain, that is to say, appointments, other than the more junior, are to retiring age which is usually the age of sixty. At the University of Khartoum, however, the appointments of expatriates are on the basis of a five-year contract with the possibility of renewal for a further five years; this is understandable since the University, which incidentally is most anxious to obtain the services of expatriates and is most hospitable to them, does not wish to block the path for its own graduates by giving appointments up to retiring age to expatriates. It may be that universities in the other countries with which this book is concerned will one day adopt this practice.

For expatriates one of the most important conditions of service relates to home leave since the most serious deprivation which they have to endure is loss of contact with home surroundings. The conditions may be summarized as follows: Hong Kong seven months leave after three and a half years; West Indies and Rhodesia each third long vacation; Malaya six months leave after three years of service; Makerere College every alternate long vacation; Ghana the long vacation three years out of every four; Khartoum, Sierra Leone and Ibadan each long vacation. Home leave always includes return passages for the members of the staff in question; conditions vary as to the extent to which passages for their wives and children are also included. These terms must be regarded as generous; the cost of passages is a heavy burden on the institutions, amounting in the case of one college to a tenth of its annual expenditure.

In the last chapter stress was laid on the difficulties which arise from academic isolation. During home leave expatriates have opportunities of making or renewing contacts with fellow workers in their field. But this is not enough; occasions arise when special leave is necessary if a teacher is to make progress with his investigations. Hence the need for study leave; all the institutions are prepared to consider applications for study leave which may not be easy to grant because of the consequential depletion of teaching strength. As recognized by the West Indies Committee study leave is still more important for locally born teachers for whom home leave does not afford opportunities of contact with other universities. As locally born replace expatriates the cost of home leave will be reduced, but unless the institutions are prepared to be generous in the matter of study leave, the locally born staff, and in consequence the institutions themselves, will suffer from academic isolation.

A visitor to any of the universities or colleges, five of which now have locally born vice-chancellors or principals, will certainly conclude that he is the fortunate spectator of one of the happiest examples of racial co-operation. But these isolated communities of teachers face difficulties. Members of the staffs mostly live in houses owned by the institutions; when, as in Hong Kong, Singapore, Khartoum, Salisbury and now to some extent at Makerere College, their houses are scattered in a large residential area, they can mix more easily with local residents than when, as in the West Indies, Ibadan, Fourah Bay and Ghana, they live within the university precincts. But in all cases the members of the staff and their families have fewer outside contacts than in a British university which is a consequence of the paucity of people outside the university or college with whom they share common interests. When people are thus thrown together there may be little need for a social club. But there is in British universities a special kind of club, the senior common room, and a senior common room with a vigorous life can be most valuable in a university. Senior common rooms exist overseas, but they do not seem to flourish; the reason is probably to be found in the special circumstances of the institutions. If a senior common room is to flourish membership must be strictly limited to teachers and senior administrators; if wives and relatives are admitted, it loses its special virtues. But if they are excluded, a senior common room does not flourish overseas because in so narrow a society an exclusive club seems out of place. The attachment of teachers to halls of residence, which is common and most effective in Ghana, is valuable, but is no substitute for a senior common room which brings all members of the staff together and enhances the consciousness of sharing common responsibilities.

The Asquith Commission hoped that appointments on secondment might help to solve the problem of staffing. Unlike visiting members from another university who may give special lectures on their own subjects but assume no duties, seconded teachers undertake teaching and administrative responsibilities. The IUC has done its best to promote secondment and to remove the obstacles which impede it; it has, for instance, set aside a sum of £15,000 to aid it. Two most valuable arrangements for regular secondment from London medical schools to the medical schools at Makerere College and Ibadan were described in Chapter 11, but in general the results of the efforts to encourage secondment have been disappointing. The reason for the small amount of success is that a member of the staff of a British university is seldom, if ever, prepared to accept secondment unless he has a guarantee that he can resume his post without loss of seniority. It is not easy for a university to give such a guarantee, for it means that, unless the department to which the seconded member belongs is expanding, the university can only offer a temporary appointment which is not likely to produce good substitute candidates. While the failure to obtain secondments in any number is regrettable, it is well to remember that, while the experience is likely to be of real advantage to the person seconded, there are limits to the benefits which accrue to the receiving institution, since it takes time to fit in and learn how teaching and administrative duties are best performed in a new environment, and since, when this has been accomplished, the term of office may be nearing its end. The situations in which secondment can be most useful are when a department needs a new impulse and when an overseas institution wishes to release a locally born member of the staff in order that he may obtain further experience abroad.

As mentioned in Chapter 2 it was very much in the mind of the Asquith Commission that everything possible should be done to bring the overseas universities and colleges within the family of Commonwealth universities. They are all members or associate members of the Association of Universities of the British Commonwealth, and this brings them welcome invitations to be represented at the periodic conferences organized by the Association.[2] But so far as the personal problems of expatriate members of the staff are concerned this recognition of their institutions does not touch the heart of the matter. What face them are academic isolation and the disadvantage under which they suffer when applying for posts in competition with candidates who are at hand and can be interviewed. The IUC has always emphasized the importance of home and study leave and has encouraged visits by senior staff from other universities. This promotes personal relations between expatriate teachers and those in other centres who work in the same field, and in this way keeps in mind the claims of expatriates for consideration when vacancies occur. The IUC has done more; it arranges for the circulation among overseas institutions of advertised vacancies in Commonwealth universities, and it drew up a scheme for an interview fund which would help to finance the cost of passages of expatriates attending interviews in connection with vacancies for which they were candidates. This scheme figured as an item deserving consideration in the agenda of the Commonwealth Education Conference held at Oxford in 1959.

A record has been kept of expatriate members of the staffs of the overseas institutions who have left to take up other posts; it shows that there have been 241 such moves, 121 to United Kingdom universities, 32 to dominion universities, 19 to foreign universities, 46 universities within the purview of the IUC, 15 to other colonial institutions of higher education, and 18 to technical and teacher training colleges in the United Kingdom. This is a very remarkable record especially when it is remembered that many of those who moved had only occupied their posts for a few years. It is evident that those who accept posts overseas need not fear that they are anchored to them. It is also evident of the academic quality of the expatriate staff; what the IUC can claim is that it has helped to make the quality more widely known. To the overseas universities and colleges this degree of mobility is double edged; losses of members of high quality are regrettable, but they serve to enhance the reputation of the overseas institutions as places where high quality is to be found.

NOTES

1. *Report of the Committee appointed to review the Policy of the University College of the West Indies*, 1958, p. 104.
2. This does not apply to the University of Khartoum; the Sudan was never within the Commonwealth.

CHAPTER 16

STUDENTS

In other chapters facts are given relating to the number of students, their selection, their subjects of study and their performance in examinations, and there is some discussion of the special difficulties which students encounter when they embark on university courses. This chapter is concerned with other aspects of student social life.

The students are young people selected from populations which, as described in Chapters 4 and 5, include different races, speak a variety of languages, inherit diverse cultural traditions and adhere to many religions. In their efforts to gain independence the peoples of the territories display a unity which is impressive; but this unity has one basis only, the determination to remove foreign domination. When this aim has been achieved the lack of other forces making for unity become apparent; if the new states are to flourish, more social cohesion than now exists is indispensable. Towards the building up of a national consciousness the universities and colleges are in a position to make a contribution of the first importance. Young people drawn from all parts of a territory and from all social classes, often belonging to different races and tribes, and speaking different languages at home, assemble to learn for three years or more; when it is remembered how restricted is the background of many students, the distant parts of their own country being often as foreign to them as Europe, it is easy to understand how eye-opening, informative and stimulating such as experience can be.

If full advantage is to accrue from bringing these young people together, they must do more than assemble to learn; they must live together. The Asquith Commission said that 'the universities should be residential' and by this they meant that students should live in halls of residence. But in England the term is used to cover a situation where all students are not living in collegiate residences; Oxford and Cambridge are called residential universities although about half the students live in lodgings. All the students of these two universities do, however, live in college for at least a year; moreover the lodgings are never far from the colleges and those who live out remain full members of a college where they can have meals and use the common rooms. In these circumstances students share, not only common teaching facilities, but also a common social life which it is the object of the residential system to secure. It is when students live in distant lodgings, scattered over a wide area, and can do little more than attend for formal education that a university cannot be called residential. For reasons which are described in Chapter 18, the situation in these territories is such that it is always difficult and sometimes impossible for students to live out if they are to have reasonable facilities for study and to be able to participate fully in student social life. This being so, the universities and colleges have from the start provided residential accommodation for students. The pre-war halls of residence in Hong Kong, Malaya and East Africa had little to recommend them in respect of dignity or amenities; for the most part the post-war halls are buildings of which any university would be proud, comfortable and well furnished, almost luxurious in Ghana and of marked architectural distinction in Ibadan.

The overseas universities and colleges have always been prepared to relax the rule that students must live in a hall if good case is shown. Recently most of them have come under pressure to admit more students than they can accommodate in their halls; this has led to some relaxation of the rule; in Malaya about 40 per cent, in Hong Kong about 15 per cent, and in Salisbury about 12 per cent live at home or in lodgings. University College, Ibadan, decided after careful enquiry that suitable lodgings could not be found in the city of Ibadan which is in any case rather far away, and has therefore decided to build less elaborate halls of residence which will serve as feeders to the main halls; the College has also considered a suggestion that it might build houses on its property and let them to tenants who would take in students as lodgers. The West Indian Committee of 1958 recommended that the residential rule should be relaxed, and that students of the College should be allowed to live in lodgings which, the Committee thought, might be available in the new suburbs. All the institutions will soon be faced with this problem since they are unlikely to find the capital needed to build halls of the existing standards which could accommodate the whole student population. The capital cost per student in existing halls varies from about £1,000 to over £2,000; it may be suggested that, rather than revert to the austerity type of pre-war hall in the search for economy, an experiment might be made by constructing hutments, forming villages within the college precincts which would require a considerably smaller capital outlay per student. The problem is further discussed in Chapter 18.

The importance of the halls in student social life differs as between one institution and another. In Ghana the halls have been elevated to form communities within the College; the system is described in Chapter 5. In the other institutions they are of less importance though everywhere the idea is fostered that they are social units and not mere dormitories; it is usual to find that members of the teaching staff are attached to a hall. In all the institutions there is an organization, usually called the students' union, of which all students automatically become members. A students' union has its constitution which sets out its aims, rights and responsibilities; the system is modelled on that found in the newer English universities. The students' union is controlled by the students, it provides valuable opportunities for student initiative, and its officers represent the student body to the authorities on matters which concern students. It is also important because it makes provision for student activities in the shape of clubs for sports, debates, music, drama and so on; if these activities are to be pursued, they must be on a college wide basis since halls do not form large enough units for these purposes. Each type of organization has its part to play; the hall is valuable as a close social organization which can bring staff and students together, but it is controlled by the authorities and tends to be paternalistic. It is not easy to adjust their roles; experience shows that the importance of the students' union varies inversely with that of the halls. In Ghana, for example, the students' union plays no large part, and in consequence the organization of sports, which the students' union alone can undertake, is less developed than elsewhere.

The University College of the West Indies was the first to build special accommodation for its students' union; University College, Ibadan, and Fourah Bay College followed suit in 1960. The University of Malaya has handed over an existing building to its union, but elsewhere the unions have to make do with inadequate premises. The universities and colleges do not seem to have put accommodation for the unions high in order of priority, and in general to have lent towards building up halls as social units. A visitor is impressed by the efforts made by students to find for the unions their proper sphere of activity; it is through the unions and the clubs attached to them that students find means for self expression. Clubs are seldom formed on a regional or tribal basis; it would not be a good sign if it were so. Interest in political problems, international as well as national, is keen but does not show itself in party political clubs; under colonial rule there is only one political aim and that is political freedom. The degree of interest shown in worldwide current affairs is very marked, and the approach to them is not doctrinnaire or on a party basis; there is an open-minded desire to be better informed which might make university authorities in other countries envious. Outside the political sphere clubs exist for a large number of activities; dramatic clubs are especially flourishing. Interest in music and the arts is evident but might well be more encouraged. At one time the students at Makerere College all spent some time in the art department; this gave obvious pleasure; more than that, it seemed evident that the students found a much-needed emotional outlet. Such an outlet seems necessary; these students are under a much heavier strain than European students, caught up as they are in surroundings which are strange, in studies that are novel and in a way of life that is unfamiliar to them.

Religious societies attract considerable membership. The Universities of Hong Kong, Malaya and Khartoum do not have their own places of worship, but churches and mosques are near at hand. In the West Indies and in East and West Africa the colleges have chapels; in Central Africa there are plans for a college. In Ghana the halls of residence have their own chapels, and at Makerere College two chapels, one Anglican and one Catholic, were part of the original building. Elsewhere the practice is for a college to set aside a plot of land within its precincts for a chapel which is built with funds provided from outside. The services are well attended; interest seems to be greater when chapels are not, as in Ghana, part of the official establishment. Chaplains, sometimes with teaching duties, may be appointed, or members of the teaching staff may assume chaplaincy duties. That it is possible to find chaplains among the staff may cause surprise, but anyone who knows the conditions in British universities is impressed by the fact that a distinctly larger proportion of the staff of the overseas colleges are active members of a church, and further that church membership is more common among the younger than the older staff. This can hardly be an accident; it must be the case that teachers with a religious outlook are especially moved to serve the cause of education overseas.

Thus the students form closely knit societies in which there is little sign of sectional segregation on any basis; groupings by race, tribe and sex might be expected but are little in evidence. The proportion of women students, who have their own halls of residence, varies widely; the percentage which women form of the total student population is 35 in Rhodesia, 33 in the West Indies, 26 in Hong Kong, 25 in Malaya, 10 in Sierra Leone, 8 in Malta, 7 in East Africa and Ghana, 6 at Ibadan and 4 at Khartoum; the corresponding figure for Great Britain is 24. Special interest attaches to race relations, and in particular to the relations between Europeans and others. In 1958 there were five British and six American students at the University of Hong Kong, and at least one president of the students' union has been British; in the University of Malaya the number of Europeans was about the same. In Hong Kong, as also at Makerere College where in 1959 there was a total of nine British and American students some of them being graduates engaged in research, the Europeans mix freely with other students. In West Africa the few British students have been graduates with research scholarships, and some of them have given useful leadership in student affairs with their experience of other universities. Rhodesia, where Europeans are in the majority, is the most interesting case; in 1960 there were 209 students including forty-nine Africans (forty-four men and five women). Within the College precincts all students live on terms of full equality, but it is only within the College that partnership, which is the official policy of the Federation, is put into practice. Outside the College the Africans are restricted as to places of entertainment, the frequenting of restaurants, the use of means of transport and in many other ways. Thus Africans belong to one world within the College and to another outside it. In these circumstances race relations, however amicable (and they are very amicable), cannot be entirely easy; members of one race are conscious of privileges and must feel awkward in consequence, while members of the other race are only too well aware of deprivations on account of which they cannot feel otherwise than resentful.

Conflict between university authorities and students can arise in various ways anywhere in the world. Political manifestations by students may lead to the breaking of university regulations and the law of the land. Trouble of this kind has been frequent at Khartoum where the students have adopted student behaviour traditional in Egypt and the Middle East. Elsewhere such trouble has not occurred, and this is remarkable since students are keenly interested in the local political situation which has often given rise to public demonstrations and sometimes to disturbances. Students in any country may organize disobedience of regulations, and there has been one serious incident of this kind: at University College, Ibadan, in 1957 the students, in spite of warnings, deliberately flouted rules, and the College was closed for a period. There is reason to believe the trouble was supported, if not instigated, from outside. Students may also indulge in childish outbreaks, sometimes destructive, which are called rags; when these affairs take place in Great Britain, or at least when they take place at the older universities, they are regarded with tolerance or amusement by the public who apparently like to hear of the boys at their pranks again. *The Times* not long ago had a picture of the head of a college in one of the older British universities watching the removal of a car from the roof of one of his buildings; vice-chancellors and principals of overseas institutions are not to be caught by photographers in such a situation since the ragging tradition, which is seldom anywhere a spontaneous exhibition of youthful exuberance but rather conformity with what is supposed to be proper for students to do, has not taken root. It may be added that the practice of subjecting freshmen to initiation ceremonies which, when it takes barbarous and disgusting shapes as in some countries, is a problem for the authorities, has given some trouble in Singapore but not in the other territories.

It is difficult to generalize about personal relations between staff and students. The fact that staff and students live in close proximity facilitates contact. A visitor receives the impression that relations are easy and friendly; he often finds students being entertained at the houses of the staff and he detects that the situation, in which the staff are situated, creates among them a strong sense of responsibility for student welfare. This manifests itself in many ways, in the provision for medical care, in the participation of the staff in dramatic performances and similar activities and in the leadership given in games and athletics. The students respond very readily and seem free of any suspicion that the colleges are exotic institutions; on the contrary, they clearly regard the colleges as national possessions of which they are proud.

In other chapters there is some description of the formal educational programme, but it is the function of universities also to encourage general education. General education is an elusive concept; it has been described as fostering interest in, and ability to discuss, problems relating to the human situation. Here all universities, especially in modern times when the demands of special education are excessive, fall short; but the situation of these overseas universities and colleges is so novel, so interesting, so perplexing, so inescapable that wider problems more readily come to the notice of staff and students alike than in a settled and traditional society. Hence the situation is more favourable to general education than elsewhere, though on the other hand the demands of special education are no less pressing and even harder to meet since the subjects and methods are less familiar.

CHAPTER 17

RELATIONS WITH GOVERNMENTS

About the relations between the governments on the one hand and the universities on the other, three questions can be asked. Have the former given to the latter adequate financial support; have they, when making grants, imposed conditions which are not compatible with university autonomy; have they acted in other ways which infringe autonomy?

The first question falls into two parts, the extent to which the need for capital was met and the adequacy of the grants for recurrent purposes. As things have turned out the help given by the British government has been limited to the provision of capital, though this was not what the Asquith Commission intended, and therefore the British government only comes into the picture when the first part of the question is put. The Sudan was never eligible for grants from C D and W sources; the government of the Sudan has provided the capital for its college, now a university, to an extent fully adequate for its needs. Ghana was eligible for grants from this source, but the British government, when authorizing the institution of a university college, made it a condition that the capital should be found by the Ghanaian government; the British government contributed only a token sum. In the matter of capital grants to its college the Ghanaian government has been generous, even lavish. The allocations made by the British government for capital purposes went to the institutions in other territories; they amount to £16,181,380 which is the sum allocated to higher education out of the total of £M.315 voted by parliament under the C, D and W Acts.[1] The following facts throw light on the extent to which this sum has met the needs of the institutions for capital. For the period 1955–9 the Colonial University Grants Committee, after consulting the IUC, informed the government that they estimated the needs of the institutions to amount to £M.8; £M.4 was allocated by the government out of the amount made available for C D and W purposes for the period. For the period 1959–64 (the two periods were made to overlap) an estimate was prepared but was not presented to the government because no opportunity to do so was given by the government; the estimate amounted to £M.9·2 for existing institutions, and a sum of £M.5·3 was allotted. Thus the sums allotted by the British government fell far below the estimated needs of the institutions for capital; but when allotting these sums, the government had in mind that the richer territories could make contributions for these purposes from their own resources. Under these arrangements there was some danger that the institutions in the richer territories might fall between two stools; this has not happened in Malaya, Singapore and Nigeria whose governments have made large contributions for capital purposes, but it did happen for a period in Hong Kong whose government, however, has recently agreed to make grants to the University. Reviewing the story it can be said that the institutions have fared moderately well in respect of capital though they could all have spent more money to advantage.

The governments of the Sudan and Ghana have been as generous over recurrent expenses as over provision for capital needs. The government of the Sudan found it possible to increase its grant to the University in a period when national finance was in difficulty; in the case of Ghana the government supported a programme which made provision for staffing and new developments ahead of teaching needs. Elsewhere the picture varies. Until very recently the University of Malta has carried on in a state of abject poverty, but Malta is fortunately an exception. The University College of the West Indies has been burdened with the heavy cost of a medical school from the start, and the restricted financial resources of the territories have made it impossible to provide for developments in other subjects which the College wished to see; but lately more support has been forthcoming. Makerere College, which has to bear the cost of three expensive professional schools, medical, agricultural and veterinary, has not been able to expand its faculty of arts, as it has long wanted to do, by making provision for languages and other subjects; expansion in the University of Hong Kong has been held back by the protracted negotiations with the government. But the overall picture is not unfavourable; the universities '(except Malta) and the colleges have certainly not been starved by lack of recurrent income. They have adopted the policy of using their income to staff existing departments adequately rather than to embark on developments at the expense of what exists; in this way they have protected the staff against an unduly heavy teaching burden and have thus demonstrated, as in other ways, their understanding of a university as a place of learning and research as well as of teaching.

All the universities and colleges are fortunate in that they can offer scholarships and bursaries provided by trusts or donors; some provide awards from their own funds. But the proportion of students supported by donor and college scholarships is nowhere large; an analysis of the students at the University College of the West Indies between 1953 and 1957 shows that the percentage benefiting from these two sources taken together was eleven, while at the University of Hong Kong in the session 1958-9 the corresponding figure was seven. It follows that, unless sufficient bursaries are available from public funds, provided centrally or locally, many applicants, whom the institutions would like to admit, cannot enter for lack of means; it also follows that, unless this is the case, it cannot be said that the governments are giving adequate financial support to university education although this form of support is directly to students and only indirectly to the university. The simplest and most comprehensive method of ensuring that poverty is no obstacle to a university education is that adopted in the Sudan. Any student admitted can apply for reduction or remission of the inclusive fee (board, lodging and tuition) of £84 a year. About a third of the students pay no fee; the rest pay a fee of from £6 to the full sum. In East Africa, Ibadan and Ghana, though the source of the funds varies as between central and local government authorities, the general position is that a student can get a grant on proof of need; at these colleges over 90 per cent of the students are in receipt of help either from public funds or from donor or college scolarships. In Rhodesia about 80 per cent of the students get a grant though the amounts seldom cover the full cost of fees and maintenance. The arrangement at Fourah Bay College is remarkable in that the Sierra Leone government pays a grant covering full costs to all local students without a means test. In all these cases support for students from public funds seem to be adequate. But in the West Indies this was not so, though the arrangements, it is understood, are now being revised. In 1957 494 students with the minimum qualifications applied for admission of whom 179 were admitted; in the case of those not admitted it was lack of funds which prevented their candidatures from going forward. In the session 1958–9 27 per cent of the students in the University of Hong Kong and 42 per cent of the students in the University of Malaya were in receipt of awards of one kind or another; in the case of Hong Kong few of the awards covered the full cost (estimated at £312 per annum), forty-eight of them amounting only to £62 a year. It would appear that provision for students from public funds was not fully adequate in these two countries. In Malta there are a few donor scholarships but no government bursaries.

In regard to the amount of financial support given by territorial governments, whether directly or indirectly, the universities and colleges have in general fared well. The question of university autonomy now arises, and governments can invade the proper autonomy of universities either by attaching conditions to grants or in other ways. University autonomy is not a self-explanatory expression and demands some consideration. In a statement issued by the British Committee of Vice-Chancellors in 1947 it was said that 'the universities entirely accept the view that the government has not only the right, but the duty to satisfy itself that every field of study which in the national interest ought to be cultivated in Great Britain is in fact being cultivated in the university system and that the resources which are placed at the disposal of the universities are being used with full regard both to efficiency and to economy'. The British government has always felt itself at liberty to institute special enquiries into the affairs of particular universities by way of royal commissions and the like. The British universities, now that the major part of their income is derived from public funds, accept a growing measure of prescription; their range

N   193

of salary scales is settled by the government and is announced in parliament. The relations between the British universities and the government are manifold, delicate and subtle; there is frequently contact between universities and the government departments. Moreover there is also interplay with professional associations, learned societies and other organizations of one kind or another. The British universities are not leading lives insulated from the outside world, official or lay, and they do not conduct their affairs guided only by an estimate of their functions founded on a monastic-like concentration on their special duties as they understand them.

The staffs of the overseas universities are rightly concerned to preserve university autonomy, and are apprehensive, and not without some reason, that the governments of the territories, which are unfamiliar with universities and their traditions, may act in ways not consonant with autonomy. But few members of the staffs have had much university experience and therefore many of them are not acquainted with the relations obtaining between the universities on the one hand and the British government and public bodies on the other; in consequence there is sometimes a disposition to regard as interference actions by a government which would not be resented in Great Britain. All this makes it most important to grasp clearly what is essential in university autonomy. This phrase is sometimes used to include the control of academic matters by teachers. In Chapter 6 the situation overseas in this respect was examined and found to be satisfactory. It is the relation between the institutions as university corporations and the governments which is here under review, and the question is whether the governments have acted so as to infringe the essential liberties of universities which are to appoint staff, to devise teaching programmes, to plan and conduct research, to award degrees as they think fit and to exercise discipline over students. In Great Britain, but seldom elsewhere, universities have the right to select from among applicants for admission those whom they are willing to take; the overseas universities also exercise this right to which there has been no challenge and with which there has been no interference.

As a preface to a review of the actions of governments as

they relate to university autonomy, one remark may be made. An observer of the situation notes that action by a government, which would not be regarded in Great Britain as interference may be interpreted as interference overseas owing to tactless handling and clumsy official procedure. Governments of these territories, whether colonial or independent, are singularly lacking in tact; action which is legitimate is made to look like aggression. One example of this is the manner in which commissions and committees of enquiry have been set up. The British government, as noted above, reserves the right to institute enquiries into university problems as and when it sees fit; but it acts after consultation and discussion. In the West Indies, following on speeches by politicians which exhibited ignorance of the University College and hostility to it, the Standing Federation Committee appointed a committee in 1957 with terms of reference, including purely academic issues, without any warning to the College, whose principal first heard of it through the press. The stage seemed set for political interference; but, as things turned out, the committee produced a report which has been of real value to the College. The events preceding the recent setting up of a commission by the government of Ghana to enquire into the affairs of the University College have been somewhat similar.

When the story of the grants made to the institutions by the British and the territorial governments, whether for capital or recurrent purposes, is reviewed, it cannot be said that the governments have used their powers in such a way as to infringe academic liberty. Conditions have not been attached to grants, which are block grants and are not itemized or ear-marked. In cases where a government has not provided enough to make possible an expensive development, such as a new professional school, favoured by a university, the government has acted within its rights since it falls to governments to decide upon major developments of policy and to determine what a country can afford. To this generalization there are one or two exceptions. In Ghana a branch of the Peoples Educational Association, for which a course had been arranged by the University College, studied the Volta River project and published a memorandum containing some criticism of the scheme. The government informed the College that its grant for adult education, which was separate from the main recurrent grant, would be stopped; the grant was later resumed. The governments of East Africa have objected to the inclusion of political subjects in adult education courses. The provision of bursaries for students is an indirect form of financial assistance to universities, and it would be an infringement of academic liberty to attach conditions relating to politics or race. No case in which the political affiliation of a student has affected a grant has been reported, but, as will presently be related, Ghanaian students, who do not support the government, have been reminded that they are attending the College at government expense, a reminder that is open to an ominous interpretation. At one time the governments of East Africa discriminated between students on racial grounds when they restricted bursaries to Africans. Reference may be made here to the very common practice of bonding students in receipt of bursaries. This practice does restrict freedom; but it was employed in Great Britain until recently, and its use by the governments is easily understood. Nevertheless staff and students complain; many bonded students, it is said, find themselves under an obligation to follow courses in which they are not interested and for which they are not fit.

The chief weapon in the armoury of a government, which wishes to impose its policy on a university, is financial; in view of what has been said, the record of the use by the governments of their financial powers, apart from minor incidents, is much to their credit. But there are other ways in which governments can interfere with academic freedom; they can, for instance, refuse entry or residence permits to those whom a university desires to have on its staff. The case of a lecturer at the University College of Rhodesia attracted much public attention; he was obliged to resign because the government refused to extend his residence permit. He had not complied with the regulations governing permits, of which he was not ignorant, and on these grounds extension was refused. Since he had acted as a correspondent of a British newspaper, it was suspected that political motives had influenced the decision of the government; but the government denied that political considerations had anything to do with the case. More recently at the same college the application of a lecturer for citizenship was refused; the lecturer in question had made his opposition to government policy well known, and the decision of the government was evidently taken on political grounds. Colonial governments have sometimes exhibited childish anxiety about the political views of teachers without proceeding to action. The authorities in Kenya were once much concerned with the fitness of a member of the staff of Makerere College to teach; it had been reported to them that the teacher in question was a follower of the late Mr Aneurin Bevan.

Ministers have sometimes expressed doubts about certain aspects of university policy and in particular about the standards demanded for entrance and for the award of degrees. These doubts relate to fundamental aspects of the Asquith programme, and fall to be considered in the next chapter where the programme is reviewed. But no pressure has been put on the institutions to change their teaching programmes or to re-direct their research. As to appointments it is not the case that governments have promoted their own candidates; but they have sometimes adopted attitudes which suggest that unless the colleges hastened to increase the proportion of locally born on the staff, they might lose favour. The colleges have not allowed themselves to be frightened into deviation from the principle of appointing the best candidate for a vacancy irrespective of origin, though the University College of Ghana has adopted the scheme of special appointments for Ghanaians which was described in Chapter 15. That University autonomy has not been invaded so far does not necessarily mean that governments understand and appreciate the reasons for maintaining it as the following pronouncements show. In the course of an address on 'The University's responsibility to society', Mr Yong Nyok Lin, the Minister of Education in Singapore, spoke of 'the so-called autonomy of the University' and said that it 'cannot possibly remain as an ivory tower, isolated from the society which sustains it and feeds it with millions of dollars a year'. He added:

'The state is to the university as an indulgent father would treat an overgrown son, who, although past 21, is however incapable of finding the means of supporting himself and therefore de-

pendent on a doting father but, at the same time, tolerated
when he loudly and spiritedly claims his "independence".[2]

The following occurs in the report of an address given by
Dr (now President) Nkrumah in 1960 to the Convention
People's Party:

' "His party", the Prime Minister declared: "is a powerful
force, more powerful, indeed than anything that has yet appeared
in the history of Ghana. It is more than a political party; it is the
living embodiment of the whole glory of our people, and its
ideology is the moral mainstay of our lives". . . . Mr Nkrumah
went on to emphasize: "The CPP is Ghana and Ghana is the
CPP". There were some people who, he said, not only chose
to forget this but went out of their way to teach others to forget
also. There were some persons, staff and students, who mis-
takenly believed that the words "academic freedom" carried
with them a spirit of hostility to the party and the government.
This was the same party of the workers and the farmers and the
same government (said the Prime Minister) whose money
had founded the university and maintained it, and who provided
them with their education in the hope that they would one day
repay their countrymen by giving loyal and devoted service
to the government of the people. The CPP could not allow "this
confusion of academic freedom with disloyal and anti-govern-
ment propaganda". In the future the party should attach the
greatest importance to the ideological education of youth.'[3]

In order to understand how such pronouncements come to be
made, it is necessary to remember the past history and present
situation in the newly independent countries. Professor Eni
Njoku, of University College, Ibadan, has given an admirable
description of the situation in Nigeria.

'There was, before contact with Western Europe, no strong
tradition of scholarship in Nigeria. There were traditional
poets, praise-singers, priests, etc. Individuals who had by their
own effort learnt the local history became important in times of
dispute. But there were no scholars in the mediaeval sense, con-

198

cerned wholly with the transmission and extension of knowledge. The modern university scholar is an entirely new type of person in Nigeria, not identified with any traditional role. The condition for such a type to flourish, such as academic freedom, is therefore an entirely new conception. Nevertheless, the principle of academic freedom has been accepted in Nigeria, not by itself, but as part of a university organization. Nigerians demanded a university as good as those existing anywhere else in the world. If academic freedom is a necessary element in such universities, then it must exist in the Nigerian institution too. . . . Although the principle of academic freedom is accepted, it is important to realize that it has to justify itself in the Nigerian context. It is not easy to argue that academic freedom is necessary in order to train the professional manpower required by the Nigerian society. On the contrary, . . . this is the very reason why an insufficiently perceptive university should be given directions by the Government to ensure that the needs of the country are met. The really cogent arguments for academic freedom, such as its being a necessary atmosphere for scholarship to flourish, although applicable to Nigeria, are derived from other situations. The scholar has not yet fully arrived in Nigeria, and the advantages to be gained by giving him freedom are not yet obvious. . . . At present it (academic freedom) is merely one of the embellishments attached in its country of origin to an imported product. It is necessary to consolidate and give local content to the principle if it is to be successfully defended in times of crisis.'[4]

The position in Nigeria prevails elsewhere in Africa, while in none of the territories outside Africa is the tradition of scholarship firmly established and the position of the scholar fully understood. When independent governments take over in these countries they do not merely find themselves burdened with the duties falling to any independent government; they are acutely aware that their countries are relatively poor and undeveloped and that they are faced by immense and urgent problems. For the supply of the higher professional skills, which these territories so greatly need, the governments look to their universities which thus have an essential part to play in official plans.

But, as Professor Njoku has said, it is not in the least apparent that, in order to produce the required supply of persons with high professional skills, academic freedom is a necessary condition of university life. Moreover some governments are tempted to think of themselves as general staffs conducting military operations; they lay down the object of the campaign which President Nkrumah defined for Ghana in the address quoted above as 'a socialist pattern of society'; they design the strategy and elaborate the tactics. They want something like a national army; any discussion initiated in the university about the merits and demerits of a 'socialist pattern of society' looks like insubordination among the officers, and any discussion of the tactics approved for this end, such as questioning the Volta River project by the People's Educational Association, looks like lack of discipline in the ranks. Hence academic freedom comes to be regarded first as unnecessary, next as a nuisance and finally as objectionable.

It is easy to see how this can come about; it is not so easy to see how the value of academic freedom in the long run can be made apparent. But the tradition of academic freedom has been carried over to these universities and colleges, and is as fully appreciated by the locally born as by the expatriate members of the staff. Professor A. A. Sandoshan, a former principal of the Singapore branch of the University of Malaya, made a vigorous reply to Mr Yong. When resigning his appointment on taking a post with the World Health Organization, he told convocation that 'universities should get government aid but should not be under government control. . . . It is the responsibility of the public to see that the need of the University to get government grants does not contribute a threat to its existence as a free institution. . . . We should keep a sharp outlook to prevent further encroachment on the University's existing autonomy'.[5] Thus the tradition of academic freedom is alive; it would not be easy to eradicate it. Governments may hesitate to restrict academic freedom since they would like to see their countries standing well in the estimation of western countries, visitors from which can help by showing their appreciation of the freedom of discussion which still exists in these territories.[6]

NOTES

1. A sum of £2,725,000 was also allocated for the colleges of arts, science and technology which come within the purview of the COCAST.
2. The *Straits Times*, June 11, 1960.
3. *The Times*, April 3, 1960.
4. Eni Njoku, 'The Relationship between University and Society in Nigeria', *The Scholar and Society*, bulletin of the Committee of Science and Freedom, No. 13, 1959, p. 83.
5. The *Straits Times*, June 12, 1960.
6. A recent incident in Malaya attracted considerable attention. The Professor of English in the University gave a lecture in which he is reported to have said that a sarong culture complete with pantun (rhymes) competitions would be as ridiculous as to bring back the maypole and the Morris dancers in England just because the present monarch happened to be called Elizabeth. 'The people must be left free to make their own mistakes, to fight that deadly battle over whether or not to enter a place of entertainment wherein lurks a juke box'. This had reference to the attempt by the government to foster a Malayan culture and to the banning of juke boxes for which the government has a strong aversion. The acting Minister for Labour and Law handed a letter to the professor in the presence of the Minister for Culture. The letter said that the professor had arrogated to himself functions 'reserved only for citizens of this country and not visitors including mendicant professors. . . . We have no time for asinine sneers by passing aliens'. . . . Should the professor again wander from the bounds of the work for which he was granted entry into Malaya, his professional visit pass would be cancelled. . . . 'You will soon be packing your bags and seeking green pastures elsewhere!' The students then held a meeting and passed a resolution, all but five of the 529 students present voting for it, which spoke of the government's attempt 'to cow an individual into silence for expressing views which do not coincide with government policy'. A day or so later the Prime Minister, Mr Lee, addressed the students and tried to smooth things over. (*The Times*, November 19, 21 and 26, 1960.) The incident is illuminating. If an Englishman were appointed to a chair in a French university and made fun of the projects entertained by M. Malraux for the advancement of French culture he might be regarded as tactless; but no such torrent of abuse and threats would

descend on his head; that it did so in Singapore shows that people in new countries can be thrown into something approaching hysteria by criticism. While illuminating, the incident was more ludicrous than serious.

CHAPTER 18

THE PROGRAMME IN RETROSPECT

About the programme drawn up in 1945 one statement can be made without fear of contradiction: it has been carried out with speed and energy. It was only in February 1946 that the government of Great Britain gave its approval to the plan; since that date two universities have been created out of previously existing colleges; in two other centres small colleges have become university colleges, while in five more centres, where there were previously no facilities for higher education, university colleges have been brought into existence. In 1945 the territories, whose needs the plan was devised to meet, were dependent but on the way to self-government. These territories have recently become, or are about to become, independent, and it is fitting to ask whether the plan was that which best suited their requirements at this important phase in their history.

When the plan was launched, it was criticized on the ground that attention should be concentrated on the lower levels of education and that development at higher levels could wait. This criticism was foreseen and answered by the Asquith Commission in the following passage:

'The situation does not present a simple issue between the claims of higher and lower education; progress at any level of education is dependent upon progress at other levels, and institutions of higher education are essential if we are to secure teachers in sufficient numbers and of a quality adequate to establish proper standards of teaching in secondary schools and if we are to be able efficiently to staff the departments of public instruction. Just as the efficiency of the secondary schools depends largely on the university, so in turn that of the primary depends on the secondary school. Indeed, the lesson to be drawn from history is quite clear even if at first sight paradoxical; it is that where education as a whole is backward, effort is most rewarding when it is directed to the higher levels. It may be remembered that the development of universities in Europe preceded the systematic organization of popular education.'[1]

Criticism of this kind is no longer heard; no one now doubts that it was the right policy in 1945 energetically to expand facilities for university education in the colonies. Attention is now focused on the insufficiency of these facilities. It is not suggested that those who were responsible, in Great Britain and overseas, for carrying out the plan could have accomplished more in the time; resources were limited and it was an uphill task to get done what has been done. The question now is, not whether it was right to launch a programme, but whether it was the right programme to launch.

'Nigerians', Professor Eni Njoku has written, 'demanded a university as good as those existing anywhere in the world'. The plan set out to satisfy this demand, and under it universities 'as good as those existing anywhere in the world' are in the making. The universities were to have ample space, dignified buildings and residences for students; the scope of studies was to be that in a British university with a full range of professional faculties; the degrees awarded were to carry the prestige of British degrees; research was to be no less important than teaching; finally the universities were to be the intellectual centres of emergent nations.

The results of carrying out this programme are to be seen in the existing universities and colleges. These institutions have come under some criticism, notably in West Africa, the West Indies and Singapore; the essence of the criticism is that universities of this kind do not sufficiently meet the needs of the countries because they cannot produce graduates as fast as they are required and because the subjects of study are restricted especially as regards courses in applied subjects which lead to vocational qualifications. To these specific complaints is often added the general complaint that these universities are exclusive, foster the rise of an elite and are insufficiently in touch with the people and their needs. These criticisms merit careful attention; they have not been made idly or out of perversity, but by those who are deeply concerned with the future of these countries. The question of the best form of university education for these countries presents a huge field of discourse, as indeed it does for all countries. Perhaps the most suitable method of giving the attention to these criticisms which they deserve is to consider particular features of the Asquith plan on which criticism has fastened because they are thought to produce the results of which complaint is made.

One feature of the plan, the residential system, has been criticized on the ground that it restricts the number of students. At present all students in the University of Khartoum and the University Colleges of East Africa, West Africa and the West Indies live in halls of residence; the University of Hong Kong operates a modified residential system under which students can live at home or in approved lodgings by special permission but must be attached to a hall; at Singapore students can live at home or in lodgings at their choice.[2] The second situation is similar to that at Oxford and Cambridge and the third to that in the newer English universities. So far as rules about residence go, the first situation limits the number of students to the number of beds, the second is more elastic but does involve limitation, while the third sets no limit. Where the first and second situations prevail the number of students could be expanded without limit (assuming that space is available) by building more halls; but it is said that the funds necessary for this purpose are not available or could be better used in other ways. Halls are expensive; the cost per student has seldom been less than £1,000 and usually a good deal more, though the cost at the hall now under construction at Ibadan will be about £600. Those who concentrate attention upon the cost of hall sometimes forget that an increase in student numbers, in the absence of any residential rules, requires increased capital expenditure on class rooms, laboratories and libraries and increased recurrent expenditure on staff and maintenance, and that, when all is taken into account, the extra capital expenditure on halls, the maintenance of which is covered by fees, does not form a relatively large item in the whole financial picture, or at least not such a large item as is sometimes believed. Moreover residence might be provided in less expensive quarters, such as groups of hutments, to the provision of which attention might well be given.

University opinion in Great Britain attaches increasing importance to residence as promoting general and social education, and all British universities are doing their best to increase the proportion of students in residence. The value of residence in these respects for students overseas is greater than in Great Britain; moreover for students overseas residence has additional value since it fosters national cohesion by bringing together young people of different races and tribes. The other side of the picture is that, when overseas students live where and how they please, they are usually much less well accommodated than British students who live at home or in lodgings. The homes of overseas students are often very poor, and in their countries there is no practice of keeping lodgings which in Great Britain provide passable accommodation. Therefore, if all residential requirements were abolished, overseas students would lose the advantages of active membership of student society; in addition many of them would live in conditions unsuitable for the mere purpose of preparating for examination. To all this more consideration might be given by critics of the residential system.[3]

It has been said that the university system, as it now operates, restricts the number of students by setting entrance requirements too high. If by that is meant that the colleges have had vacancies which they could not fill for lack of qualified applicants, it is a mistake. Only in two colleges, and then only for short periods, have there been unfilled beds. At one time at the University College of the West Indies, there were vacancies; this was not because there were insufficient applicants with the necessary qualifications to fill them; it was because, though qualified applicants largely exceeded the number of vacancies, many of them could not enter the College because they were poor and because of the scarcity of government bursaries. The University College of Ghana had vacancies for two or three years, but this was the result of a reorganization of the schools; the schools developed sixth forms which meant that for two years or so those who would have entered the College remained at school. In other words minimum entrance qualifications have not been set at a point which led to vacancies. The position is the other way round; there is an excess of applicants with minimum entrance qualifications over vacancies, and this excess is rapidly increasing. So long as this is so, a lowering of minimum entrance requirements would not increase the number of students.

It is also said that the output of graduates is restricted because the achievement, as tested by examination, needed for the award of degrees is unnecessarily high. An example of this line of criticism is contained in a despatch in *The Times* setting out the views of the government of Singapore.

'The argument is that colonial universities have produced graduates whose qualifications are well above, and often far removed from, the ordinary needs of the community, and whose numbers are hopelessly inadequate. They form a small elite who have graduated for the most part in the English language, history, geography, "and the more innocuous fields of human learning", as Mr Lee Kuan Yew, the Prime Minister, has put it. They are not engineers or technologists, and too few have become doctors and dentists.

If the government gets its way, this will now change. More students will go to university and be turned out as graduates with lower qualifications, while only honours students and the academically brilliant will pass on to standards comparable with the best abroad.

"I acknowledge", Mr Lee has said, "that it would be a temporary necessity, albeit unpleasant, creating unhappiness for those striving for ideal standards, that we should lower the requirements before one gets a general degree or diploma, before one begins to serve the community, if for no other reason than that you must train them (students) in large numbers. And I also suggest that perhaps for the outstanding, for those who are likely to make a contribution to human knowledge, these absolute standards could be maintained. In any society you find your need is greatest for the average, but progress and absolute high standards are finally attained by your above average."

Other countries, declared the Prime Minister, were taking

this course. The Indonesians, the Chinese and the Indians were all producing graduates, many of whom by absolute European or British standards, would not be completely qualified engineers, draughtsmen, architects, geologists, and so on. High standards had been maintained in British colonial universities, but only for the few. Last year, for example, the University of Malaya expected to produce only six dentists for all Malaya, with the result that a host of unqualified technicians who learnt by trial and error had to be allowed into the profession for work such as filling cavities.'[4]

Mr Lee's remarks suggest that he may be under a misapprehension concerning the place of the professional faculties in the overseas universities; as was shown in Chapter 9, great efforts have been made to build up these faculties. But that is a minor point. He is concerned with a problem of the first importance for the less developed countries; they have not got graduates, especially professional graduates, in anything like sufficient numbers, and the output of graduates from the universities is not meeting their urgent needs. His remedy is to reduce the achievement now demanded for the award of a degree; he is exceptional among the critics of degree standards since he recognizes the value of high aims in the case of gifted students for whom he would leave a loophole.

Since the great need, as Mr Lee says, is for professional graduates, attention may be concentrated upon professional degrees. If, by lowering degree standards, it were made possible to graduate in a shorter period, the supply of graduates would be increased; by reducing the length of a course from three to two years the output goes up by fifty per cent (in the University of Malaya the course in pharmacy lasts two years, in engineering three, in dentistry five and in medicine six). Thus by shortening the courses the output could be appreciably increased without adding to the staff, the buildings or the equipment. Mr Lee would also like to see an increase in the number of students which would require additional teaching facilities.

About this programme two things may be said of which the first relates to Mr Lee's anxiety that the universities should adjust their arrangements with the needs of the 'average' student in mind (the average student is not the same as the average person of student age). But this is what universities already do since they only admit those who have a good prospect of gaining a degree, and a degree in a professional subject is in effect a certificate of competence to practice. Thus competence to practice at existing levels is within reach of the 'average' student; it is true that, if there were a large increase in the number of students, the quality of the 'average' student might fall, but in that case some students might not have the capacity to gain a degree at the reduced standard in the shortened period. For the able students universities offer the opportunity of winning honours, but professional degrees do not as a rule carry honours, and in the University of Malaya none do so. The second point is that there are what may be called international standards for professional qualifications; inexact and unsystematized as these standards are, it is nevertheless quite clear that, as a result of this programme, professional degrees in Malaya would fall into the second rank.

To the proposal to replace courses leading to the present levels of professional competence by courses leading to lower levels there are powerful objections. The universities would not be able to claim that they were 'as good as those existing anywhere in the world'. It would not be easy to attract staff of high quality, and in consequence the universities would decline in strength as centres of research. The needs of the 'average' student would not be better met; in fact he would be in a worse position insofar as he was aiming below his capacity. If these objections to lowering standards are valid, the programme for the less developed countries which need more graduates is to develop the existing universities and add to their number. There are those who say that the expansion needed would cost more than these countries could bear and that the results would come too slowly. As to expense it is sometimes forgotten that any alternative programme would be costly; as to delay it is unfortunately true that no programme can achieve what is needed in a short space of time. Nevertheless so urgent is the need for more professional services that methods of alleviating the position should be investigated. It would be well worth while to explore the possibility of increasing the number of those who render ancillary professional services and of providing partial training in engineering and other professions somewhat as suggested by Mr Lee; the availability of such people in large numbers, working under fully trained practitioners, could enable the benefits of professional skills to be spread more widely. Before it could be said how far the benefits of professional services could be extended in this manner, a careful survey would have to be made of the situation in each profession. As an example of what is in mind reference can be made to medical services. It is sometimes said that it is intolerable to have to wait for the appearance of a corps of fully qualified doctors before an effective drive can be made to reduce infant mortality and therefore that the aim should be to turn out less fully qualified practitioners who could be produced more quickly. But, putting aside the argument against lowering standards, would this be as effective as increasing the number of those in the ancillary medical vocations—of nurses, midwives and health visitors, especially if their services were organized under the general direction of fully qualified practitioners? There is in Great Britain the interesting case of the opticians. There were never enough occulists to attend to the needs of those with defective eyesight, and the ancillary profession of opticians emerged and has received statutory recognition. The Asquith Commission thought there was 'need for large numbers of a grade of medical staff with training inferior to that of a qualified medical practitioner but more extensive than that of a nurse',[5] and consideration might well be given to the creation of new ancillary medical services as well as to the expansion of those in existence. This is merely intended to suggest that in one profession the need of the community for its services could be more extensively met than at present without ceasing to educate fully qualified practitioners whose general supervision is indeed necessary if the ancillary services are to be efficient. The same may hold for other professions. But it does not follow that training for the ancillary vocations should be provided in universities; in fact there are reasons why such training should be given outside the university, and these reasons are explained below when considering another criticism made of the present university programme.

It is said that the present scope of university studies is too limited. This criticism is heard in West Africa where the American land grant colleges have attracted attention and are held out as models which the overseas universities might well follow. These colleges were instituted under the Morrill Act of 1862 and received support from the federal government in the shape of grants of land on condition that they placed emphasis on agriculture and the 'mechanic arts'. At that time many Americans, under the influence of Jacksonian democracy, thought that existing colleges were too conservative, aristocratic and traditional, and were therefore out of touch with the people and their needs. The new colleges had as their motto 'serving the people'. Sixty-nine institutions now appear in the list of land grant colleges; an inspection of the list does not show that they share features which distinguish them as a group from other colleges; only some of them make a point of emphasizing the persistence of the original intention which lay behind the movement.[6] It is the original programme which attracts sympathetic interest.

When we ask in what respects those who are attracted by the land grant college idea would like the overseas colleges to be modified, the answer seems to be that they want to see new courses of a practical kind included in the programme, to bring the universities into closer touch with the people and to change their atmosphere so that they ceased to figure as institutions for a privileged elite. How this might work was shown in the course of an address given by Dr Azikiwe who is known to be interested in the land grant college idea.[7] He was describing the possible organization for a university in the eastern region of Nigeria. There would be five faculties offering degree courses and twenty-six institutes offering diploma courses; among the latter would be courses in architecture, commerce, domestic science, dramatics, fine arts, journalism, librarianship, music, nursing, pharmacy, public administration, secretarial studies, social work and surveying; there would also be facilities for gaining diplomas in such subjects as accountancy and engineering. The range of subjects, some vocational and others non-vocational for which diplomas would be available, is very wide; facilities for studying these subjects are little developed in the territories, and this constitutes a serious gap in their educational systems. Dr

Azikiwe proposes to fill the gap by making it a function of universities to provide these facilities. It would not appear that he is concerned to lower degree standards or to offer degree courses in subjects for which degrees are not now available. His intention is greatly to widen the scope of subjects which can be studied in universities; that he is concerned with an urgent problem no one can doubt. What needs consideration is whether his method of solving it is best.

Universities do not act in an arbitrary fashion when they design their programmes; they are prepared to offer courses in all subjects which can be studied in depth if the intention is to study them in depth. This guiding principle may seem inexact, but universities, conforming with British and European continental models, find no difficulty in applying it in practice. Hence these universities attract people with certain aptitudes, interests and tastes, and develop an environment favourable to studies of this kind. In educational, as in other matters, there is value in the division of labour, and therefore, before Dr Azikiwe's proposal is adopted, very careful consideration should be given to other possible methods of filling the gap that he has detected. In the next chapter this matter is further pursued; there it will be asked whether, in order to meet the very urgent needs of these countries, it is necessary to extend the range of university studies and responsibilities.

It is not only because universities form a convenient umbrella, ready for use, that Dr Azikiwe and others want to place these studies under that shelter; they think that the universities should be brought into closer touch with ordinary people and immediate practical concerns from which they are now remote. This is summed up in the common complaint that the universities form an elite. The essential feature of an elite is that it is composed of the pick of a group, and unless all who want to go to a university were allowed to enter, the university population and the graduates who emerge must form an elite. In western society graduates merge in the community, but in societies most members of which live in very humble circumstances and few form a middle class, students and graduates are isolated by their attainments, interests and mode of life; on this account many are remote from their families, even from their wives, since few women possess the attainments or share the interests of graduates. The position of the small graduate group is difficult; they have to endure social isolation. But it cannot be charged against the graduates that they are ignorant of, or oblivious to, the problems of their communities; a good case could be made for saying that they are among the most devoted citizens. Therefore there is no case for attempting to recall students and graduates to their social duties by associating them with students whose studies are more directly practical; as for social isolation it is perverse to lay the blame on universities since it is an inescapable, but fortunately only a temporary, phenomenon. But in connection with this whole subject the overseas universities, while preserving all the essential features of university life, would do well to see that the trappings and unessentials do not take the shape of exotic importations tending to create unnecessary barriers between themselves and the local way of life.

Since this chapter is concerned with the services rendered by universities through their graduates to society, the results of two surveys, planned to discover the occupations of former students, may be summarized. An indication of the careers followed by graduates of a university which has had time to develop its professional faculties is provided by figures from the University of Hong Kong whose professional schools have been in existence for some time. Replies to a questionnaire revealed that graduates were found in occupations in the following order of importance, medicine, education, engineering, architecture and commerce, to mention only the first five; the policy followed in other overseas universities and colleges is like that in Hong Kong in respect of the development of professional education, and it may therefore be expected that when their professional faculties have become established, most graduates will be found in similar employments.[8]

An analysis has been made of the occupations followed by old students of Makerere College who had entered up to 1953.[9] This record, which covers about 1,700 old students, includes very few graduates the first of whom only appeared in 1953, and refers to a period when the studies were at a lower level and their range far more restricted than now. But the analysis yields interesting results. Of the past members, 542, or just under a third, had taken up teaching, 103 were in the government agricultural service (in addition 27 were substantial farmers), 117 had entered medicine, 72 were in business, 62 in administration and 79 in clerical and similar employment. There were also among the old students 65 chiefs, including 6 paramount chiefs, 16 major chiefs and 43 lesser chiefs. The prime ministers of the kingdoms of Ankole, Toro and Bunyoro and two ministers in the government of the Buganda kingdom were also included. Surely a very remarkable testimony to the influence of the College. Another important fact emerged: 719 old students were working for central governments and 162 for local governments. Though figures are lacking, it is the case that a large proportion of old students of other colleges are in government service. In all countries the higher ranks of government service are excluded, at least by convention, from any active connection with political movements, but in these territories it is often a condition of government service that any connection with politics is banned. So far as the political life of the community is concerned, this has the effect of sterilizing a considerable proportion of those with higher education. In this way through no fault of the universities, the influence which these graduates can exert on political life is restricted; in conversations with students a visitor may often detect frustration because they foresee that their careers will condemn them to remain spectators of the political scene.

An observer, pondering over these criticisms, may well turn his eyes to the University of Khartoum. That University was built upon the Asquith plan. Since 1956 it has been entirely free to refashion itself. It has not done so and does not propose to do so; it advances along existing lines. It adheres to the residential principle, it has not lowered its standards and it has not enlarged its range of studies beyond the limits prevailing in European univerities. It commands the confidence of the government and the people; it is a national institution embodying national aspirations. This provides some reason for thinking that in its essential features the plan was sound, since the needs of the emergent nations are much alike. Nevertheless these countries are in urgent need of a very much larger number of graduates, and especially of professional graduates, and the next chapter is devoted to the problem how this need can be met.

NOTES

1. *Report of the Commission on Higher Education in the Colonies*, 1945, p. 12.
2. It is understood that the University of Khartoum is thinking of adopting the Hong Kong practice. It would appear from remarks made by the Principal of the University College of the West Indies that he would like to abolish all residential requirements (*The Daily Gleaner*, May 25, 1960).
3. Ghanaian experience is illuminating. There are four junior technical institutes which have always been fully residential. Between 1953 and 1957 technical institutes were set up at Tarkwa, Takoradi, Kumasi and Accra, and were originally non-residential. It was found that satisfactory accommodation in lodgings was not available for students living outside these towns for whom residential accommodation has now been provided.
4. *The Times*, July 18, 1960.
5. *Report of the Commission on Higher Education in the Colonies*, 1945, p. 62.
6. See E. D. Eddy, *Colleges for our Land and Time*, 1957.
7. An Address delivered by Dr Azikiwe at Michigan State University, July 10, 1959.
8. R. F. Simpson, *A Survey of Employment and other Facts relating to the Graduates of the University of Hong Kong*, 1958.
9. J. E. Goldthorpe and M. Macpherson, 'Makerere College and its Old Students', *Zaire*, Vol. XII, 4, 1958.

CHAPTER 19

THE FUTURE

The Asquith Commission said that the university colleges
should become universities without undue delay, and thought
that this would happen before the territories became independent. Independence has come earlier than was foreseen, and
it is by accident that the colleges have become ripe for university
status at about the time of independence. There is no necessary
connection between the assumption of university status and independence; the University College of Ghana has retained its
status as a university college for more than three years after
independence. While the elevation to university status is an
important event in the history of the colleges, the attainment of
self-government by the territories is of far greater importance
not only to them but also to the universities since it places responsibility for university policy on the successor governments.

Already two developments have taken place in territories with
self-government (in the case of Nigeria after internal self-
government had been attained but before independence). In
accordance with a plan agreed before independence the Federation of Malaya has set up a branch of the University of Malaya
near Kuala Lumpur which will shortly become a university; it is
interesting to note that this new centre will follow the pattern
of the University of Malaya in respect of standards and scope of
studies, and that no radical innovations are proposed. The legislature of the Eastern Region of Nigeria founded the University
of Nigeria in 1955; its academic aims, as set out in the Act, are
similar to those of University College, Ibadan. But in certain
respects its programme departs from that hitherto followed.
The Act in its original form declared that there would be facul-

ties of arts, science, medicine, law, engineering and theology, and institutes dealing with a large number of subjects, including fine arts, fishery, journalism, librarianship, music, physical education, and social work. The Act was amended in 1956 making the establishment of all the faculties and institutes permissive rather than mandatory. In 1959 a site was found for the University near Nsukka, a town with 5,000 inhabitants about forty miles north of Enugu, the capital of the Eastern Region. There is ample room for development on the site which has much to recommend it from the scenic point of view. The University opened in 1960 with some 250 students of arts subjects; Michigan State University and the University of London are giving help and advice at the request of the University.

Thus the new era has begun; moreover it has begun at a time when the need for more graduates and therefore of more students, always very much in the minds of those engaged in carrying out the Asquith plan, is now universally recognized as very pressing. In Great Britain there is one university student for every 500 of the population; the corresponding figure, omitting students in other countries, in Nigeria is in the region of 20,000, in Ghana 9,000, in the West Indies and Malaya 4,000. But these figures represent only the present achievement of the Asquith plan; the existing universities and colleges are growing rapidly in size; University College, Ibadan, has doubled its numbers in four years. The ultimate achievement will be much greater, and another way of looking at the situation is to take note of the provision of universities in relation to population. In Great Britain there is one university (including the University College of North Staffordshire) to every 2·3M of the population; the corresponding figure for Nigeria is 35M (not counting the University of Nigeria because it was founded after the attainment of internal self-government), for East Africa 8·5M, for Ghana (not counting the Kumasi College of Technology) 6M and for Hong Kong and the West Indies 3M. It is plain that the provision of universities in most of the territories lags behind that in Great Britain and that, even after existing universities have become full to their ultimate capacity, there will be, in many of the territories, need to found new universities. But such is the demand for more graduates that, in territories where the provision is least adequate, thought should be given at once to the creation of more universities.

Of all the territories Nigeria has least provision for university education in relation to population; it was therefore most appropriate that the problems of Nigeria should be studied by an authoritative commission. The Commission on Post-School Certificate and Higher Education in Nigeria (called the Ashby Commission after its chairman Sir Eric Ashby) was appointed in 1959 and reported in 1960.[1] It had nine members, including the chairman, and was Nigerian-Anglo-American in composition having three members from each country. The report is of great importance because it presents the views of an international Commission on the desirable extent of university provision and the appropriate shape of university education in one of the less developed countries; since the problems are much alike in all such countries, the recommendations of the Commissioners have wide relevance. Their views are of special interest to those who have been in any way concerned with the building up of university education in the territories since 1945 because it is not difficult to infer from their recommendations how far in their judgment the foundations which have been laid are sound.

The report is very comprehensive since the Commissioners found it necessary to overstep the terms of reference and to include primary and secondary education; all that needs to be said here about their recommendations concerning these subjects is that they are directed to building up secondary education which, as compared with primary education, is less advanced. The proposals of the Commission relating to the number and siting of new universities can be briefly summarized by saying that they recommend the foundation of new universities at Zaria and Lagos which would give Nigeria four universities, one in each region and one in federal territory.[2] This would provide places for 7,500 students by 1970 when there would be one university student for rather less than each 5,000 of the population; much could be said, and no doubt will be said, as to whether this is the right amount of provision and whether it would be in the right places. There is also the question how the necessary funds for capital and recurrent costs can be found. But from the point of view of this book these problems can be left aside because interest centres on the constitution, organization, standards and scope of study recommended for the new universities. Is it proposed to multiply universities more or less on present lines or to found universities on some new pattern? In other words is it the view of the Commission that the Asquith programme was rightly designed?

A word may be first said about the manner in which new universities are to be brought into existence in Nigeria. Under the federal constitution higher education is on the concurrent list though University College, Ibadan, is scheduled as a federal responsibility. The Commission are anxious that the Nigerian university system should be co-ordinated, and foresees that 'private groups, and perhaps municipal authorities, may in due course wish to establish universities. Regional governments would therefore be wise to adopt policies to govern the right to award degrees'.[3] The Commission recommend the institution of a National Universities Commission which would among other duties investigate proposals for new universities which desire federal grants and would advise the federal government whether they should be approved for grants. They also suggest that the National Universities Commission should prepare a memorandum of agreement for consideration by the regional governments which would include 'the adoption of a common pattern of legislation to cover the ways in which universities may be established, the minimum standards needed for the right to award degrees and the requirements of eligibility for federal support'.[4] By such means the Commission hope to check the foundation of universities which would not be of the type which they recommend, or, if they were, would be in excess of needs or not sited at appropriate places.

As to university government the Commission wrote as follows: 'We recommend that each university should be governed by its own autonomous Council, which should have undisputed control over the affairs of the university: the appointment of staff, the content of the courses, and the admission and examination of students. The Council of University College, Ibadan, presents a good model of an effective governing body'.[5] In other words the method of government, recommended by the Asquith Commission and put into practice in all the colleges, is endorsed.

On the question of standards the Commissioners put their view in the following passages: 'Universities are unlike other educational institutions: they have bonds of loyalty not only to the country which supports them, but also to the international company of universities all over the world. This double loyalty is essential because a nation's university degrees, like its money, must have currency in other nations. Through a tradition which is six centuries old, universities like to recognize one another's degrees and open their doors to one another's members, for this is the only way international standards in science and scholarship can be maintained. . . . A university which did no more than serve the demands of its own community would never gain respect from its sister universities abroad; it would not attract staff of high intelligence; its graduates would not be welcome in other centres of learning. There is no room in the academic world for a university which does not set itself international standards'.[6] 'University standards are an indispensable anchor for the whole intellectual and professional life of Nigeria; if this anchor drags, Nigeria will fail to take her rightful place among the nations'.[7] In these most emphatic terms the Commission express their support for the policy in relation to standards which was adopted by those who have been responsible hitherto for the new foundations.

The Commissioners went on to say that 'a much greater diversity of demand is likely to be made on Nigerian universities than on their British counterparts. We believe that Nigerian universities should meet this demand on one condition: that what is required of them is indeed greater diversity and not lower standards'. They give seven examples of 'changes of attitude to university work' thought by them to be desirable. There should be a degree of BA (Education) with teaching practice in vacations.[8] The curriculum of the engineering course should be 'down-to-earth' and be flexible enough to accept sandwich-course students, but the standard of the degree should 'be equivalent to that required for membership of the professional engineering institutions of the United Kingdom.'[9] The agricultural course should include home economics and training for those who will undertake extension work. There should be a degree in law which would form the passport to the legal profession. Extra-mural work should be extended. There should be a department or institute of African studies mainly concerned with research.[10] Medical and veterinary degrees should cease to be 'tied to the requirements of overseas professional organizations'; the courses could then be adjusted to Nigerian needs.'[11]

The desirable 'change of attitude', which the Commissioners clearly regard as the most radical, relates to professional qualifications in accountancy, banking, insurance and company secretaryship. In Great Britain these qualifications are gained by passing the examinations of professional associations. The Commissioners recommend the institution of a Bachelor of Commerce degree in which the chief specialization would be 'accountancy, banking, company secretaryship, government, insurance and transport.'[12] This is not a complete departure from British practice, but coupled with this recommendation is the proposal that the courses should be sandwich courses, office based, which is an innovation, but not necessarily a departure from the principle that university courses should take the form of study in depth.[13] It could be argued that what is proposed for these professions is, broadly speaking, that which now obtains for the medical profession; the courses would include 'clinical' training, and the degree would constitute a professional qualification.

There is nothing in these proposals for diversifying the curriculum which conflicts with the principle which has hitherto guided the programme of the university colleges, namely that the subjects included in university courses should be capable of study in depth and should be so studied. Technical institutes, of which there are now four in Nigeria, would provide education below university level; they would offer courses in sub-professional subjects. This implies that, in the opinion of the Commission, a number of subjects, for which provision could be made in the institutes proposed for the University of Nigeria, should be assigned to the technical institutes. In short it is proposed to diversify university studies, but not to depart from the university tradition hitherto followed.

University schemes of study are always in course of modification in the light of experience and of changes in conditions. When the new colleges were founded local conditions were little known and there was no accumulation of experience. There is now the experience of some ten years upon which to draw, and the recommendations of the Commission are based on it. These recommendations are directed to Nigeria but are, as was said, of wide relevance. It is interesting to note that the specific proposals made by the Commission had already been the subject of discussion in the colleges and that action had been taken along these lines in certain cases. Royal College, Nairobi, had already designed courses in accountancy and allied subjects, the University College of Ghana had instituted a degree in law, African studies were receiving increasing attention while the extension of extra-mural work was held back only by lack of special government aid. The recommendations are to be regarded as an encouragement to the colleges further to pursue policies already adopted or contemplated, and not as criticism of the past carrying the need for decisive change in outlook.

The Commission are anxious to see a larger place given to public health, preventive medicine and paediatrics in the medical course, and this may well be desirable. But they seem to misunderstand the position which has prevailed hitherto. 'We say emphatically that they (medicine and veterinary science) both suffer in Nigeria through a mistaken, but understandable, belief that standards of attainments for Nigerians practising in Nigeria must be acceptable to the bodies which legislate for Englishmen practising in England'.[14] But this was not a mistaken belief; in a colony the only passport to professional practice is a qualification recognized in Great Britain. This is a fact of which the colleges had to take account; the locally born wanted access to the higher ranks of professional practice, and if the colleges were to satisfy this very reasonable demand they had to devise courses leading to a British qualification. Perhaps the Commission mean that the colonial system was at fault, but they have used language which appears to impute blame to the colleges and others concerned with the Asquith programme.

The Commission indicate certain changes that they regard as desirable in the medical course, but they employ wording and make a proposal which are not easy to harmonize with the passages quoted above in which they lay great emphasis on standards. 'The best', they say when speaking of medical education 'becomes the enemy of the good'. By the best in this context no one has ever meant more than the attainment of an international standard, and if the Commission have it in mind that medical attainments in Nigeria shall be below that standard, they are departing from their own principles. But they do seem to have this in mind because they recommend the institution of a locally recognized qualification for those who fail to qualify for medical degrees. They do not say what status the locally qualified would have, but if their status were to be that of a medical graduate, the standards of the Nigerian medical profession would be undermined. It is possible that the locally qualified would perform ancillary or sub-professional services, and if so the proposal is in line with the suggestions made in Chapter 18 which are intended to indicate how professional services could be extended to meet the needs of the community. The treatment of the problem of medical education by the Commission, which had no medical member, is puzzling.

The Commission recognize that universities at Ibadan, Zaria and Nsukka must be residential; it is a noteworthy fact that the University of Nigeria at Nsukka, the first to be founded under purely African auspices, is designed to be residential, and this is an effective reply to those critics who have represented the residential principle as a costly fad imported from abroad. These three universities would share much in common; but expensive faculties should not be duplicated beyond necessity, and each university would specialize in one or more directions. The university proposed for Lagos would be of a different character. 'At Lagos it is possible to think of a non-residential institution'.[15] There would be a school of commerce and business administration, and a school of economics and social science; in the former students would study for the degree of BComm. mentioned above. There would be evening as well as day students. The University would offer correspondence courses directed to a degree of BA in a limited number of subjects which can be taught well by correspondence. So far as overseas territories are concerned the programme for the university in Lagos is novel in respect of residence, the limited academic programme, the admission of part-time (evening) students, and correspondence courses, but it involves no departure from the fundamental principles, so far followed, in respect of standards and the nature and kind of studies provided in universities. Part-time students would have daytime occupations, and so too would most full-time students for whom courses would be arranged on a sandwich basis; for them it is reasonable to waive residential requirements since they would have their own homes and would mostly be above normal student age. It would clearly be valuable to offer such facilities in Lagos, the commercial centre of the country. No one doubts that attendance for instruction is to be preferred to correspondence courses; but the latter are a great deal better than nothing, and, if confined to those in employment who cannot enter one of the other universities, have much to recommend them. The Commissioners point to the United States where experience has shown the value of correspondence courses; they might also have referred to Australian experience. The Universities of Queensland and New England conduct correspondence courses for degrees on a large scale; in the latter University, where the system is most carefully organized, the work is carried out by regular members of the staff and not by people specially appointed for the purpose, and this is a most valuable feature of the system. On the basis of this experience it can be said that correspondence courses could be a useful adjunct to university facilities in Nigeria.

Finally the Commissioners recommend that the new universities should seek sponsorship. 'The new Nigerian universities', they say, 'will be at a great disadvantage in attracting staff, and in establishing currency for their degrees, if they do not seek sponsorship from well-established universities overseas. . . . The sponsorship need not be onerous either for the new university or its sponsor; but if a well-established overseas university is to underwrite with its prestige a new Nigerian university we would expect the sponsoring university to have a place on its Council, to be consulted about the general pattern of courses, to appoint some of the examiners and to be assured that the university has a sound constitution and reliable sources of finance'.[16] The system of special relationship was designed to give the prestige of London University to the colleges; 'it has been', the Commission say, 'of inestimable benefit that University College, Ibadan, started under the wing of London University; a standard has been set for higher education which other developing countries may envy'.[17] But since the new universities will confer their own degrees from the start, as is certainly desirable, this system is no longer applicable. The Commission are no doubt right in thinking that the new universities would benefit from the prestige which sponsorship would confer on them, but sponsorship by one university is not the only way to achieve this end. Sponsorship by two or more universities would be possible, but would probably create difficulties. An alternative, which might be considered, would be to appoint a board of academic advisers, not representing one university, but selected for their experience and their eminence in their subjects.

It is most fortunate that when the first phase in the development of university education is drawing to a close, authoritative commissioners have surveyed the future needs of Nigeria. After a most careful assembly of the relevant facts they have produced a programme which will be studied with great attention; to carry it out will be very expensive, and, as the Commissioners emphasized, international aid will be necessary. But this book is the story of achievement during the first phase, and it is therefore of the greatest interest to find that international commissioners of great experience, who are not motivated by any paternal sentiments for the Asquith plan, propose what is in effect a great expansion of university facilities on the lines which guided development during the first phase.

Since the problems of all less developed countries are much alike, it is probable that equally authoritative international commissions, appointed to report on the situations in other territories, would propose that university development should follow lines similar to those recommended for Nigeria. Existing universities and colleges would be advised to diversify their studies, and probably also to introduce correspondence courses in preparation for degrees, but otherwise to continue as at present, while new universities would be encouraged to model their constitutions and programmes on the precedents set by the former. It is most unlikely that there would be support for those who advocate some new type of university which would aim at lower standards and would include sub-professional training; such proposals attract sympathy because many people are disposed to look for mistakes in colonial policies and to find an example in the foisting onto emergent peoples of a university system which suits older peoples. But it is not shown why this system does not suit emergent peoples; it is certainly no compliment to them to recommend that they should aim at standards lower than the highest. There is no more logic in holding that new peoples should have novel universities than there is in the passage which inspired Dr Johnson's famous parody. But when the critics and the doubters point to the small number of graduates which the universities and colleges have so far produced, a reply is called for from those who hold that in principle the present system is sound.

The outstanding fact is that the number of students in all the existing institutions is far below the total which they could accommodate without exceeding the number beyond which their student population should not grow. Hence the obvious policy is rapidly to expand numbers in the existing colleges and universities. If this were done in Hong Kong, Malaya (with its prospects of two universities), and in the West Indies (with two branches for its college) there seems to be no immediate need for new foundations. In Ghana there is the problem of the Kumasi College of Technology, which is recognized by London University as preparing for degrees in engineering; the College might be brought within a federal university, or it might be raised to the status of a university along with the University College. If the University of East Africa were to come into being with three constituent colleges, there would be no need for more university provision for some time to come. The future of Central Africa is clouded by uncertainty about its political organization, but owing to the paucity of secondary schools for Africans, there will be for some years ahead an insufficient supply of African candidates, with qualifications for admission to a university, to justify a new foundation. Only in Nigeria is it urgent that new universities should be founded at once.

In all these territories a problem must be faced, namely how to ensure that the power to award degrees is conferred only on institutions whose financial resources are adequate, whose constitutions are proper to a university, and whose standards and range of studies conform with the programme agreed to be fitting for universities. This problem arises, not only when governments have it in mind themselves to expand university provision, but also when local authorities and private organizations develop ambitions to found universities, which may happen at any time. It is therefore very necessary that governments should clear their minds concerning the task which awaits them; in this, as in many other spheres, that of economic policy for instance, governments need informed advice; arrangements should be made under which such advice is available to them, and a convention should be established that it is sought before action is taken. Where the constitution is federal, and education is a function assigned to the concurrent legislative list as in Nigeria, special difficulties arise; the Ashby Commission have suggested how they could be overcome in that country. Appendix 8 contains a sketch of the procedures in use in certain English-speaking countries.

The importance of controlling the power to grant degrees cannot be exaggerated. It is only by control that four essential aims can be achieved; first that university provision is designed to conform with national needs so far as national finance makes possible; secondly that universities do not come into existence in unsuitable places with insufficient equipment and inferior teaching facilities; thirdly that the possession of a degree denotes a minimum standard of achievement in the absence of which a degree has little or no significance; fourthly that this standard has international currency. By achieving the fourth aim the less developed countries can join on a basis of equality with the more developed countries in world-wide intellectual endeavour. For some time to come the less developed countries must remain poorer than the more developed countries in material things; in things of the mind they can achieve the highest standards here and now provided that they set this as the aim for their universities.

NOTES

1. *Investment in Education*, the Report of the Commission on Post-School Certificate and Higher Education in Nigeria, 1960.

2. A reservation by one of the Nigerian members of the Ashby Commission recommends an additional university for each region, bringing the total to seven.

3. *Investment in Education*, loc. cit., p. 34.

4. ibid., p. 34.

5. ibid., p. 46.

6. ibid., p. 31.

7. ibid., p. 22.

8. This would not be an innovation in British university practice. The University College of North Staffordshire offers a degree of BA with diploma in education.

9. *Investment in Education*, loc. cit., p. 23.

10. The Institutes of Economic and Social Research were described in Chapter 14; this proposal would continue and extend the Nigerian institute since it would deal with 'African history, and antiquities, its languages, its societies, its rocks and soils and vegetation and animal life'. (*Investment in Education*, loc. cit., p. 23.) The present policy is to integrate the existing institute with the relevant teaching department.

11. *Investment in Education*, loc. cit., p. 23.

12. ibid., loc. cit., p. 121.

13. The BSc (Economics) degree of the University of London permits specialization in money and banking, accounting and government while transport is an optional subject.

14. ibid., p. 23.

15. ibid., p. 121.

16. ibid., p. 26.

17. ibid., p. 25.

APPENDIX 1

THE COMMISSION ON HIGHER EDUCATION IN THE COLONIES

MEMBERS

Lord Justice Asquith, PC (Chairman)
Sir Donald Cameron, GCMG, KBE
Sir Alexander M. Carr-Saunders, KBE, FBA
H. J. Channon, Esq, CMG
Sir Fred Clarke
Sir James Duff
The Lord Hailey, PC, OM, GCSI, GCMG, GCIE
Sir James C. Irvine, KBE, FRS
Sir Richard Livingstone
R. Marrs, Esq, CMG, CIE
Dame Lillian Penson, DBE
Miss Margery Perham, CBE
Sir Raymond Priestley, MC
Professor J. A. Ryle
Sir Richard Southwell, FRS
J. A. Venn, Esq, CMG
Professor A. V. Hill, CH, OBE, FRS, was prevented by force of circumstances from continuing as a member of the Commission.
Mr D. W. Malcolm was Secretary until May 1944, when he was succeeded by Mr S. Robinson.

APPENDIX 2

THE INTER-UNIVERSITY COUNCIL FOR HIGHER EDUCATION OVERSEAS

Membership

Representative Members	University represented	Date of Membership	Offices held with dates
Si George Allen, CBE	Malaya	1949–52	Executive Committee 1952–6
Professor R. C. Baskett, OBE		1952–6 (Deputy)	
Professor C. P. Beattie	Belfast	1946–50	
Professor G. H. Bell	Sheffield	1958–	
Professor N. Bentwich, OBE, MC	St Andrews	1957–	Executive Committee 1960–
Professor J. W. Blake	Jerusalem	1946–8	
Professor A. H. Bunting	North Staffordshire	1954–	Executive Committee 1960–
Sir Sydney Caine, KCMG	Reading	1959–	
	Malaya	1952–6	
Sir Alexander Carr-Saunders, KBE, FBA	London	1946–56	Vice-Chairman 1946–51 / Chairman 1951–6 / Vice-Chairman 1957– / Executive Committee 1946–
		1957–(co-opted)	
D. G. Christopherson, OBE, FRS	Durham	1960–(previously co-opted 1956–60)	Executive Committee 1958–
Professor C. V. Christie	London	1952–5	
Dr J. W. Cook, FRS	Exeter	1954–	Executive Committee 1956–
Professor L. J. Davis	Glasgow	1947–	
Professor V. W. Downs	Cambridge	1960–	

Representative Members	University represented	Date of Membership	Offices held with dates
Professor A. N. Duckham, CBE	Reading	1957–9	Executive Committee 1946–7
Sir James Duff	Durham	1946–60 (then co-opted 1960–)	1959–
The Very Rev G. S. Duncan, OBE	St Andrews	1952–4	
Professor L. E. S. Eastham	Sheffield	1946–58	Executive Committee 1949–58
Sir Ifor Evans	Wales	1946–52	
J. S. Fulton	Sussex	1960–(previously co-opted 1957–60)	Executive Committee 1958–
Sir William Hamilton Fyfe	Aberdeen	1946–8	
Professor M. Grant, OBE	Edinburgh	1950–6 1959	
Dr W. W. Grave	Cambridge	1950–52	
The Hon Robert V. Galea, OBE	Malta	1946–8	
B. L. Hallward	Nottingham	1948–	
Dr T. C. Hunt	London	1955–	
J. B. Hunter, CBE, MC	London	1948–51	
Sir James C. Irvine, FRS	St Andrews	1946–52	Chairman 1946–51 / Executive Committee 1946–51
Dr D. G. James	Southampton	1952–	
Sir Ivor Jennings, KBE, FBA	Ceylon	1946–8	
Dr Brynmor Jones	Hull	1956–	
Dr B. Mouat Jones	Leeds	1946–8	
Professor J. MacMurray, MC	Edinburgh	1946–50 1956–8	Executive Committee 1960–

231

Representative Members	University represented	Date of Membership	Offices held with dates
Dr J. A. Manché	Malta	1948–	
Sir Charles Morris	Leeds	1948–	Vice-Chairman 1956–57 / Chairman 1957– / Executive Committee 1949–
Professor Noah Morris	Glasgow	1946–7	
Sir Philip Morris, KCMG, CBE	Bristol	1946–	
Professor F. H. Newark, CBE	Belfast	1950–	
J. H. Nicholson, CBE	Hull	1954–6	
Sir Alexander Oppenheim, OBE	Malaya	1957–	
Dame Lillian Penson, DBE	London	1957–(previously co-opted 1946–57)	Executive Committee 1946–9 / 1951–
Sir Raymond Priestley, MC	Birmingham	1946–52 (then co-opted –58)	Vice Chairman 1951–6 / Executive Committee / 1946–58
Sir William Pugh, OBE, FRS	Manchester	1946–50	
Dr L. T. Ride, CBE	Hong Kong	1949–	
Professor H. G. Sanders	Reading	1951–4	
Sir Folliott Sandford, KBE, CMG	Oxford	1958–	Executive Committee 1960–
Dr D. J. Sloss, CBE	Hong Kong	1946–9	Executive Committee 1951–7
W. T. S. Stallybrass, OBE	Oxford	1946–8	
Dr A. B. Steel, OBE	Wales	1952–	
Professor R. H. Stoughton	Reading	1946–51	Executive Committee 1947–51 1955–7
Sir Thomas Taylor, CBE	Aberdeen	1954–7 1948–	

Representative Members	University represented	Date of Membership	Offices held with dates
Sir Henry Thirkill, CBE, MC	Cambridge	1953–60	Executive Committee 1954–60
Sir Arthur Thomson, MC	Birmingham	1952–	
Professor W. J. Tulloch, OBE	St Andrews	1954–7	
Sir Douglas Veale, CBE	Oxford	1949–58 (then co-opted –60)	Executive Committee 1951–60
Dr J. A. Venn	Cambridge	1946–50	Executive Committee 1946–7
Professor C. H. Waddington, CBE, FRS	Edinburgh	1959–	
Professor C. W. Wardlaw	Manchester	1950–	
Professor E. G. White	Liverpool	1956–	
Dr C. H. Wilson	Leicester	1954–	Executive Committee 1955–
Sir Robert Wood, KBE, CB	Southampton	1952	
Professor J. G. Wright	Liverpool	1946–56	

Ex-Officio Member	Date of Membership	Offices held with dates
Sir Christopher Cox, KCMG	1946–	Executive Committee 1946–

233

Co-opted Members	Date of Membership	Offices held with dates
Sir Robert Aitken	1955–	Executive Committee 1955–7
Sir Eric Ashby	1955–7 1958–	
Professor C. E. Carrington	1955–	Executive Committee 1946–
Sir Alexander Carr-Saunders, KBE, FBA	1957–(previously London)	Executive Committee 1958–
D. G. Christopherson, OBE, FRS	1956–60 (then Durham)	Executive Committee 1947–60
Professor T. H. Davey, OBE	1946–	Executive Committee 1946–7,
Sir James Duff	1960–(previously Durham)	1959–
J. S. Fulton	1957–60 (then Sussex)	Executive Committee 1958–
Sir David Hughes-Parry	1952–5	
Sir Willis Jackson, FRS	1955–8	
Sir Ivor Jennings, KBE, FBA	1948–	Executive Committee 1958–
Dr J. F. Lockwood	1958–	
Sir Keith Murray	1954–	Executive Committee 1946–9
Dame Lillian Penson, DBE	1946–57 (then London 1957–)	1951–
Miss Margery Perham, CBE	1946–	Executive Committee 1949–
Sir Raymond Priestley, MC	1952–8 (previously	Vice-Chairman 1951–6
	Birmingham 1946–52)	Executive Committee 1946–58)
Professor S. G. Raybould	1955–	
Sir Arthur Trueman, KBE, FRS	1947–52	Executive Committee 1947–9
Sir Douglas Veale, CBE	1958–60	Executive Committee 1951–60
	(previously Oxford 1949–58)	

234

Secretaryship

Secretaries

	Offices held with dates	
Dr W. Adams, CMG, OBE	Secretary	1946–55
J. D. McCormack	Assistant Secretary	1959–
I. C. M. Maxwell	Assistant Secretary	1952–9
	Secretary	1959–
P. F. Vowles	Assistant Secretary	1948–51
Dr S. J. Worsley, MC	Secretary	1955–9

Librarianship

Library Advisors

	Date
Dr R. Offor	1947–60
J. H. P. Pafford	1960–

Holders of Offices in the Universities and Colleges

Universities	Vice-Chancellor	Chairman of the Council	Registrar	Librarian
Malta	1946–8 Professor R. V. Galea 1948– Dr J. A. Manché	The Chancellor	1946–50 J. L. Pace 1950–3 E. Serracino Inglott 1953– L. M. Pace	1946–53 Professor J. Aquilina (Hon Librarian) 1953–9 J. Cassar Pullico 1959– Professor Mgr P. P. Saydon (Hon Librarian)
Hong Kong	1946–9 Dr D. J. Sloss 1949– Dr L. T. Ride	The Vice-Chancellor	1946–8 S. V. Boxer 1948– B. Mellor	1946–50 Mrs M. E. M. Ring 1950–60 Mrs D. Scott 1960–1 G. N. Bonsall (Act'g Librarian) 1961– H. A. Rydings
Malaya	1949–52 Sir George Allen	(a) Chairman of Council 1949–51 Sir Roland Braddell	Singapore Division 1949–54 W. D. Craig	Singapore Division 1951–59 E. H. Clark

1952–6	Sir Sydney Caine	1951–3	Sir Onn bin Ja'afar	1955–7	M. Brown	1959–	Miss J. M. Waller
1957–	Sir Alexander Oppenheim	1954–7	Dr Haji Mohamed Eusoff	1957–8	W. Burton		*Kuala Lumpur Division*
		1958–9	Dr Yang Teramat Mulia Tunku Ya'acob		*Kuala Lumpur Division*	1959–	W. J. Plumbe
				1959–	H. D. Lewis		

(b) *Chairman of Central Council* 1959–

Kuala Lumpur Division
1959– Foo Yeow Yoke

The chair at alternate meetings is taken by the Chairmen of the Divisional Councils, Singapore and Kuala Lumpur.

(c) *Chairman of Divisional Council:*

Singapore Division
1959– Dr Tay Teck Eng
Kuala Lumpur Division
1959– Haji Mustapha Albakri

| Khartoum | 1956–8 | Dr M. Grant | 1956– | Dr Abdel Halim Mohammed | 1956 | G. C. Wood | 1956 | M. Jolliffe |
| | 1958– | Sayed Nasr el Hag Ali | | | 1956– | Sayed Ahmed el Mardi Gobara | | |

University Colleges	Principal	Chairman of the Council	Registrar	Librarian
Khartoum	1951–6 L. C. Wilcher 1956 Dr M. Grant	1951 Arthur Gaitskell 1951–6 Sayed Ibrahim Ahmed Ibrahim 1956 Dr Abdel Halim Mohammed	1951–56 G. C. Wood	1951–6 M. Jolliffe
Makerere	1949 Dr W. D. Lamont 1950– Bernard de Bunsen	1949–53 Sir Reginald Robins 1953–5 Sir Joseph Hutchinson 1955–8 Sir Ronald German 1958– Sir Donald MacGillivray	1949–52 Lt-Col A. Scragg 1953– Paul Vowles *College Secretary* 1955–61 A. Tattersall	1949–54 Miss J. Larter 1954– H. Holdsworth
Ibadan	1948–53 Dr K. Mellanby 1953–6 Dr J. T. Saunders 1956–60 Dr J. H. Parry 1960– Dr K. O. Dike	1948–51 Dr K. Mellanby 1951–8 Sir Sydney Phillipson 1958– Sir Francis Ibiam	1948–51 F. P. G. Hunter 1951–3 W. A. Husband 1953–7 S. O. Biobaku 1957–60 J. D. Irwin 1960– N. K. Adamolekun	1948– W. J. Harris

Ghana	1948–57	D. M. Balme	1948–51	Sir Leslie M'Carthy	1948–52	G. I. Smith	1948–	Miss A. E. Walker
	1957–	Dr R.H.Stoughton	1951–	Sir K. Arku Korsah	1952–	M. Dowuona		
West Indies	1949–52	Sir Thomas W. J. Taylor		The Chancellor	1949–	Dr H. W. Springer	1949–54	H. Holdsworth
	1953–8	Dr W. W. Grave					1955–	W. E. Gocking
	1959–	Dr W. Arthur Lewis						
Rhodesia & Nyasaland	1955–	Dr Walter Adams	1955–58	L. M. N. Hodson	1955–6	Langham Murray	1955–	D. A. Clarke
			1958–	Rt Hon the Viscount Malvern	1956–	J. D. Angus		
Sierra Leone (Fourah Bay College)	1959–60	Dr J. J. Grant	1959–60	The Hon Mr Justice S. B. Jones	1959–60	A. Wainwright	1959–	R. S. Burkett
	1960–	Dr Davidson S. H. W. Nicol			1960–	F. O. Hooley		
Royal College, Nairobi	1960–	Dr J. M. Hyslop	1960–	P. J. Rogers	1960–	G. W. Manfield	1960–	D. A. R. Kemp

HIGHER EDUCATION IN CEYLON BEFORE 1945

In Ceylon, as so often is the case, provision for medical education preceded that for any other form of higher education. A medical college was founded in 1870, for which local benefactors provided the capital for buildings; it was recognized as a colonial medical school under the Medical Act of 1886. A law college followed, and by the end of the century legal and medical education of full professional standard was available in Ceylon.[1] But Ceylonese who sought degrees had to enter Indian universities, and this led to the formation early in the present century of a Ceylon University Association. As a result of its efforts a committee, appointed in 1911, recommended the foundation of a university college; in 1913 the executive council resolved that a university college should be set up. The outline of a scheme was submitted to the Board of Education in London; in reply the Board asked whether it was a university or a university college which was in mind, where it was to be located and whether it would include oriental studies. Sir Robert Chalmers, the Governor of Ceylon, answered that the site would be in Colombo, that oriental studies would find a place in the curriculum and that he hoped for affiliation with the University of Oxford. The University was approached, and in 1914 a degree was passed requiring the Hebdominal Council to appoint a committee for the purpose of co-operating with the government of Ceylon in the establishment and maintenance of a college of university rank in Colombo.[2] After the war the government of Ceylon returned to the scheme and founded Ceylon University College which was opened in 1921. The problem of degrees settled itself; the University of London had opened an examination centre in Ceylon in 1907 where external students could sit for external degrees, and students of the College took advantage of those facilities. It had been intended that the status of the institution as a university college should be short, and plans were made to raise the College to the rank of a university. By 1925 a draft ordinance, incorporating the College as a university, had been prepared after discussion with the committee of the Hebdominal Council which was reconstituted in 1921. At that point no further progress was made for many years; a prolonged controversy arose over the question of the site, and in addition attention became focused on the constitutional problems involved in the ambition of the colony for independence. Nevertheless the College developed rapidly under the energetic direction of the Principal; honours courses for degrees were instituted in 1922, student numbers rose and between 1921 and 1941 580 graduated. Finally in 1942 the University of Ceylon was created; the University College and the Medical College, losing their separate identities, became faculties of the University.

1. Sir Ivor Jennings, 'The Foundation of the University of Ceylon'. *University of Ceylon Review*, Vol. IX, No. 3, July 1951, p. 148.
2. ibid., p. 154.

EXTERNAL DEGREES AND AFFILIATION

Certain British universities possess powers which enable them to make their degrees available to students in colleges overseas. These powers are of two kinds, that to award external degrees and that to affiliate another institution.

By the power to award external degrees is meant the possession of authority to confer degrees upon candidates upon whom no compulsion to attend an approved place of instruction is necessarily imposed. The University of London obtained this power as a result of a long and involved story the outline of which is as follows. The foundation in 1826 of what is now University College, London, and in 1828 of King's College, London, led to a demand that their students should be able to proceed to degrees. Various plans designed to achieve this end met with insuperable obstacles until 1836 when the University of London was created by royal charter. In this body teachers had no part. It was in effect wholly controlled by civil servants who designed the syllabuses, set the examinations and awarded degrees; they had authority to draw up a list of institutions which were empowered to issue certificates to such of their pupils as wished to enter for the examinations for which only those with certificates could sit. The list was issued in two parts; in the first part were the institutions entitled to issue certificates to candidates for degrees in arts and laws, and these institutions had to be in the United Kingdom; in the second part were the medical institutions entitled to submit candidates, and these latter institutions might be 'in foreign parts'. The first calendar of the University was published in 1844, and in the second part of the list are found the University of Malta and the Military Hospital in Ceylon. Thus began the long association of London University with higher education overseas. In 1850 a supplementary charter made possible the inclusion in the first part of the list of institutions in 'possessions abroad' and in 'territories under the Government of the East India Company.'

The manner in which this system worked roused strong criticism chiefly because of the irrational selection of institutions for inclusion in the list. A new charter of 1858 made drastic changes; the list was abolished and it became possible for candidates to sit for examinations irrespective of whether they had attended any institution for instruction. This was the beginning of the London external system in the sense defined above. Until 1863 the right to sit for examinations was confined to candidates in the United Kingdom; in that year to the words 'United Kingdom' were added the words 'and elsewhere'. Thus the new system was extended without geographical limitation. Up to 1900 there was no distinction between 'internal' and 'external' degrees; one of the consequences of the transformation of the University in that year was the creation of this distinction. What this distinction is and how the University employs its powers to award 'external degrees' to students of colleges in special relation has been described in Chapter 3.

The Ashby Commission, as mentioned in Chapter 19, has recommended that the proposed university in Lagos should offer degrees to those who follow its correspondence courses. Since it does not appear that those who took advantage of these facilities would be under compulsion to make any attendance at the university, the recommendation means that the university should have power to award external degrees.

All British universities, other than London, are restrained from awarding degrees to those who have not attended for instruction. These restraints may be found in basic constitutional documents, in which case special procedure would be needed to remove them, or in regulations which could be abolished almost overnight. But it is of no importance whether or not the restraints are entrenched because no university has any wish to be rid of them. But it is not always the case that attendance must be within the walls of the university; some universities have power to recognize attendance at other institutions, and such institutions are said to be affiliated.

In 1879 the University of Cambridge, having received memorials from Nottingham, Hull and Sheffield, asking for association with the University, obtained statutory powers to recognize 'any college or institution within the United Kingdom or any part of the British dominions, being a place of education in which the majority of students are of the age of seventeen at least', as 'an affiliated college' on certain conditions including 'that the University shall be represented on its Governing Body and should undertake the conduct of its examinations or part of them as the University shall from time to time determine'. The effect of this was to entitle a person, who had successfully completed a three years' course at an affiliated college, to proceed to the final tripos examination and to the BA degree at the end of two years instead of the usual three years. The conditions quoted above were waived in a number of cases and were deleted in 1894. After 1950 a list of affiliated institutions was no longer published, and recognition is now of degrees rather than of institutions, but the privileges of an 'affiliated student' remain the same as those conferred on the members of the earliest affiliated institutions. Affiliation of this kind allows a limited amount of exemption from intra-mural attendance.

The special conditions which were an original feature of the Cambridge scheme are of interest, for they resemble the conditions which the Ashby Commission have suggested as appropriate to be included in any arrangement under which an established university might agree to sponsor a new Nigerian university. But sponsorship, as contemplated by the Ashby Commission, would be fundamentally different from affiliation; the Nigerian university would award its own degrees. The intention of sponsorship is to secure for a new foundation the backing of its standards by the prestige of an established university and not to grant special privileges at the sponsoring university to students of the sponsored institution.

The University of Oxford took action in 1880 similar to that described above for Cambridge with similar consequences. The only institutions affiliated were colleges in the United Kingdom. When the government of Ceylon and Makerere College applied for assistance in 1914 and 1940 respectively, their requests were not dealt with under the affiliation statute; the Hebdominal Council set up advisory committees to help them. The advisory committee for Ceylon, which was revived after the first world war, gave useful assistance, but there is no record of any meeting of the committee set up for Makerere College. The one tangible result of the approach of the College to the University of Oxford was the placing of the coat of arms of the University over the main entrance to the College where it is still to be seen.

In 1875 the University of Durham took Codrington College, Barbados, into affiliation, and in the following year also Fourah Bay College, Sierra Leone; it was laid down that students of those colleges could be admitted to the examinations of the University. At that time the charter of the University neither gave power to affiliate nor placed any restrictions upon affiliation; it was a very nebulous document. In 1908, by which time other universities had come into existence whose statutes regulated affiliation, new statutes were promulgated which permitted the University to affiliate 'any College or like Institution within the United Kingdom or any part of the British Dominions'. The present statute (1937) tightens the procedure since, after maintaining the affiliation of the two colleges, it lays down that 'no other College or Institution shall be affiliated to the University except under a statute made on its behalf'.

Other British universities also have power to affiliate. The clause in the charter which confers this power requires that it be exercised in accordance with ordinances. The universities usually frame their ordinances so as to restrict the exercise of this power both geographically and in relation to the length of attendance at an affiliated institution which can be recognized as exempting from attendance at the university. This is the position at the University of Birmingham (December 1960). But the power need not be so restricted, and it is understood that the University of Birmingham has under consideration the promulgation of an additional ordinance which will enable it to recognize attendance at the proposed medical school of the University College of Rhodesia and Nyasaland as exempting from any attendance at the University.

NANYANG UNIVERSITY

In the section on the University of Malaya in Chapter 4 mention was also included of Nanyang University. This University was founded in Singapore under the companies ordinance of the colony, and, as explained in Appendix 8, it is probable that, if the incorporation had been challenged, it would have been declared invalid as far as the power to award degrees is concerned. In 1959 the University was incorporated by an act of the local legislature, thus putting its status on a firm basis. The initiative came from a group of wealthy Chinese residents who wanted to provide university education for Chinese students who had insufficient command of English to enter the university of Malaya. Criticism of the new University led to the setting up of a commission consisting of the vice-chancellor of the University of Western Australia and four other members representing American, Chinese and Dutch university traditions. The Commission reported in 1959; 'we regret', they said, 'that we must report adversely on the academic standards of Nanyang University; we further regret that we cannot at present in good conscience recommend that the degrees of Nanyang University should be automatically recognized by the Government of Singapore as being comparable with the degrees awarded by other universities which are now so recognized'. (*Report of the Nanyang University Commission*, 1959, p. 27.)

There are now about 2,000 students of whom all but one (a Malay) are Chinese; teaching is mostly in Mandarin, and the subjects taught do not extend beyond arts, science and commerce. The government of Singapore has announced its policy in relation to the University which has been stated as follows. 'We will not shirk our responsibility of supporting wholeheartedly the re-organization of Nanyang University and backing it with adequate finance.' But 'academic standards must be raised'. A review committee appointed by the government 'clearly indicated that something is basically wrong with Nanyang University. . . . In its four years of existence Nanyang University suffered many setbacks but none more crippling than the lack of expert planning and advice. A group of shrewd businessmen started the University with a great deal of intitiative but a university is an organization for learning and research and not a business enterprise. . . . Perhaps out of consideration for financial stability, quality has been sacrificed in the interest of quantity. . . . The curriculum shows a lack of systematic planning and proper co-ordination.' Therefore 'before any grant can be made, government must be assured that government funds are well spent and properly accounted for and that proper standards in regard to academic staff and teaching are maintained'. Nevertheless the government had decided to employ Nanyang graduates and to recognize the university's degrees as equivalent to the pass degrees of a recognized university. (The *Straits Times*, February 11, 1960.)

STUDENTS IN OTHER COUNTRIES

The following figures have been assembled from various sources. They must be regarded as no more than indications of the situation. Students are defined in different ways; the figures probably include some who ought to be excluded and certainly omit others who ought to be included. But they serve to indicate that the number of those coming from the less developed countries who seek higher education in the United Kingdom, the United States, Canada and Australia is large.

Home Country	United Kingdom 1959–60	United States 1959–60	Canada 1958	Australia 1959	Total
Hong Kong	253		546	338	1,137
Malaya and Singapore	380	247		1,182	1,809
Nigeria	883	265			1,148
Ghana	354	167			521
West Indies	568	1,640	804		3,012
East Africa	575	221			796
Central Africa	133	27			160
Sierra Leone	107	39			146
Cyprus	146				146
Mauritius	140				140
Other Countries	204	3			207
Total	3,743	2,609	1,350	1,520	9,222

THE CREATION OF UNIVERSITIES

In Chapter 19 it was pointed out that the procedure by which universities are brought into existence is important since, only if the procedure is appropriate, is it possible to ensure that universities will conform with national needs. Some description was given of the procedure which is recommended for Nigeria by the Ashby Commission, and it may be useful to sketch briefly the procedure in use in some other countries.

In the United Kingdom the right to grant the power to confer degrees, an essential privilege of a university, is a prerogative of the Crown. Apart from the Universities of Oxford and Cambridge which came into being before the conception of a university was formulated, all British universities were created by royal charter with the exception of the University of Durham which owes its birth in 1832 to an Act of Parliament, that is to the crown in parliament. All petitions for royal charters are considered by the Privy Council which takes informed advice, and, in the case of a petition for a new university, that of existing universities; since the institution of the Universities Grants Committee in 1919, the advice of that body is also sought. The Privy Council would not recommend the crown to issue a charter if that step were not in accordance with advice from these quarters. This procedure therefore provides assurance that the objects described above as desirable are secured.

Stress is laid on the power to confer degrees because any definition of a university includes this power among the attributes of a university. The Oxford English Dictionary defines a university as follows: 'the whole body of teachers and scholars engaged, at a particular place, in giving or receiving instruction in the higher branches of learning; such persons associated together as a society with definite organization and acknowledged powers and privileges (especially that of conferring degrees)'. Though the point has not been decided in the courts, it would appear that in the United Kingdom a body of persons, incorporated as a university by competent authority though without a specific power to confer degrees, would nevertheless be entitled to confer them. The University of Durham was created by an Act of Parliament in 1832 in which no mention was made of degrees; in 1835 the authorities of the University took legal opinion and were advised that degrees could be awarded. (C. E. Whiting, *The University of Durham*, 1932, p. 58.)

All doubts were removed in 1837 by the issue of a royal charter giving degree granting powers. When the self-styled University of London, now University College, London (self-styled because it was not empowered to call itself a university by charter or statute) proposed to seek a charter, the law officers advised that the grant of a charter would carry degree-giving powers even if no mention of degrees were made in the charter. (H. H. Bellot, *University College, London*, 1929, p. 221.) On the other hand the conferment of degree-giving powers does not make an institution into a university. St David's College, Lampeter, received a royal charter in 1827; the charter gave the College a limited power to confer degrees but did not style the College as a university. When the College claimed a declaration that it was a university, it was unsuccessful. ('St David's College, Lampeter *v*. Ministry of Education', *All England Law Reports*, 1951, vol. I., p. 559.) Under its charter of 1883 the Royal College of Music has limited powers to confer degrees, and the Archbishop of Canterbury can confer 'Lambeth degrees'—a right supposed to be derived from one of the powers of his predecessors as *legatus natus* of the pope which survived the Reformation. But neither the Royal College nor Lambeth Palace has claimed to be a university.

In the countries of western continental Europe a different procedure provides a similar assurance. In these countries, as in Great Britain, the creation of universities is a function of the central government, but in Canada and Australia, which have federal constitutions, it is a function of the provinces or states. (The federal government of Australia is directly responsible for the Australian Capital Territory over which it has full powers. In the exercise of these powers it has created the Australian National University.) There is a strong case for holding that, while educational provision up to the university stage is a proper function for the latter, it is otherwise in regard to universities. Unlike schools universities serve the nation and not a geographically defined section of it, and therefore it should be the function of the central government to determine their number and sites. There are other arguments in support of this contention; it is important that universities should not come into existence unless they have the intention to aim at certain standards of work for which sufficient staff and facilities of the necessary quality are indispensable, but the achievement of national standards can only be secured by the central government. Moreover the central government is everywhere in the best position to obtain informed advice where university problems are under consideration, and in new countries, without an ancient university tradition, sources whence this advice can be sought are scarcer than in the older countries, which means that such advice is not readily accessible to provincial and state governments in new countries even if they recognize the need to seek it. The experience of Canada under a federal constitution, which assigns responsibility for universities to the provinces, is illuminating. The Atlantic provinces, with a population of well under two million, have no less than fifteen independent degree-giving colleges and universities, a provision clearly in excess of needs; this has been realized, and in the four western provinces legislation limits universities to one in each province.

The federal governments of Canada and Australia can, however, exercise an indirect influence over the creation of universities, because they can, and now do, make grants to universities, and provincial and state governments would hesitate to take steps which would not attract grants. But in Canada the federal grant is on a fixed formula, and passes to the universities through the Canadian Universities Foundation which is no more than an agency of the federal government; the system does not enable the federal government to influence university policy; it does no more than relieve the provincial governments of a part of the cost of their universities. The federal government of Australia, however, has recently set up the Australian Universities Commission, the members of which are well informed about the academic world. The Commission advises the federal government as to the financial needs of the universities and allocates to them such money as the federal government provides for the purpose. Under this procedure the development of the Australian University system, including the creation of new universities, will be guided by the informed advice rendered to the federal government, and it is likely that the creation of universities will be controlled to much the same extent and purpose as in Great Britain. Of the territories under consideration in this book, the West Indies, Rhodesia and Nyasaland, and Nigeria have federal constitutions which, in the cases of the West Indies and Rhodesia, assign university education to the exclusive federal list while that of Nigeria places university education on the concurrent list. The National Universities Commission, proposed by the Ashby Commission, is designed to do for Nigeria what the Australian Universities Commission will do for Australia.

In the United States education falls to the component elements of the federation. The federal government gives no gr nts to universities and is therefore unable to bring influence to bear on university provision. But new universities can be created, not only by acts of the state legislatures, but also by incorporation under a procedure which corresponds to that under the British Companies Act. The following passage describes how this works out in the United States:

'The states differ greatly in the qualifications that are required before a group can obtain a charter to operate a college or university. In some states, as in New York, the authority is assigned to the state department of education . . . and the Board of Regents; these agencies have set up relatively high standards which must be met before a new institution may be issued a charter. In many of the states, however, no standards whatever are maintained, and any group that can put up a few dollars to pay the cost of its incorporation or can persuade the state legislature to issue a charter, can obtain the authority to grant all kinds of academic degrees, without reference to the facilities or equipment they may have for such purposes. In very few states, moreover, is there any supervision of non-publicly controlled institutions after they have once been established. The lax provisions for the issuance of institutional charters, and the virtual absence of supervision over the quality of the programmes maintained in existing institutions in most states have led to the operation of many fraudulent institutions often known as "diploma mills", which sell degrees, diplomas and credentials at a price to unwary or unscrupulous customers. . . . In many instances . . . the enterprising managers of such institutions peddle their bogus degrees and credentials to persons in foreign countries who are unfamiliar with the fact that control over higher education in the United States is lax enough to permit such fraudulent operation'. (*American Universities and Colleges*, American Council of Education, 7th edition, 1956, p. 21.).

It follows that, when in a federal state the federal government exercises no influence over the creation of universities by its component parts, and when in addition it is possible for universities to come into being under procedure analogous to that under the British Companies Act, there is not that degree of control over the grant of power to award degrees which is essential if the objects set out in Chapter 19 are to be achieved. In Appendix 6 it was said that the incorporation of Nanyang University under the companies ordinance of Singapore was almost certainly invalid because,

Singapore being then a colony, the right to grant degree-giving powers was the prerogative of the crown. It is important that, when colonial territories achieve independence, it should not become possible to obtain degree-giving powers by this kind of procedure. Under the constitutions of Nigeria, the West Indies, Rhodesia and Nyasaland the incorporation of companies is on the exclusive federal legislative list which goes some way to making it unlikely that this will happen.

STUDENT NUMBERS IN OVERSEAS UNIVERSITIES AND COLLEGES
October 1960

University or College	Men	Women	Total
Royal University of Malta	224	19	243
University of Hong Kong	1,035	370	1,405
University of Malaya ⎱Singapore	1,259	443	1,702
⎰Kuala Lumpur	505	149	654
University of Khartoum	1,320	55	1,375
Makerere College, the University College of East Africa	844	68	912
University College, Ibadan	1,173	79	1,252
University College of Ghana	638	47	685
University College of ⎱Jamaica	577	315	892
the West Indies ⎰Trinidad	67	—	67
University College of Rhodesia & Nyasaland	136	73	209
Fourah Bay College, the University College of Sierre Leone	269	33	302
Royal College, Nairobi	285	48	333
Total	8,332	1,699	10,031

INDEX

Achimota College, 25, 26, 37, 76, 81, 82, 148.

Advisory Committee on Education in the Colonies, 28.

Advisory Committee on Native Education in Africa, 28.

Adult Education, 154–61, 221, 222.

Affiliation by universities, 243–5.

Agriculture, education for, 146, 147.

Air conditioning, 117, 118.

Appointment of staff, 43, 173–82.

Architecture, education for, 150.

Area needed for universities and colleges, 114, 115.

Art teaching, 70, 71, 186.

Ashby Commission, composition of, 218; proposals of, 218–24.

Asquith Commission, survey made by, 17; appointed, 29; programme of, 34–41; programme in operation, 42–50; and West Africa, 75; and West Indies, 93; views on finance, 97, 103; views on constitutions, 105, 106; views on medical education, 140; and engineering, 147; and agriculture, 146; and adult education, 154; views on salaries, 177; views on second-ment, 180; views on student residence, 183; views on levels of education, 203; and Ashby Commission, 225; membership, 229.

Association of Universities of the British Commonwealth, 173, 181.

Autonomy of universities and colleges, 39, 105, 193–202.

Azikiwe, Dr, 211, 212.

Benefactions to universities and colleges, 99, 100.

Bookshops, 162.

British Council, 155.

British National Book Centre, 165.

British West Indies, education in before 1945, 27, 28; see also University College of the West Indies.

Bursaries for students, 192, 193.

Cambridge School Certificate, 23, 119.

Cameron, Sir Donald, quoted, 25.

Cantlie, Sir James, 18.

Capital grants to universities and colleges, 97–9.

Careers of graduates, 213, 214.

Carnegie Corporation of New York, 44, 160, 176.

Cartmel-Robinson, Sir Harold, 87.

Ceylon, University of, 20, 92, 241, 242.

Channon, Professor H. J., 29.

Chapels, 24, 69, 80, 84, 187.

Clifford, Sir Hugh, quoted, 31.

Climate, problems presented by, 116–18.

Codrington College, 27.

Colonial Development and Welfare, 30, 43, 45, 66, 75, 86, 97, 98, 99, 142, 162, 171, 178, 190, 191.

Colonial Social Science Research Council, 171, 172.

Colonial University Grants Committee, 40, 42, 45, 46, 97, 190.

Commission of Enquiry on the University of Malaya, 110.

Commission on Higher Education in the Colonies, see Asquith Commission.

Commission on Higher Education in East Africa, see De La Warr Commission.

Commission on Higher Education in Malaya, see McLean Commission.

Commission on Higher Education in West Africa, see Elliot Commission.

Commission on Post-School Certificate and Higher Education in Nigeria, see Ashby Commission.

Committee appointed to review the policy of the University College of the West Indies, 96, 175, 176, 179, 185, 195.

Commonwealth Universities Exchange Scheme, 44.

Convocations, powers of, 107.

Copyright privileges, 165.

Correspondence courses, 222, 223.

Cost of education, per student, 40, 103.